The Many Faces of Multilingualism

Trends in Applied Linguistics

Edited by
Ulrike Jessner

Volume 33

The Many Faces of Multilingualism

Language Status, Learning and Use Across Contexts

Edited by
Piotr Romanowski
Martin Guardado

ISBN 978-1-5015-2729-6
e-ISBN (PDF) 978-1-5015-1469-2
e-ISBN (EPUB) 978-1-5015-1451-7
ISSN 1868-6362

Library of Congress Control Number: 2020940232

Bibliographic information published by the Deutsche Nationalbibliothek
The Deutsche Nationalbibliothek lists this publication in the Deutsche Nationalbibliografie;
detailed bibliographic data are available on the Internet at http://dnb.dnb.de.

© 2022 Walter de Gruyter Inc., Boston/Berlin
This volume is text- and page-identical with the hardback published in 2020.
Typesetting: Integra Software Services Pvt. Ltd.
Printing and binding: CPI books GmbH, Leck

www.degruyter.com

Contents

Notes on contributors —— VII

Li Wei
Foreword: Multilingualism in Context —— XI

Piotr Romanowski
Chapter 1
Introduction: The Many Faces of Multilingualism —— 1

Part I: (Socio)Linguistic Aspects of Multilingualism

Piotr Romanowski
Chapter 2
The Polish Linguistic Map: An Overview of Minority Languages in the Education System —— 11

Edenize Ponzo Peres, Kyria Rebeca Finardi and Poliana Claudiano Calazans
Chapter 3
Language Contact, Maintenance and Conflict: The Case of the Guarani Language in Brazil —— 25

Martin Guardado
Chapter 4
"My Gain Would Have Been Their Loss": Key Factors in the Heritage Language Socialization and Policies of a Middle-class Mexican Family in Canada —— 39

Hiroki Hanamoto
Chapter 5
Gesture Sequences and Turn-taking Strategies in Communication Settings in the Multilingual Philippines —— 63

Anna Khalizova
Chapter 6
The Phenomenon of Code Alternation by Multilingual Speakers —— 85

Part II: Pedagogical Aspects of Multilingualism

Asunción Martínez-Arbelaiz, Isabel Pereira
Chapter 7
Identity and Language Proficiency in Study Abroad: A Case Study of Four Multilingual and Multicultural Students —— 109

Anna Szczepaniak-Kozak
Chapter 8
The Influence of the Mother Tongue and L3 on Learning Pragmatics in EFL among Poles —— 127

Vita Kalnbērziņa
Chapter 9
Curriculum Reform in Latvia: A Move from Multilingual to Plurilingual Education —— 145

Antoinette Camilleri Grima
Chapter 10
Pluralistic Approaches in Foreign Language Education: Examples of Implementation from Malta —— 163

Natalia Barranco-Izquierdo, M. Teresa Calderón-Quindós
Chapter 11
Interlingual Education in the Classroom: An Action Guide to Overcoming Communication Conflicts —— 187

Vimbai Mbirimi-Hungwe
Chapter 12
Transcending Linguistic Boundaries in Higher Education Pedagogy: The Role of Translanguaging and Lecturers —— 207

Martin Guardado
Chapter 13
Bringing it all Together: Multilingualism in Family, Society and Education —— 223

Subject Index —— 233

Notes on contributors

Natalia Barranco Izquierdo has a PhD in Didactics of Language and Literature and is currently teaching at the School of Education and Social Work of the University of Valladolid, Spain. Her main research interests are methods of teaching and learning English as a foreign language and early acquisition of a foreign language. She has published several papers on mediation as a communication language activity and early foreign language teaching.

Poliana Claudiano Calazans is a High School Language professor and coordinator in the Guarapari, ES, Brazil. She has a PhD in Linguistics from the Federal University of Rio de Janeiro with research on indigenous languages. In 2019, she participated in a training by Capes at Fanshawe College in Canada.

María Teresa Calderón Quindós is Associate Professor of English at the University of Valladolid, teaching General English at the School of Education and Social Work. In 2005 she was awarded by AESLA (Spanish Association of Applied Linguistics) for her work on Cognitive Poetics. Her most relevant work in the field appears in *Annual Review of Cognitive Linguistics,* John Benjamins (2005). She has also done research in English literature and foreign language education.

Antoinette Camilleri Grima is full professor of applied linguistics at the University of Malta. She teaches language pedagogy and she has published several books and articles in internationally refereed journals on intercultural competence, educational sociolinguistics, learner autonomy and bilingual education. She has authored two radio series in Maltese as a foreign language, and has coordinated a number of Council of Europe workshops in the area of modern languages.

Kyria Rebeca Finardi is a professor in the Department of Languages, Culture and Education (DLCE) and a researcher in the post-graduate programs of Education (PPGE) and Linguistics (PPGEL) of the Federal University of Espirito Santo (UFES). She is also the former President of the Brazilian Association of Applied Linguistics (ALAB).

Martin Guardado is a Professor of applied linguistics and sociolinguistics at the University of Alberta. He obtained his PhD from the University of British Columbia specializing in language education and heritage language socialization. Additional active research includes EAP, TESL, TBLT, interlingual family language policies, and Náhuat Pipil Indigenous language revitalization in El Salvador.

Hiroki Hanamoto holds a PhD in Sociolinguistics awarded by Kansai University, Japan. He is Associate Professor in the Department of Science and Engineering at Tokyo Denki University. He mainly researches issues related to multimodal interaction using interactional resources such as gesture and embodied action in English as a lingua franca (ELF) contexts. He has published articles in international journals and written book chapters in various areas of ELF interactions.

Vita Kalnbērziņa obtained her PhD from Lancaster University, UK. She presently holds an Associate Professor's position at the University of Latvia and works as a curriculum and examination expert at the Ministry of Education and Science of Latvia. Her main interests are language acquisition, language testing and intercultural communication.

Anna Khalizova studied German, English, Spanish languages, literature and pedagogy at Moscow State Linguistic University (MSLU). After graduation, she started her PhD project at Albert-Ludwigs-University in Freiburg, Germany, and she completed it in 2017. She was a DAAD-scholarship holder at the University of Duisburg-Essen. She worked as a research assistant at the University of Freiburg. Presently, she is a research assistant at the University of Koblenz-Landau and Goethe University Frankfurt. Her research interests are multilingualism, intercultural communication, conversation analysis, multimodal analysis, language didactics, German as a second/foreign language.

Asunción Martínez Arbelaiz has been the language coordinator for University Studies Abroad Consortium since 2001, where she designs, administers and assesses different courses of Spanish as an additional language. She also teaches in the European Master in Multilingualism and Education and is part of the research group Elkarrikertuz, both at the University of the Basque Country, Spain.

Vimbai Mbirimi-Hungwe is a lecturer in the Department of Language Proficiency at the Sefako Makgatho University of Health Sciences in South Africa. She has just completed her PhD. Her research focuses on the use of translanguaging, reading comprehension and collaborative learning at the tertiary level. She is an upcoming researcher who has contributed with two book chapters and a few peer-reviewed journal articles.

Isabel Pereira received a PhD in SLA from the University of Illinois at Urbana Champaign, Department of Spanish, Italian and Portuguese, in 1996. She works as Assistant Director of NYU Madrid in charge of the language program, and she teaches Spanish at different levels. Her areas of interest include curricular development and second language research as well as second language acquisition and language pedagogy in study abroad.

Edenize Ponzo Peres, is a professor of the Department of Languages and in the Post Graduate Program of Linguistics (PPGEL) of the Federal University of Espirito Santo, Vitória-ES, Brazil. She is currently pursuing her second PhD with research on indigenous and heritage languages and communities at the Catholic University of Minas Gerais.

Piotr Romanowski holds a PhD in Linguistics. He is Assistant Professor at the Department of Applied Linguistics, the University of Warsaw. His main research interests include bilingual and multilingual education, sociolinguistics, and foreign language teaching and learning. He is the Chief Editor of the *Journal of Multilingual Theories and Practices* (Equinox Publishing), and the founding member of *MultiLingNet*. He has authored over forty papers, one monograph and co-edited five other volumes. He has guest lectured in the UK, the USA, Canada, Brazil, Chile, Taiwan, South Africa, New Zealand.

Anna Szczepaniak-Kozak is Associate Professor at the School of Languages and Literatures at Adam Mickiewicz University (AMU) in Poznań, Poland and the Deputy Editor in Chief for *Glottodidactica. An International Journal of Applied Linguistics*. Anna's main research interests are within the field of applied linguistics, particularly interlanguage pragmatics and teaching-oriented studies of hate speech. She is the author of three books, the co-editor of six monographs, and the author of more than fifty scholarly papers. In years 2014–2016, she conducted research and training activities in a project financed by the European Commission titled RADAR (Regulating Anti-Discrimination and Anti-Racism). In 2019, she received the AMU Rector's award for outstanding academic achievements.

Li Wei
Foreword: Multilingualism in Context

The recent realisation in the international academic community of the significance of multilingualism in sociocultural, educational and cognitive terms has come as something of a surprise to the very many communities across the globe where multilingualism has always been an integral part of people's everyday life. This is evidently due to the presence of large numbers of 'misplaced' populations who speak languages other than the assumed indigenous ones. These speakers are usually labelled as 'migrants, 'refugees', or 'ethnic minorities.' Over time, their languages become called 'community' or 'heritage' languages. The designation of a language and its speakers with one of these labels has serious consequences on the status of the language and the community in society. Policies and practices that are designed to support the minoritized languages and social groups usually assume that their status is a real one rather than imposed by society. For instance, in Britain and the United States where English is the dominant language, people who have roots in another country are often designated as English-as-an-additional-language (EAL) speakers. EAL children are expected to struggle in the mainstream educational system. They need help with English. And if they do achieve well in schools, they will be celebrated as examples of success.

Multilingualism is a human phenomenon; it is evidence of human beings' capacity to learn and use multiple languages. The learning and use of multiple languages presume access to them. But access may not be equal. To understand multilingualism, one must look at the specific historical, sociocultural, environmental and material conditions on access to languages for the individuals and communities concerned. Only in doing so can we understand the status of different languages in society and the implications of the designated status of the language for its speakers in society. Migration, which has hugely intensified across the globe in recent decades, is another condition that impacts on access to languages. The recent and ongoing migratory processes have not been balanced in the sense that it is often people from under-developed parts of the world migrating to the more developed countries and regions, though this is relative and by no means universal. The status of language and its speakers as a result of migration is a politically sensitive topic for exploration and has serious implications for policy and practice.

Li Wei, University College London, United Kingdom, E-mail: li.wei@ucl.ac.uk

The educational impacts of multilingualism are a major concern for both the speaker and the system. Some people are able to maintain all the languages in their repertoire, and in fact, in some cases can even increase the number of languages they can learn and use. Others give up the languages they acquired in childhood and replace them with other languages that they use in their everyday communication. Reasons for language maintenance and language shift or attrition are complex and multiple. They are a fascinating topic for research. How the educational system responds to multilingualism is another hotly debated issue. The idea and ideal of education for all, or inclusive and equitable education, are put to real tests in the presence of diverse multilingual learners. Whilst many have argued that multilingualism is a rich and important resource for learning, it is fair to say that most of the so-called bilingual education programmes that exist in the developed world especially are educational programmes for people who are already bilingual rather than aiming to support learners to become bilingual or maintain their bilingualism and multilingualism. Institutional and policy support for multilingual pedagogies is still lacking.

The present volume is a welcome addition to the expanding body of literature that explores issues of diverse contexts of multilingualism and the implications for education. It is also an invitation to further research on these and other issues in an ever-changing world.

Piotr Romanowski
Chapter 1
Introduction: The Many Faces of Multilingualism

Multilingualism is a complex phenomenon that can be studied from different perspectives in disciplines such as linguistics, psycholinguistics, sociolinguistics and education to name but a few from a wide array of fields (Cenoz 2013). As much as multilingualism is a common phenomenon globally, there is a lot of divergence in defining the concept. The unifying focus in research is an interest in individuals and communities that use a number of languages (Aronin and Hufeisen 2004). There are many definitions of multilingualism. For example, Li Wei (2008) defined a multilingual individual as "anyone who can communicate in more than one language, be it active (through speaking and writing) or passive (through listening and reading). The European Commission (2007: 6) has provided a well-known definition of multilingualism: "the ability of societies, institutions, groups and individuals to engage, on a regular basis, with more than one language in their day-to-day lives".

A multilingual is a person who has the ability to use three or more languages, either separately or in various degrees of code-mixing. Those languages are used for various purposes, competence in each varying according to such factors as register, occupation, and education. Multilinguals may not have equal proficiency in or control over all the languages they know (Kemp 2004). The term 'plurilingual' is also applied by some researchers, including the Francophone tradition, to indicate individual as opposed to societal multilingualism (Aronin and Ó Laoire 2004). Plurilingualism is not in every aspect different from multilingualism. It needs to be stated that plurilingualism is first and foremost a term that describes sociolinguistic phenomena in contact situations, where people use two, three or more languages in interactions, as does multilingualism (Marshall and Moore 2016). Perhaps the most notable key point of distinction found in the literature between the *pluri* and the *multi* centres on notions of the social and the individual. Accordingly, we can consider multilingualism (the study of societal contact) and plurilingualism (the study of individuals' repertoires and language agency) (Beacco and Byram 2007, Gajo 2014, Moore and Gajo 2009).

Piotr Romanowski, University of Warsaw, Poland, E-mail: p.romanowski@uw.edu.pl

Research in multilingualism has had an important boost recently and it is one of the most intensely investigated areas of applied linguistics today due to academic interest in globalization and multilingual work environments (Lüdi, Höchle Meier and Yanaprasart 2016; Meyer and Apfelbaum 2010). The ubiquity of multilingualism in private and public interaction is unprecedented worldwide. At the individual level, some of the most researched areas are: the cognitive outcomes of multilingualism (Schwieter 2016); the relationship between language and thought in multilingual speakers (Bylund and Athanasopoulos 2014); multilingual language processing (Bikel and Zitouni 2012); and cross-linguistic interaction in the multilingual brain (Cenoz, Hufeisen and Jessner 2001; Gabryś-Barker 2012; De Angelis, Jessner and Kresic 2015). At the societal level, multilingualism has been examined in relation to globalisation, human mobility, education, and the effect of new communication techniques. Some of the most relevant areas are: multilingualism as a social construct (Fishman 1991[2014]; Stavans and Hoffman 2015); multilingual identities (Pavlenko and Blackledge 2004; Block 2006; Blackwood, Lanza and Woldemariam 2016); multilingual practices (Li Wei and Zhu Hua 2013; Lanza and Lexander 2019) and multilingualism (Grucza, Olpińska-Szkiełko and Romanowski 2016); multilingual education (Gorter, Zenotz and Cenoz 2013; Otwinowska and De Angelis 2014; Garcia, Lin and May 2017; Romanowski and Jedynak 2018), multimodality (De Saint-Georges and Weber 2013) and new technologies (Kelly-Holmes and Milani 2013; Deumart 2014).

There exist almost 7,000 languages in the world and about 200 independent countries (Lewis 2009). It is not only that there are more languages than countries but also that the number of speakers of different languages is unevenly distributed, meaning that speakers of smaller languages need to speak other languages in their daily lives. Multilinguals can be speakers of a minority indigenous language (e.g., Navajo in the United States, Maori in New Zealand, or Welsh in the United Kingdom) who need to learn the dominant language. In other cases, multilingual speakers are immigrants who speak their first language(s) as well as the language(s) of their host countries. In some cases, languages are learned as they spread internationally, and it is believed that they open doors to economic and social opportunity. This is currently the case with English, which is the most widespread language, and it is very common as a school subject and as a language of instruction in schools and universities worldwide (see, e.g., Kirkpatrick and Sussex 2012). Several factors, as indicated earlier, have contributed to the current visibility of multilingualism – among them, globalisation, transnational mobility, and the spread of new technologies are highly influential in different political, social, and educational contexts. In the 21st century, the internet facilitates multilingual communication across great distances, both synchronously and asynchronously. Multilingual communication is multimodal and instantaneous in a variety of modalities. At the same time, globalisation has increased the value of both: societal and individual multilingualism. Speaking different languages has an added value. As Edwards (2004) pointed out, speaking English can be necessary, "but the ability to speak other languages nonetheless ensures a competitive edge". Given its growing importance in modern society, multilingualism has increasingly attracted attention in applied linguistics as can be seen from the titles of articles, books, and academic conferences using the term multilingualism.

The aim of this volume is to showcase diverse perspectives and methodologies in the research on multilingualism. The book presents a range of perspectives and methods including qualitative, quantitative, critical and textual approaches–all within the area of societal and individual multilingualism. It also seeks to promote interdisciplinary research which connects various areas of investigation. We invited manuscripts from diverse research perspectives and language communities so as to provide rich insight into the phenomena of multilingualism and multilingual education. Hence, the disciplinary spectrum represented here includes linguistics, applied linguistics, psychology, neuroscience, sociology, and education. The chapters' discussions are anchored in the literature on early bi-/multilingualism, bi-/multilingual language development, education, competencies, literacy, identity, communities, work environments, later-learned additional languages, language maintenance and attrition.

The discussion of the different cases can provide useful examples of how multilingualism functions across diverse contexts and how multilingual education has been successfully implemented. The study of multilingualism as reported in the 11 chapters of the volume demonstrates the intersection of the social and individual perspectives as multilingualism is taught and enacted in educational settings around the world. Of major significance are the many diverse concepts defined and thoroughly discussed across the pages of the present volume, i.e. minority, language contact, code alternation, multilingual identity, interlingual education, translanguaging, etc. A minority is to be understood as a group numerically inferior to the rest of the population of a particular country, which is in a non-dominant position, and whose members, although being nationals of the country, possess ethnic, religious or linguistic characteristics differing from those of the rest of the population (Capotorti 1979). In various settings minority and majority languages come to contact. Language contact is the social and linguistic phenomenon by which speakers of different languages interact with one another, leading to a transfer of linguistic features. Two languages or codes can come to contact by means of code alternation, too. Code alternation describes the alternating use of two recognisable grammatical systems (Muysken 1997). Yet one might think that there is no difference between code alternation and code-switching. However, these are two different ways of thinking about language output, where the first relates more to the grammatical form and the second to the communicative function. Both concepts seem to exist in multilingual speakers, or speakers who have constructed the so-called multilingual identity. This notion describes speakers who have developed an awareness of their own linguistic repertoire. Multilingual identity formation can be viewed in terms of learners' active involvement in the language learning process who can constantly (re)negotiate their own identity, both in and out the classroom (Fisher et al. 2018). The term of interlingual education is somehow related to the issue of multilingual identity formation. It is defined as the social process of facilitating the building of knowledge, competences and values through the active use of several languages in the learning process (Yamamoto 2001). Finally yet importantly, translanguaging frequently observed in interlingual education, having a clear pedagogical dimension – sometimes questioned and viewed as a re-conceptualisation of code-switching or code alternation – shaping a multilingual speaker's identity and being part of their life, referring to both majority (prestigious) and minority languages, hence affecting language contact (Garcia and Li Wei 2014).

As such, this volume, composed of eleven chapters, has been divided into two thematic parts. The first part, "(Socio) Linguistic Aspects of Multilingualism", is devoted to the role of heritage and minority languages as well language contact and language policies. It consists of five chapters where each one of them has clear theoretical grounds and is supported by detailed examinations of the evidence. The blending of the voices outlined by the contributors are grounded in experience in different geographical regions allowing the reader to see how multilingual themes are tackled in Poland, Brazil, Canada, Japan, and Germany. The second part: "Pedagogical Aspects of Multilingualism" focuses on a series of contextualised studies related to multilingual classrooms with diverse research designs applied in different educational settings, such as: Spain, Poland, Latvia, Malta, and South Africa. The chapters focus on the numerous and heterogeneous relations between languages and look at international student internships, projects, and study-abroad programs as well as the latest thinking on the role of higher education in developing multilingual programs, with a unique emphasis on newer voices from such places as: South Africa. The authors also report on the curricula and reforms, and foreign language education. Last but not least, they give an insight into multilingual school settings showcasing successful examples of educational institutions where rates of multilingualism have soared.

The first part opens with Piotr Romanowski's contribution to the volume, a detailed overview of minority languages in the Polish education system has been provided. The author outlines changes in legislation both at national and EU levels pertaining to minorities and their respective languages. He then presents the scope of teaching in minority languages, as both a subject of study and medium of instruction, by drawing on the results of the 2018/2019 Education Report drawn up by the Polish Statistics Office. The question that Edenize Ponzo Peres, Kyria Rebeca Finardi and Poliana Claudiano Calazans address in the third chapter seeks an answer to the problem of how to preserve multilingualism in Brazil through elaborating on language policies that promote understanding and tolerance among cultures, languages and identities. The authors describe the social history of Guarani – a language spoken by one of Brazil's many indigenous groups. In addition, their study is motivated by the observation that most public education in Brazil is offered in Portuguese leading to the exclusion of native languages and jeopardising their cultures. Based on his ethnographic study, in the subsequent chapter Martin Guardado examines a Mexican-Canadian family's language ideologies and heritage language practices. Drawing on data from participant observation, naturalistic linguistic interactions, and interviews, Chapter 4 encompasses a deep analysis of how the parents attempted to socialise their children into particular ideologies and identities. Hiroki Hanamoto, in Chapter 5, explores the functions performed by gesture sequences and turn-taking strategies in the Philippines. He elaborates on the function of negotiation serving as a possible solution to overcoming communication differences, misunderstandings and enhancing clarity in the course of interaction in multilingual settings. This part closes with Chapter 6 authored by Anna Khalizova, who draws our attention to the phenomenon of code alternation among multilingual speakers. She based her investigation on an audio and video corpus of form-based data collection interviews in an enrolment office at a German university, which are part of the enrolment procedure for international students. In her study, strong cultural diversity is visible due to the fact that students originate from almost fifty countries and German and English are used in the conversations.

The second part begins with a chapter by Asunción Martínez-Arbelaiz and Isabel Pereira who investigate the relationship between identity and language proficiency development among multilingual and multicultural students in study-abroad programmes. The authors of Chapter 7 indicate the role of identity in the SLA research observed in various social contexts affected by global mobility and the social positioning of self and others. In Chapter 8, Anna Szczepaniak-Kozak delves into the issue of pragmatic features transferred from one language to another. She analysed interference errors on the bases of English, Polish and German and concluded that they were predominantly driven by the students' mother tongue. The contribution by Vita Kalnberzina addresses the issue of language curriculum reform in Latvia. In her work (Chapter 9), Kalnberzina examines the results of state examinations in foreign languages in relation to the plurilingual repertoire level descriptors applied in accordance with the new 2018 Common European Framework of Reference promoted by the Council of Europe. Antoinette Camilleri Grima discusses pluralistic approaches in foreign language education based on examples from her own country, Malta, in Chapter 10. She highlights the existence of a paradigm shift in foreign language pedagogy and stresses the ubiquity in the present-day education system of learners who are equipped with competence in two or three languages and the experience of cultures different from their own. The chapter that follows, by Natalia Barranco Izquierdo and M. Teresa Calderón Quindós, concentrates on the necessity of developing intercultural and interlingual competence in schools, based on European policies on education and immigration. The authors of Chapter 11 offer useful advice on how to solve communicative conflicts among students in a multicultural classroom arising due to the presence of two or more tongues and diverse home cultures. In addition, they attempt to provide school teachers with an action guide to minimise these conflicts in the school environment. The body chapters of the volume end with a chapter by Vimbai Mbirimi-Hungwe, who examines the significant role of translanguaging in higher education. In Chapter 12 she argues that translanguaging should be advocated in the teaching of content subjects (Maths, Statistics, Physics and Computer Science) for the benefit of students, and English-only pedagogies in teaching content in all subject areas are not the best alternative.

With this volume the editors hope to have successfully responded to the voices of wider research communities. The present collection seems needed as the number of publications in the field of multilingualism is still insufficient. It is worth reiterating that because a wider spectrum of topics is being examined in this book, the editors sincerely hope that the findings discussed in the collection might contribute to the better understanding of "multilingual themes" omnipresent in our contemporary, globalised, yet still very differentiated and diverse world.

References

De Angelis, Gessica, Ulrike Jessner & Marijana Kresic. (eds.). 2015. *Crosslinguistic Influence and Crosslinguistic Interaction in Multilingual Language Learning*. London: Bloomsbury Academic.
Aronin, Larissa & Britta Hufeisen. (eds.). 2004. *The exploration of multilingualism. Development of research on L3, multilingualism and multiple language acquisition*. Amsterdam: John Benjamins.
Aronin, Larissa & Muiris Ó Laoire. 2004. Exploring Multilingualism in Cultural Contexts: Towards a Notion of Multilinguality. In Charlotte Hoffmann & Jehannes Ytsma, (eds.). *Trilingualism in Family, School and Community*. Clevedon: Multilingual Matters.

Beacco Jean-Claude & Michael Byram. 2007. *From linguistic diversity to plurilingual education: Guide for the development of language education policies in Europe.* Strasbourg: Council of Europe.
Bikel, Daniel & Imed Zitouni. 2012. *Multilingual Natural Language Processing Applications.* Indianapolis: IBM Press.
Blackwood, Robert, Elizabeth Lanza & Hirut Woldemariam. (eds.). 2016. *Negotiating and Contesting Identities in Linguistic Landscapes.* London: Bloomsbury Academic.
Block, David. 2006. *Multilingual Identities in a Global City.* Basingstoke: Palgrave Macmillan.
Bylund, Emanuel & Panos Athanasopoulos. 2014. Language and thought in a multilingual context: The case of isiXhosa. *Bilingualism: Language and Cognition 12 (2)*, 431–441.
Capotorti, Francesco. 1979. *Study on the Rights of Persons Belonging to Ethnic, Religious and Linguistic Minorities.* New York: United Nations.
Cenoz, Jasone. 2013. Defining Multilingualism. *Annual Review of Applied Linguistics 33*, 3–18.
Cenoz, Jasone, Britta Hufeisen & Ulrike Jessner. (eds.) 2001. *Cross-linguistic Influence in Third Language Acquisition: Psycholinguistic Perspectives.* Clevedon: Multilingual Matters.
Cenoz, Jasone & Durk Gorter. 2015. *Multilingual Education: Between Language Learning and Translanguaging.* Cambridge: Cambridge University Press.
Deumert, Anna. 2014. *Sociolinguistics and mobile communication.* Edinburgh: Edinburgh University Press.
Edwards, Viv. 2004. *Multilingualism in the English-speaking world.* Oxford: Blackwell.
European Commission. 2007. Final Report: High Level Group on Multilingualism. Luxembourg: Office for Official Publications of the European Communities. Retrieved from https://op.europa.eu/en/publication-detail/-/publication/b0a1339f-f181-4de5-abd3-130180f177c7
Fisher, Linda, Michael Evans, Karen Forbes, Angela Gayton & Yongcan Liu. 2018. Participative multilingual identity constriction in the languages classroom: a multi-theoretical conceptualisation. International Journal of Multilingualism. https://doi.org/10.1080/14790718.2018.1524896
Fishman, Joshua A. (ed.). 1991 [2014]. *Advances in the Study of Societal Multilingualism.* Berlin: Walter De Gruyter.
Gabryś-Barker, Danuta (ed.). 2012. *Cross-linguistic Influences in Multilingual Language Acquisition.* Dordrecht: Springer.
Gajo, Laurent. 2014. From normalization to didactization of multilingualism: European and francophone research at the crossroads between linguistics and didactics. In: Conteh Jean and Gabriela Meier (eds.). *The Multilingual Turn in Languages Education: Opportunities and Challenges.* pp. 113–131. Clevedon: Multilingual Matters.
Garcia, Ofelia & Li Wei. 2014. *Translanguaging: Language, Bilingualism and Education.* New York, NY: Palgrave Macmillan.
García, Ofelia, Angel Lin, & Stephen May. (eds.). 2017. *Bilingual and Multilingual Education.* Dordrecht: Springer.
Gorter, Durk, Victoria Zenotz & Jasone Cenoz. (eds.). 2013. *Minority Languages and Multilingual Education: Bridging the Local and the Global.* Dordrecht: Springer.
Grucza Sambor, Magdalena Olpińska-Szkiełko & Piotr Romanowski. (eds.). 2016. *Advances in Understanding Multilingualism.* Frankfurt/ Main: Peter Lang Academic Publishers.
Kelly-Holmes, Helen & Tommaso M. Milani. (eds.). 2013. *Thematising multilingualism in the media.* Amsterdam: John Benjamins.

Kemp, Charlotte. 2004. Defining multilingualism. In Larissa Aronin & Britta Hufeisen. (eds.)., *The exploration of multilingualism. Development of research on L3, multilingualism and multiple language acquisition*. Amsterdam: John Benjamins.

Kirkpatrick, Andy & Roland Sussex. (eds.). 2012. *English as an international language in Asia: Implications for language education*. Berlin: Springer.

Lanza, Elizabeth & Kristin Vold Lexander. (2019). Family language practices in multilingual transcultural families. In Simona Montanari & Suzanne Quay (eds.)., *Multidisciplinary Perspectives on Multilingualism: The Fundamentals*, pp. 229–252. Berlin: Mouton de Gruyter.

Lewis, M. Paul. (ed.). 2009. *Ethnologue: Languages of the world*. Dallas: SIL International. Retrieved from http://www.ethnologue.com/

Li, Wei. 2008. Research perspectives on bilingualism and multilingualism. In Li Wei & Melissa G. Moyer (eds.), *The Blackwell Handbook of Research Methods on Bilingualism and Multilingualism*, pp. 3–17. Oxford: Blackwell.

Li, Wei & Hua Zhu. 2013. Translanguaging identities: creating transnational space through flexible multilingual practices amongst Chinese university students in the UK. *Applied Linguistics 34 (5)*, 516–535.

Lüdi Georges, Katharina Höchle Meier & Patchareerat Yanaprasart. (eds.). 2016. *Managing Plurilingual and Intercultural Practices in the Workplace: The case of Switzerland*. Amsterdam: John Benjamins Publishing Company.

Marshall, Steve & Danièle Moore. 2016. Plurilingualism amid the panoply of lingualisms: addressing critiques and misconceptions in education. *International Journal of Multilingualism, 15*, 19–34.

Meyer Bernd & Birgit Apfelbaum. (eds.). 2010. *Multilingualism at work. From policies to practices in public, medical and business settings*. Amsterdam: John Benjamins Publishing Company.

Muysken, Pieter. 1997. Code-switching processes. Alternation, insertion, congruent lexicaliztation. In Putz, Martin (ed.), *Language choices. Conditions, constraints, and consequences*, pp. 361–380. Amsterdam: John Benjamins Publishing Company.

Otwinowska, Agnieszka & Gessica De Angelis. (eds.). 2014. *Teaching and Learning in Multilingual Contexts: Sociolinguistic and Educational Perspectives*. Clevedon: Multilingual Matters.

Pavlenko, Aneta & Adrian Blackledge. (eds.). 2004. *Negotiation of Identities in Multilingual Contexts*. Clevedon: Multilingual Matters.

Romanowski, Piotr & Małgorzata Jedynak. (eds.). 2018. *Current Research in Bilingualism and Bilingual Education*. Dordrecht: Springer.

De Saint-Georges, Ingrid & Jean-Jacques Weber. (eds.). 2013. *Multilingualism and Multimodality. Current Challenges for Educational Studies*. Rotterdam: Sense Publishers-Springer.

Schwieter, John W. (ed.). 2016. *Cognitive control and consequences of multilingualism*. Amsterdam: John Benjamins Publishing Company.

Stavans, Anat & Charlotte Hoffman. 2015. *Multilingualism*. Cambridge: Cambridge University Press.

Yamamoto, Masayo. 2001. *Language use in interlingual families: A Japanese-English sociolinguistic study*. Clevedon: Multilingual Matters.

Part I: (Socio)Linguistic Aspects of Multilingualism

Piotr Romanowski
Chapter 2
The Polish Linguistic Map: An Overview of Minority Languages in the Education System

Abstract: The present chapter discusses the multiethnic and multilingual character of Poland – a country that has been regarded as monolingual due to the existence of only one official language. A myriad of factors resulting from the presence of 13 minorities in Poland shape and affect the present-day education system. In this chapter, I outline the changes in the legislature both at national and the EU levels regarding national, ethnic, and regional minorities. I then present results from the 2011 national census, which shed light on the numerous nationalities to which the inhabitants of Poland claim to belong. Finally, yet importantly, I present the scope of teaching in minority languages, as both a subject of study and medium of instruction, by drawing on the results of the 2018/2019 Education Report prepared by the Polish Statistics Office.

Keywords: ethnic minorities, regional minorities, national minorities, minority languages, Poland, education

1 Introduction

There are over 38 million citizens of the Republic of Poland living in Poland. A vast majority of them – 95% – have declared Polish to be their native language. The remaining 5% articulate their familiarity with Polish, however, officially they constitute part of the so-called national and ethnic minorities (Komorowska 2013). Hence, to some extent, it may be stated that Poland is a uniform state in terms of ethnicity and has the lowest percentage of minorities in the EU.

If we look at the history, the territory of the Republic of Poland has always been inhabited by a much higher percentage of national and ethnic minorities, which points to its huge linguistic diversity (Moskal 2004). Before the Third Partition of Poland in 1795 about 40% of the population consisted of national and ethnic minorities. In those times, the territories of Lithuania, Belarus, most

---

Piotr Romanowski, University of Warsaw, Poland, E-mail: p.romanowski@uw.edu.pl

of present-day Ukraine and Poland were part of one state or a union of states (the Polish-Lithuanian Commonwealth, 1385–1795). This country was also often referred to as the Republic of Many Nations, which clearly demonstrated the multilingual landscape of the former Poland.

Between World War I and World War II (1918–1939), after Poland regained the independence as much as 33% of its citizens declared a different ethnicity. They inhabited over half of the country's territory (Majewicz and Wicherkiewicz 1998). According to Kersten (1989) the population of Poland at the time consisted of Ukrainians and Russians (15%), Jews (9.5%), Belarusians (3.5%), Germans (2%) and other minorities (3%). These numbers decreased dramatically to only 3% after World War II, meaning that Poland became a one-nation and monolingual state, which was the result of border-shifting, migration, and the holocaust (Dąbrowska 2014). In the Polish People's Republic, the country that was created after World War II, the government adopted a policy against linguistic and ethnic minorities, which was typical of the whole Eastern bloc and the newly-created countries of Eastern Europe at the time.

Currently, the largest minority groups in Poland are German, Ukrainian, and Belarusian, and the smallest ones are Slovak, Czech, Armenian, Tatar, and Karaim (Pisarek 2011). As far as regional languages are concerned, Kashubian is spoken in the north of the country – a language celebrating its revival.

There are two research questions addressed in this paper: 1/ What minority languages exist in the Polish education system?, and 2/ What is the scope of teaching in minority languages? Divergent minority contexts will be discussed throughout the chapter in order to inform readers about the status of particular languages as well as strengthen their general role and visibility.

2 Defining "minority"

No consensus has been reached as to how minorities should be defined in international law, since the issue has to be approached from a different perspective in each case (Baranowska 2014). Article 27 of *the International Covenant on Civil and Political Rights* (1966) stipulates that persons belonging to ethnic, religious, or linguistic minorities shall be granted the right to avail of their own culture, practise their own religion, and use their own language in states or territories where such minorities exist. A major distinction between national and ethnic minorities is to be made, though. The first group identify themselves with a nation organised in their own state (e.g., the Hungarian language spoken in

Slovakia or Romania) whereas the latter one does not (e.g., the Frisian language spoken in the Dutch province of Fryslân in the Netherlands) (van Dongera, van der Meer, and Sterk 2017).

In the 1970s, Capotorti (who used to work for the United Nations) made another attempt to provide a definition of the term "minority":

> A group numerically inferior to the rest of the population of a State, in a non-dominant position, whose members–being nationals of the State–possess ethnic, religious or linguistic characteristics differing from those of the rest of the population and show, if only implicitly, a sense of solidarity, directed towards preserving their culture, traditions, religion or language. (1979, 14)

Given that Poland is situated in the European context, Capotorti's (1979) definition seems to be the most satisfactory. However, there is still an ongoing debate in some countries about whether a minority group needs to be linked historically to a certain territory or not in order to be defined as such (Hoffman 2007).

2.1 The legal regulations concerning minorities and their languages

The legal status of minorities and their languages is outlined both at the level of national and international acts. The principal document regulating the status of minorities in Poland, including linguistic minorities, is the *National and Ethnic Minorities and Regional Language Act* of 6 January 2005, which is the first legal act of its kind in the post-war history of Poland. According to the Polish law, nine national and four ethnic minorities exist in Poland. Further, the speakers of Kashubian are recognised as a linguistic minority (although not a national, nor an ethnic one) due to the fact that this language is considered regional (Pisarek 2011). Similarly, the status of the Silesians, from the south of Poland, and their language, Silesian, has been disputed for a long time. The Polish authorities do not acknowledge their rank as a national group, but a regional one.

Poland is rightly regarded as a country actively involved in the protection of minority groups' rights. It is a signatory of the *European Charter for Regional or Minority Languages* (1992) and the *Framework Convention for the Protection of National Minorities* (1991). In addition, minorities are protected in Poland by the *Constitution of the Republic of Poland* (1997) (Article 35), which grants them many rights related to their languages, education, and culture.

2.2 The linguistic map of minorities in Poland

With the ratification of the *European Charter for Regional or Minority Languages* by the Republic of Poland in 2009, the following languages were recognised as minority languages: Armenian, Belarusian, Czech, German, Hebrew, Karaim, Kashubian, Lithuanian, Lemkian (often referred to as Ruthenian), Romani, Russian, Slovak, Tatar, Ukrainian, and Yiddish. Within this category, there are languages of national groups whose state is outside the territory of a particular country; thus their standard varieties are official languages of other countries, e.g., Belarusian, Czech, German, Lithuanian, Russian, Slovak, and Ukrainian. Further, since the remaining eight languages (Armenian, Hebrew, Karaim, Kashubian, Lemkian, Romani, Tatar, and Yiddish) are not spoken by indigenous groups inhabiting their traditional lands in another state, their languages do not possess the official status of state language(s).

In other words, Armenian, Belarusian, Czech, German, Hebrew, Lithuanian, Russian, Slovak, Ukrainian, and Yiddish were labelled as languages of national minorities, while Karaim, Lemkian, Romani, and Tatar were labelled as languages of ethnic minorities. In addition, Armenian, Hebrew, Karaim, Romani, and Yiddish are also often referred to as diaspora languages. It should also be pointed out that some sources list these languages as non-territorial languages (Pisarek 2011).

Lastly, another interesting issue pertains to the role of regional languages. Regional languages are spoken by indigenous groups, and because of their relationship to the official/majority languages, they are sometimes regarded as dialects of official languages although the issue is debatable and controversial. Four languages spoken in Poland can be found within this group: Kashubian, Silesian, Lemkian, and Wilamowicean (Moskal 2004).

2.3 Speakers of minority languages in numbers

It is hard to determine precisely how many people and how many speakers of particular minority languages inhabit the territory of Poland as there is a divergence between the data submitted by the representatives of minorities and the results of the 2011 national census. In addition, respondents sometimes declared they were members of two different nations and linguistic communities. The matter was further complicated by respondents who claimed to have a nationality other than Polish without specifying which one they held.

It is also assumed that a declaration of nationality signifies a declaration of a particular native tongue, although I will outline some discrepancies below.

Chapter 2 The Polish Linguistic Map: An Overview of Minority Languages

The results of the 2011 national census revealed that a uniform national identity dominates among the citizens of Poland (36,522,221 people, or 94.8% of the total population). A non-Polish national/ ethnic identity was voiced by 1.5% of the people (596,303 citizens) and within this group 45,899 people identified with two nationalities. Dual citizenship was declared by 917,339 inhabitants (including Polish 871,440, or 2.3%). According to the 2011 National Census, in general, the Polish national identity (both uniform and dual) was expressed by 37,393,651 citizens (97.1% of the total population).The results of the 2011 national census, as far as the minorities are concerned, are presented in Table 2.1.

Table 2.1: Minorities According to the 2011 National Census.

MINORITIES IN NUMBERS BY DECLARED NATIONALITY		
NATIONAL MINORITIES	Armenian	3,623
	Belarusian	46,787
	Czech	3,447
	German	147,814
	Lithuanian	7,863
	Russian	13,046
	Slovak	3,240
	Ukrainian	51,001
ETHNIC MINORITIES	Karaim	346
	Lemkian	10,531
	Romani	17,049
	Tatar	1,916
REGIONAL MINORITIES	Kashubian	232,547

It is assumed that indicating the place where particular national and ethnic minorities reside might be of significance in this study. The results of the 2011 national census showed that most representatives of minorities inhabit the country's major cities: Warsaw, Cracow, Gdańsk, Katowice, and Wrocław, and the provinces along the Polish borders. The provinces with the highest density of minorities are Pomeranian in the north, and Silesian and Opole in the south (around 10% of all the people are located in each). As Pomeranian Province is where the Kashubians live, it is interesting to note that this regional minority resides mainly outside of major urban centres; instead, they live along the province from the north to the south in small towns and cities and villages. The German minority resides in the other two provinces located in the south of Poland, along the Czech border. This is also where Silesian is spoken, however it has not yet been recognised officially, contrary to Kashubian; hence, there have been disputes over its legitimacy for several decades. It is worth emphasising though that according to the results of the 2011 census, Silesian has over 500,000 speakers in both provinces. Podlasian Province in the north-east of Poland reached about ca. 7–8% of Belarusian and Lithuanian speakers. This province borders Belarus and Lithuania, so it is no surprise that the two minority groups are found there. The Ukrainian minority is well represented in four provinces: Subcarpathian and Lublin in the south-east, as well as Warmia-Masuria in the north-east and Pomerania in the north. That the highest density of Ukrainians can be found in the first two provinces (around 5%) is unremarkable, due to their geographical location along the border with Ukraine. The other two provinces in the north are the result of shifting borders and resettlement following World War II. Speakers of Romani are dispersed all over the country and settle in large urban centres as well as small towns, particularly in Greater Poland, Świętokrzyskie, and Łódzkie Provinces – all situated in the centre of Poland. The Romani are also represented in the south-east of Poland, in Subcarpathia. The density estimates about 1% in each of the four provinces. Finally, the Lemkians are found in four provinces. Two of them, Subcarpathia and Lesser Poland in the south-east, are where they have lived for three generations. The other two provinces of Lower Silesia and Lubusz Land, situated in the south-west along the borders with the Czech Republic and Germany, are the regions where they were resettled after World War II, having been displaced and stripped of their land in the south-east of Poland. Lemkians reside in Lower Silesia, however, ca. 2% and Lubusz Land with 1%. The highest numbers of Russian minority speakers have been noted in the largest Polish cities of Warsaw, Cracow, and Łódź where they are estimated to make up around 0.5% of the total population.

Interestingly, the 2011 national census provided some additional information on the complexity of national and ethnic identities. It was the first time after World War II Polish citizens had been allowed to express their dual nationality and/or identity. Further, similarly to the 2002 national census, the respondents were interrogated about the language they used at home. As a result, 948,523 people reported using languages other than Polish (176,520 speakers of one or two non-Polish languages), or switching between another language and

Polish (772,003 speakers). The most widely spoken minority/ ethnic or regional languages were Kashubian (108,140), Belarusian (26,448), Ukrainian (24,539), and Russian (19,805). The data also showed that other languages than Polish were spoken by a larger group of respondents when compared to the number of people who declared either a non-Polish or dual national/ ethnic identity (917,339) (Rykała 2014).

Finally, yet importantly, the issue of mother tongue was first highlighted in the 2011 national census (previously it was included in the national census of 1931). This aspect shed light on the problem of national and ethnic minorities in Poland. Mother tongues were not regarded as identical to languages spoken at home. The mother tongue was the first language one learnt. A non-Polish mother tongue was declared by 333,892 speakers – Silesian (140,012), German (58,170), Ukrainian (28,172), Belarusian (17,480), and Russian (17,048). Hence, there were fewer declarations regarding non-Polish mother tongues than languages used at home. This discrepancy can be explained in most cases by declaring more than one language spoken at home when compared to one mother tongue (Rykała 2014).

3 Minorities and their languages: Problems and challenges

As indicated in the introductory part of this chapter, Polish is the country's official language and there are no autonomous regions that would envisage the official use of other languages in public domains. The *National and Ethnic Minorities and Regional Language Act* specified how the freedom granted by *the Constitution of the Republic of Poland* could turn into practice the issues related to education, bilingual signage, local administration, media, and cultural life (Brohy et al. 2019). The legislature offers very favourable conditions for the promotion of minority languages in Poland. However, the situation of each minority group and their language is not as positive as state law suggests it might be.

Most minority languages suffer from problems with their ethnolinguistic vitality to varying degrees (Brohy et al. 2019). The German minority, which is the largest national minority in Poland, faces problems with the intergenerational transmission of their language, which means that their children do not acquire German at home, but they start learning it at school. The Ukrainian, Belarusian, Lithuanian, Lemkian, and Kashubian minorities have the most balanced status as the majority of them speak their minority language. However, with increased mobility, these groups are also potentially in danger of disrupting intergenerational language transmission practices and possibilities. The smallest minority groups either no longer use their languages (Tatar, Karaim), have very few speakers (Czech, Slovak, Yiddish and Hebrew), or are the new immigrants rather than the traditional minority members (Armenian, Russian). The Romani community, due to the non-territorial nature of their language, finds it hard to exercise the right to use it with the local authorities, which is also the case with Armenian, Yiddish, and Hebrew.

The right to use minority languages enshrined in Polish law should theoretically help reverse these negative intergenerational trends and foster the use of minority languages (Brohy et al. 2019). In practice it is each minority community's ability to exert pressure on the local authorities that might lead to a change. Another obstacle halting the promotion of minority languages in Poland is low levels of popular awareness of their existence. The average Polish citizen has very little knowledge about the multiethnic and multilingual nature of the Polish society, and so stereotypical or even hostile attitudes towards otherness are common. Therefore, it becomes clear why exercising the rights enshrined in the legal framework experiences problems with implementation.

3.1 Minority languages in the education system

It is also important to note that the members of national and ethnic minorities as well as communities using a regional language (e.g., Kashubian) are required to learn Polish. If they choose to, minorities may also participate in activities and classes aimed at maintaining their minoritised language and culture. A minority language can become the language of instruction or a second language of instruction (in bilingual education). Alternatively, it can function as a non-compulsory subject. A class may be established for as few as seven pupils interested in learning a language at their parents' request. In the case of dispersed minorities, minority language teaching may be organised in inter-school groups with sizes between three and 20 pupils (Poszytek et al. 2005).

The state funds, staffs, and otherwise coordinates minority language teaching and learning in Poland. In some cases, children are supposed to learn almost all school subjects in their minority or regional language at all levels of compulsory education (Brohy et al. 2019). Currently, however, Lithuanian and Ukrainian are the only minority languages offered as languages of instruction. The German minority has been struggling to establish bilingual education but with no success. There is also the option of learning regional or minority languages as school subjects in the case of Belarusian, Kashubian, Lemko, and Ukrainian.

As Wicherkiewicz (2005) has observed, Polish Lithuanians are in fact the only minority group in the country who have developed a fully bilingual school curriculum: from pre-school education up to the university level. All the minority language schools in Podlasian Province offer bilingual education in Polish and Lithuanian; however the amount of hours provided in both languages varies according to the school type. There are schools with Lithuanian as the language of instruction where all the subjects except for the Polish language and literature, history, geography, and foreign languages are taught in Lithuanian, with Lithuanian language and literature being taught for four hours a week. The curriculum in bilingual schools also includes courses in the history and geography of Lithuania (one hour per week). On the other hand, schools with Lithuanian as an additional language exist, too. In this case, all the subjects are taught in Polish, and Lithuanian is treated as a subject taught for three hours per week.

The majority of Ukrainians reside in the following six provinces: Warmia-Masuria, Pomerania, Western Pomerania, Lower Silesia, Podlasie, and Subcarpathia. Lemko/ Ruthenian people, on the other hand, are present in Lower Silesia and Little Poland – the latter being the original habitat of that minority group. Wicherkiewicz and Syrnyk (2006) explain that all schools available in the provinces listed above offer classes in Ukrainian or Lemkian/ Ruthenian and/or bilingual education in Polish and Ukrainian. The curriculum is similar to the one adopted for Lithuanian as it provides learners and their parents with some choices. Schools with Ukrainian as a language of instruction offer most subjects in Ukrainian except for Polish language and literature, history, geography, and foreign languages. Ukrainian language and literature is taught four times per week. These schools also make it possible for learners to study the history and geography of Ukraine for one hour a week. Schools that offer Lemko/ Ruthenian as an additional language teach all other the subjects in Polish, whereas Lemko/ Ruthenian is taught as a separate subject for three hours a week.

The Belarusian minority, similarly to the Lithuanian one, resides mostly in the Podlasian Province. Unfortunately, the number of pupils learning Belarusian and learning in Belarusian is decreasing. In the 1960s the number of those learning Belarusian reached 12,000. In comparison, in the 2007/2008 school year, it had dropped to 3,000. There are bilingual kindergartens that offer instruction in both Polish and Belarusian. It is possible to learn Belarusian as an additional subject in primary and secondary schools; however there are no institutions where Belarusian would be a language of instruction (Barszczewska 2009). This makes the role of Belarusian weaker in the education system when contrasted with the roles performed by Lithuanian and Ukrainian.

3.2 Minority languages in the education system in numbers

The teaching of minority, ethnic, and regional languages takes place across the whole education system, and it involves all types of educational institutions from kindergarten to post-primary schools. According to Article 17 of the *National and Ethnic Minorities and Regional Language Act* of 6 January 2005, nine national minority languages, four ethnic minority languages, and one regional language are recognised in Poland.

Table 2.2: Distribution of school types and languages.

	Belarusian	Kashubian	Lithuanian	Lemkian	German	Slovak	Ukrainian
Total	1065						
Primary Schools	27	328	7	25	569	7	91
Total	70,664						
Primary School Students	1,757	17,048	363	208	49,402	164	1,355
Total	76						
Lower Secondary Schools	3	29	1	1	36	0	4
Total	804						
Lower Secondary Schools Students	60	228	2	0	473	0	14
Total	71						
Upper Secondary Schools	6	35	2	0	14	0	13
Total	1,909						
Upper Secondary Schools Students	445	962	67	0	157	0	265

A total number of 73,400 children attended all education levels: primary, lower- and upper-secondary, post-primary in the 2018/2019 school year (Education Report in 2018/19 School Year). These educational institutions offer either all instruction in a minority, ethnic, or a regional language or a possibility to learn one of these languages. There were 70,664 pupils in 1,065 primary schools, 804 pupils in lower-secondary schools in 76 lower-secondary schools, and 1,909 students in 71 upper-secondary and other post-primary schools (see Table 2.2).

German is the language of the largest national minority in Poland. 569 primary schools all over the country offered education for the German minority, which accounted for 53.4% of all primary schools educating children in the languages of national and ethnic minorities. The German minority comprised 69.9% of the total number of pupils in all primary schools for national and ethnic minorities. The same tendency is visible for lower-secondary schools, which were eliminated in the 2018/2019 school year according to the 2017 Education Reform. The primary school cycle was extended by two years and re-establishing the two-tier education system that had existed prior to 1999 (Romanowski 2019). 47.4% of lower-secondary schools provided education in German as a minority language while only 8.2% of students were from the German minority (14 schools).

38.2% of schools offered education in Kashubian (the only regional language whose status has been acknowledged). The popularity of Kashubian in the education system is increasing year by year. The highest proportion of students is in primary education where 17,048 students were learning this language in 328 schools in the 2018/2019 school year. Those learning Kashubian in lower-secondary schools accounted for 28.4% of all the pupils. A clear dominance of this language is observed in upper-secondary education where 962 students, out of all 1,909 minority language students at this level, were those who enrolled in learning Kashubian.

Another notable phenomenon refers to studying Belarusian with a high number of students enrolled at the primary level of education (27 schools and 1,757 students). A similar trend is true for Ukrainian, however the number of primary schools is much higher (91) though the number of students is lower (1,355). This may suggest that the learners of Ukrainian are more dispersed than those of Belarusian.

Despite having a strong position in Poland, Lithuanian is taught in seven primary schools attended by 363 students (0.5% of all the pupils at this level). It is also interesting to bring up the situation of Slovak, which according to the data, has only started to be taught. It only exists in seven primary schools educating 164 pupils in total.

The remaining learners belonged to the Lemkian minority and accounted for 0.2% of the total number of students (Education Report in 2018/19 School Year).

4 Concluding remarks

Although Poland is officially a monolingual country, it celebrates the multi-ethnicity and multilingualism of its minorities as it has adhered to the various regulations regarding ethnic, national and regional minorities at both national and international levels. It has also generously offered financial support towards the development of education for children in minority groups, as is apparent in the results of the 2011 national census. In addition, the data of the Education Report in 2018/2019 School Year also show that the status of the major minority groups has been recognised and that their languages are represented in the education system.

What is interesting in Poland is that members of different minority groups vary in terms of their attitude towards their language. Kashubians place significant symbolic value on their regional language, just as the Lithuanians, Lemkians, and Germans do with their mother tongues. Other minority groups suffer the loss of their languages (e.g., Karaims and Tatars). However, the most serious sociopolitical problem connected with linguistic minorities in Poland may be related to the status of the present-day Silesian dialect. Due to the presence of over 530,000 Silesians in the provinces of Silesia and Opole, its promotion to the position of a regional language may be the next likely step that would, at the same time, solve the issue of partial recognition.

As Gorter, Zenotz and Cenoz (2013) report minority language groups have a strong local dimension. Most of them are spoken in a limited area of a country or sometimes across the borders of more than one state. Although the use of minority languages can be contested, their speakers treat them as part of their identity and a vehicle of everyday communication. Minority groups perceive education as a safeguarding force for the revival or the development of their languages. The state usually promotes national cohesion through strong propagation of the standard majority language for general use, often at the expense of minority languages. This is also experienced in Poland. As has been outlined in the present paper, today in their struggle for survival various minority groups try to obtain a place in the educational system, e.g. Ukrainian in the case of Poland. Policy makers need to understand that education is no longer about teaching one language, i.e. Polish. If we employ teaching a minority language, we may initiate bilingual education, because our aim is not to replace the majority language completely, but have and use both languages alongside.

References

Baranowska, Grażyna. 2014. Legal regulations on national and ethnic minorities in Poland. *Przegląd Zachodni*, No. 2, 35–48.

Barszczewska, Nina. 2009. Język białoruski w Polsce: historia i stan obecny [Belarusian in Poland: History and its Present State]. *Acta Polono-Ruthenica* 14, 339–351.

Brohy, Claudine, Vicent Climent-Ferrando, Aleksandra Oszmiańska-Pagett & Fernando Ramallo. 2019. *European Charter for Regional and Minority Languages. Classroom Activities*. Strasbourg: Council of Europe.

Capotorti, Francesco. 1979. *Study on the Rights of Persons Belonging to Ethnic, Religious and Linguistic Minorities*. New York: United Nations.

Dąbrowska, Anna. 2014. Multilingual education in Poland. *EFNIL*, 121–126.

van Dongera, Rixt, Cor van der Meer, & Richt Sterk. 2017. *Research for CULT Committee – Minority languages and education: best practices and pitfalls*, European Parliament, Policy Department for Structural and Cohesion Policies, Brussels.

Education Report in the 2018/2019 School Year. 2019. Warsaw/Gdańsk: Statistics Office, accessed: 25th April 2020. https://stat.gov.pl/en/topics/education/education/education-in-the-20182019-school-year,1,15.html

Gorter, Durk, Victoria Zenotz & Jasone Cenoz. (eds.). 2013. *Minority Languages and Multilingual Education: Bridging the Local and the Global*. Dordrecht: Springer.

Hoffman, Rainer. 2007. Minorities, European Protection. In *Max Planck Encyclopedia of Public International Law*. Oxford: Oxford University Press.

Kersten, Krystyna. 1989. Polska – państwo narodowe. Dylematy i rzeczywistość [Poland – a National State. Dilemmas and Reality]. In Marcin Kula (ed.), *Narody. Jak powstawały i jak wybijały się na niepodległość?* [Nations. How They Came into Being and Stepped out to Independence] Warsaw: PWN.

Komorowska, Hanna. 2013. Multilingualism: Its open and hidden agendas. *Studies in Second Language Learning and Teaching* 3 (4), 463–482.

Majewicz, Alfred F. & Tomasz Wicherkiewicz. 1998. Minority Rights Abuse in Communist Poland and Inherited Issues. *Acta Slavicalaponica* 16, 54–73.

Moskal, Marta. 2004. Language minorities in Poland at the moment of accession to the EU. *Noves SL, Journal on Sociolinguistics*, Spring-Summer, 1–11.

Pisarek, Walery. 2011. The relationship between official and national languages in Poland. In Gerhard Stickel (ed.), *National, Regional and Minority Languages in Europe*. pp. 117–122, Frankfurt/ Main: Peter Lang Verlag.

Poszytek, Paweł, Maria Gorzelak, Anna Dakowicz-Nawrocka, Grażyna Płoszajska, Barbara Kujawa, Stanisław Dłużniewski, Tomasz Płoszaj, Beata Trzcińska, & Lucyna Grabowska. 2005. *Country Report. Language education in Poland*. Warsaw: Ministry of National Education.

Romanowski, Piotr. 2019. A Comparative Study of CLIL Trajectories in the Polish System of Education. *English Language Overseas: Perspectives and Enquiries* 16 (2), 63–76.

Rykała, Andrzej. 2014. Mniejszości narodowe i etniczne w Polsce z perspektywy geografii politycznej [National and Etnic Minorities in Poland from the Perspective of Political Geography]. *Acta Universitatis Lodziensis. Folia Geografica – Socio-Oeceonomica* 17, 63–112.

Wicherkiewicz, Tomasz. 2005. *Lithuanian. The Lithuanian language in education in Poland*. Leeuwarden: Mercator Education.

Wicherkiewicz, Tomasz & Marko Syrnyk. 2006. *Ukrainian and Ruthenian. The Ukrainian and Ruthenian language in education in Poland*. Leeuwarden: Mercator Education.

Edenize Ponzo Peres, Kyria Rebeca Finardi and Poliana Claudiano Calazans

Chapter 3
Language Contact, Maintenance and Conflict: The Case of the Guarani Language in Brazil

Abstract: The main objective of this study was to examine whether the indigenous language of Guarani, spoken in the state of Espirito Santo (ES) in Brazil, showed traces of shift to Portuguese or whether it remained intact. In this chapter, we examine which social factors contributed to the maintenance or loss of this language. We begin by describing the linguistic panorama in Brazil, focusing on Guarani. We discuss Guarani in contact with the majority/official language Portuguese, and review the relevant sociolinguistics and language contact literature. We then analyze interviews with Guarani from ES in relation to the Language Vitality and Endangerment Document (UNESCO 2003). The overall results of the study suggest that the Guarani maintain their language despite the contact with Portuguese and the challenges posed by it.

Keywords: Language contact, Guarani people in Espirito Santo, Guarani Mbya language, language maintenance

1 Introduction

While many people think Brazil is a monolingual country, it is in fact a multilingual country with dozens of immigrant and indigenous languages spread throughout many communities where Portuguese is not the native language (Finardi 2017). With a continent-size territory and population of more than 205 million people, Brazil is bordered by the Atlantic Ocean to the East and Spanish-speaking nations to the West. Brazilians have yet to recognize and preserve the country's multilingualism by reflecting on and elaborating language policies that promote

---

Edenize Ponzo Peres, Kyria Rebeca Finardi, Federal University of Espirito Santo, Vitória, ES, Brazil, E-mail: eponzoperes@gmail.com, E-mail: kyria.finardi@gmail.com
Poliana Claudiano Calazans, High School, Guarapari, ES, Brazil,
E-mail: polianazans@hotmail.com

https://doi.org/10.1515/9781501514692-003

understanding and tolerance among cultures, languages and identities. Most schools, for instance, only offer English as a foreign language.

It is estimated that more than six million people lived in Brazil when the Portuguese colonizers arrived in the year (1500) (Grupioni 2001; D. Silva 2009). Among these six million, it is estimated that some 1.5 million Guarani were spread over 350,000 square kilometers (Brandão 1988). Currently, the Guarani are one of the largest indigenous groups in South America, located in Argentina, Bolivia, Brazil and Paraguay, though there is no consensus on their number. According to the magazine *Guarani people, great people! Life, earth and future* (Revista da Campanha Guarani, 2007), there are approximately 250,000 Guarani people, which is similar to the estimate of 225,000 Guarani in South America, provided at the Continental Meeting held in Porto Alegre, Brazil, in April 2007 (America Latina en Movimiento [ALAI] 2007: n.p.).

According to the 2010 Census of the Brazilian Institute of Geography and Statistics (IBGE, 2010), there are 896,900 indigenous people in Brazil, or 0.4% of the total population. Of this total, 67,523 were Guarani: 43,401 of the Kaiowa group, 8,596 of the Nhandeva group, 8,026 of the Mbya group, and 7,500 declared to be only Guarani without any further specification. An inventory of the Guarani Mbya Language done in 2010 detailed that the Guarani are located along the country's coastline from the south, starting in the state of Rio Grande do Sul (RS), and are found as far as state of Mato Grosso do Sul (Morello and Seiffert 2011). According to the same inventory, the 269 indigenous people living in the state of ES in 2010 lived in three villages: Boa Esperança, Três Palmeiras and Piraquê-AçuMirim, located in the rural municipality of Aracruz, but close to the urban area of the municipality.

This study describes the social history of the Guarani language spoken by indigenous people in the state of ES based on the theoretical and methodological assumptions of Contact Language and the work of authors such as Appel and Muysken (1996), Baker and Jones (1998), Coulmas (2005), Fishman (1967), and Weinreich ([1953] 1970), to name a few. In addition to UNESCO (2003) language vitality and endangerment document, in relation to Guarani, we assess the factors that have helped the Guarani to keep their language alive, despite its proximity to Portuguese-speaking Brazilians and the prejudice and pressure to replace their language with Portuguese.

To investigate the maintenance/loss of Guarani in a bilingual community in the state of ES, we refer to the literature reviewed in dialogue with our observations of this community and the analysis of interviews carried out in 2013 with 35 Mbya Guarani in three villages located in the municipality of Aracruz. We asked questions about the Mbya Guarani's perceptions regarding the maintenance/loss of their language and issues related to their history and religion. Our focus on these aspects addresses a gap in our knowledge about the Guarani language in Brazil, in particular concerning the sociolinguistic situation of Guarani language in the state of ES, and the language policies that preserve linguistic diversity in the state.

In what follows, we begin by tracing the history of the arrival of the Guarani in the state of ES and then focus on the history of the Mbya Guarani language. Then we analyze the sociolinguistic situation of the Mbya Guarani language, based on the Language Vitality and Endangerment document (UNESCO 2003), interview data from Calazans' (2014) master's thesis, and findings from studies of language contact.

2 The Mbya Guarani and their arrival in the state of Espirito Santo

After living for more than 150 years in the Jesuit missions, the Guarani people divided into two groups: one which joined the rural population of Paraguay and another which fled into the South American woods, joining other independent indigenous groups. According to historians, their tribal life was shattered due to the socioeconomic and epidemic problems that plagued many indigenous populations (Ribeiro 2010). Theirs is a story of struggle and resistance embedded in the very term *Guarani*, which means 'warrior people'. According to Teao (2009), the Mbya Guarani, who now live in the state of ES, left Paraguay and headed towards Argentina. By the 1940s, part of the group had settled in the Brazilian state of Rio Grande do Sul and then migrated to other states, always moving towards the north and along the coast.

The migration process of the Guarani following the Atlantic coastline is linked to their search for perfection. There is a common belief among the Guarani in the existence of a *Land without Evil* (Brandão (1988); M. Silva 1999) – a perfect land which, according to their ancestors, can only be reached by crossing the *great water*. According to Brandão (1988), "whatever the interpretation given to [this] place (....), it is always towards the east, the sea, and the Atlantic coast of Brazil" (14). For historians, this sought-after part of Brazil represents not only a land of plenty, but also an unspoiled place with a sense of eternity, a time of salvation when the bad earth will be destroyed. During their long migration up the Brazilian coast, the Guarani formed villages. Survivors of this journey came to the state of ES around the 1970s, following the preaching of their spiritual leader Tatantin Roa Retée. A group settled on the southern coast of the state and another followed the leader Tatantin who, coming across the bay of Santa Cruz in Aracruz, spotted the Land without Evil (M. Silva 1999: 32).

The land, however, was not entirely without evil, as predicted by their spiritual leader. Even before the arrival of the Guarani, the Tupinikim, an indigenous people who lived – and still live – there were already facing problems related to the exploitation of the native forest such as the soil impoverishment caused by eucalyptus plantations established by non-indigenous people. Thus, a conflict between the Guarani and various invaders began and perhaps still continues today. The indigenous people interviewed for this study describe how the lack of natural resources prohibit the Guarani from expressing the full extent of their values and culture.

Today indigenous lands in the region are protected by laws and, as in other states of Brazil, the Guarani culture remains preserved in the state of ES. Guarani people work in their small-scale farms and in the trade of handicrafts, maintaining close and constant contact with their non-indigenous Brazilian neighbors. They have kept most of their ancestors' customs and traditions, including the language.

3 Linguistic contact and the maintenance of the Mbya Guarani language

Many factors can lead a minority language to be maintained or replaced by majority languages. Studies on language contact (see, for example, Appel and Muysken 1996; Baker and Jones 1998; Coulmas 2005; Couto 2009; Fasold 1996; Heredia 1989; UNESCO 2003; Weinreich 1970) have found that many political, social, cultural and linguistic factors affect the maintenance or loss of a given language in that community.

Among the factors that affect the use of a minority language in a given community, pointed out by researchers in the area of language contact referred to in the previous paragraph, are the existence of institutions that conduct their services in the minoritized people's mother tongue (L1), cultural and religious ceremonies in the L1, nationalistic aspirations as a language group, and the existence of strong relationships of identity with the language and native culture (see, for example, Appel and Muysken 1996; Coulmas 2005; Couto 2009; Fasold 1996; Weinreich 1970). Other factors that affect the use of a minority language are in which domains the majority language is used as well as the number of speakers of a given language in relation to recent and/or continuing migration (Couto 2009; Heredia 1989); close proximity to the homeland and ease of travel to homeland (in the case of immigrant languages) (Appel and Muysken 1996); homeland language community intactness (in the case of immigrant languages) (Appel and Muysken 1996); stability in occupation (Couto 2009); L1 standardization and the existence of a written form (Weinreich 1970); international status of the home language (Megale 2005); home language literacy used in the community and with the homeland (in the case of immigrant languages) (Coulmas 2005); and flexibility in the development of the home language (e.g., limited use of new terms from the majority language).

The Language Vitality and Endangerment document (UNESCO 2003: 7–17) proposes nine factors to assess the vitality of a language:
1. intergenerational language transmission;
2. absolute number of speakers;
3. proportion of speakers within the total population;
4. trends in existing language domains;
5. response to new domains and media;
6. materials for language education and literacy;
7. governmental and institutional language attitudes and policies;
8. attitudes of community members towards their own language;
9. amount and quality of documentation.

Based on the items listed above in the Language Vitality and Endangerment document (UNESCO 2003), we analyzed the vitality of the Guarani language in the state of ES. With that aim, the villages of Boa Esperança, Três Palmeiras and Piraquê-Açu Mirim, located in Aracruz on the north coast of the state were analyzed with the help of researchers from the Federal University of Espirito Santo. The testimonies collected from residents of those communities were reported in a previous unpublished study carried out by one of the authors of this chapter (Calazans 2014). The research findings related to the factors listed in the UNESCO document (2003) are described in depth in the next sections.

3.1 Intergenerational language transmission

The UNESCO document (2003: 7) states that: "The most commonly used factor in the evaluation of the vitality of a language is whether or not it is being transmitted from one generation to the next". To support this factor, the Inventory of the Guarani Mbya Language (Morello and Seiffert 2011) and Calazans (2014) report on the transmission of the Guarani language to younger generations in the state of ES. According to the Inventory, among the 11 heads of families surveyed that have children, 10 (91%) said they teach them the Guarani language, and among the four couples with grandchildren and one great-grandchild, all of the children learned Guarani (Morello and Seiffert 2011). When the question was whether the head of the family wanted to teach Guarani to future generations, the answers were all positive. Calazans (2014) also asked questions regarding the transmission of the Guarani language given the constant contact between indigenous and non-indigenous people, including through media tools in that community. Based on the 35 interviews, she concluded that the Guarani transmit their language to their children. Portuguese is learned at school or by contact with non-indigenous people and is used with people from outside the village. According to Calazans (2014: 120, our translation): "FK, an elder Guarani confirms that children in preschool are not able to speak Portuguese and adds that he has frequent conversations with Guarani children about the culture of their ethnicity, so that they do not let themselves be influenced by the Brazilian culture when they have access to it in school". This example shows the importance of their language, which, according to the older members of the village, could ensure the survival of Guarani or at least postpone its displacement by Portuguese.

As stated before, in 2010, the Guarani Mbya language inventory counted 269 indigenous people concentrated in three villages in Aracruz. In these villages, inventory takers visited 13 families, among which 11 were monolingual in Mbya Guarani and two were bilingual in Mbya Guarani and Portuguese. On the other hand, 269 Guarani corresponded to 0.33% of the population of Aracruz, which in 2010 was 81,832. Given that the villages are close to urban centers, many indigenous people maintain constant contact with whites and their culture.

3.2 Trends in existing language domains and response to new domains and media

Data obtained from the 35 informants in Calazans (2014) indicate that there was a consensus among them that Portuguese is to be used only with individuals who do not speak Guarani, i.e., indigenous people from other ethnic groups and white people. Similarly, when the informants were asked about the language they speak at home with other indigenous people, they all said that they speak Guarani, though in other areas outside the village, they need to use Portuguese, due to the constant pressure from the majority language.

When it comes to new areas where the minority language is used, the UNESCO document (2003: 11) suggests that "while some language communities succeed in expanding their own language into the new domain, most do not. Schools, new work environments, media, including broadcast media and the internet, usually expand the scope and power of the dominant language at the expense of endangered languages".

In the case of the Mbya Guarani language, it has not been used in any new domains, there are no newspapers circulated in the community written in Guarani, nor are there radio or television programs in that language, positioning it as irrelevant and/or stigmatizing it, and thus putting it at a greater risk of extinction.

3.3 Materials for language education and literacy

According to the UNESCO document (2003: 12), "Education in the language is essential for language vitality". The Guarani language has status as an official language in Paraguay and as a co-official language in Bolivia and in certain South American cities, such as the Brazilian city of Tacuru, in the state of Mato Grosso do Sul. In these locations, there are written texts and materials for teaching Guarani such as grammar books, Portuguese-Guarani and Spanish-Guarani dictionaries and textbooks for teaching Guarani as an additional language (L2). However, in the state of ES, there are relatively few educational materials available in Guarani. Therefore, teachers aiming to give students differentiated bilingual education work with self-produced materials in Guarani. Teachers also use materials in Portuguese, though emphasis is placed on the Guarani-language materials.

3.4 Governmental and institutional language attitudes and policies, including official status and use

According to the Vitality and Endangerment Language document (UNESCO 2003: 13), the linguistic ideology of the state may inspire linguistic minorities to mobilize their population toward the maintenance of their languages or to force them to abandon them. These linguistic attitudes can be a powerful force both for the promotion and loss of their languages.

Brazil, at many times during its history, has reduced the freedom to use any language other than Portuguese. As an example, we have the Decrees of 1938 and 1939, prohibiting foreigners residing in the country to speak their native languages (which at the time were associated with *enemy* countries during the preparation for World War II). However, in 2006, important steps were taken towards the recognition of minority languages in Brazil, culminating in the creation of the *Record Book of Languages* by the Congress. As a result, in December, 2010, Decree 7387 was signed establishing the National Inventory of Linguistic Diversity, which aims at mapping and characterizing languages besides allowing heritage languages to contribute to their continuity and recovery (Instituto do Patrimônio Histórico e Artístico Nacional, 2010).

Also in 2010, and for the first time in Brazilian history, a census carried out by the Brazilian National Geography and Statistics Institution (IBGE 2010) asked questions about Brazilian indigenous peoples and the languages spoken by them, such as: "Do you consider yourself indigenous?", "What is your ethnic group or people you belong to?", "Do you speak indigenous language(s) at home?", "Which one(s)?" and "Specify the indigenous language(s) and the amount of Portuguese you speak at home". Collecting these data was the first step toward challenging the belief that Brazil is a monolingual country. Because of these governmental actions and policies, some immigrant and indigenous languages (including Guarani) now have co-official status in certain Brazilian municipalities.

Regarding the education of young Guarani in their mother tongue, in the villages studied there are two local elementary schools with indigenous teachers, selected, trained and paid by the Municipality of Aracruz. This was an important community achievement because before 2001, professionals working in indigenous schools were mostly non-indigenous. In these schools, children communicate and are taught in Guarani during the first four years of schooling, with the use of didactic materials produced by their teachers. There, the oldest person in the community participates in the classes, teaching along with teachers to pass down knowledge of their culture, such as medicinal plants, animal and plant species, traditional food, crafts, body painting, Guarani songs, etc. (Calazans 2014; Teao 2009). From the fifth school year on, Guarani is taught as a school subject with a Guarani teacher, since the other teachers are indigenous Tupinikims, who speak only Portuguese. Although Portuguese language instruction is not fully accepted in the community, many Guarani believe it is through education in the dominant language that they will gain a better understanding of existing legislation and will be better equipped to protect their rights.

After the Guarani finish elementary school, students complete their studies outside the village in officially monolingual schools which are often insensitive to the different linguistic and cultural realities of their students, thus causing a high dropout rate. The Guarani are now demanding a secondary school in their villages, which would offer continuity for what is already being taught in indigenous schools as a way to prevent language shift, violence, and other forms of prejudice towards indigenous people (Calazans 2014).

Finally, with respect to the use of minority languages in public, in Guarani villages there is no circulation of spoken or printed media in Guarani, nor is it used in the administration or in public buildings in Aracruz.

3.5 Community members' attitudes toward their own language

The Language Vitality and Endangerment document (UNESCO 2003: 14) presents four attitudes that a community can have in relation to their language:

> They may see it as essential to their community and identity and promote it; they may use it without promoting it; they may be ashamed of it and, therefore, not promote it; or they may see it as a nuisance and actively avoid using it. When members' attitudes towards their language are very positive, the language may be seen as a key symbol of group identity.

The studies of Mbya Guarani reviewed in this work (Calazans 2014; Morello and Seifert 2011) investigated the reasons why the Guarani people might want to maintain their language. According to the Inventory of the Guarani Mbya Language (Morello and Seifert 2011: 68), the main reason given by respondents was "to keep the language of the people/custom/culture/tradition". Some variation on this response was given by 68% of respondents in the state of ES.

In the investigation of maintenance factors of the Guarani language in the villages in the state of Espirito Santo, Calazans (2014) focused on issues such as pride among the Guarani, which aligns with self-esteem and linguistic loyalty. 92% of the adults Calazans (2014) interviewed considered Guarani to be the most beautiful language, and 8% cited other languages but did not include Portuguese. Among the children, 31% said that the Guarani language was the most beautiful, 4% said it was Portuguese and 65% did not answer the question. A second question: "If there was a Guarani soccer team and if it played against the Brazilian team, who they would cheer for?" yielded the following results: 67% would cheer for the Guarani team, 22% for the Brazilian team, and 11% for neither.

In the testimonies of indigenous people collected by Calazans (2014), pride for being Guarani is evident in the data and may explain why the Guarani, regardless of age, do not change their culture or abandon their language, despite the fear of violence and prejudice associated with it. Loyalty to the Guarani language and culture also comes from another factor in language maintenance: religion. In each village there is a house of prayer, the Opy, where most Guarani go every night. Among the informants in Calazans (2014), 75% said they are religious, following the Guarani religion and patrons in the prayer house. The services consist of prayer, dance and songs in the Guarani language. There, too, the young are taught by elders about the importance of maintaining ethnic identity, history, and culture. The testimony below, from MOS, a male adult, sheds light on the work in the house of prayer:

> In the house of prayer we learn in theory and in practice through songs and dances to revere the God Creator which has healing powers given to the healer, the shaman who heals with medicine and spiritual healing. Also we learn how to live on earth, how to respect nature, to respect each other (. . .). So we have much respect for the forest, the rivers, the people, right? That is why God spared the lives of the Guarani.

Thus, religion is an important aspect guiding the way of life for the Guarani people interviewed by Calazans (2014). The Guarani consider the religious word as a gift with mythical powers of primordial connection to the spiritual world. Hence the intrinsic relationship between religion and language. In short, the interviews carried out in Calazans' (2014) study show that pride and loyalty are important factors for the Guarani and their language, helping to protect it against threats from Portuguese.

3.6 Amount and quality of documentation

As we have stated throughout this chapter, the Guarani language (in its varieties) is spoken by thousands of people, being the official or co-official language in some countries in South America. As such, it has been widely documented (e.g., in written texts and audio and video recordings). It also appears in educational materials such as books as the L1 and L2, including e-books. In the case of the Mbya Guarani, the Inventory (Morello and Seifert 2011) interviewed and recorded this variety, which is available, unedited, in a CD that accompanies the printed book version of the inventory. Although the villages of Aracruz do not have this material, it can be easily accessed and/or obtained by the Municipal Department of Education. Thus, it can be suggested that the Guarani language has sufficient documentation to be able to survive for many more generations. The question of how resilient it will be is partly a question of the approaches and policies used to protect and promote this language.

4 Conclusion

This chapter sought to analyze the sociolinguistic situation of the Guarani language in the multi-ethnic (indigenous communities, afro descendants, and European immigrants (Peres 2014, 2017)) state of Espirito Santo. The analysis of interviews from Calazans (2014) as well as the observations carried out in the communities showed that the Guarani have a strong sense of pride in and loyalty to their language and culture. They view their language as a mark of ethnic identity and advocate for its preservation.

The Guarani are able to preserve their language in two main ways. The first way is through the use of Guarani in domestic situations and conversations between natives of the same community, such as in ceremonies and religious gatherings carried out in the prayer houses. Religion is the fundamental link between contemporary Guarani and their ancestors. Elder Guarani teach their children the importance of loyalty to their ethnic identity through religion. The second way is in the community's sense of continuity, which enables the Guarani language and culture to continue to be passed down from one generation to the next. Such continuity could be accomplished by the incentive, on the part of the governmental organizations, to maintain the use of Guarani within the family domain. We also find that the media in the villages (e.g., television, radio, internet etc.), the proximity of indigenous territory with urban areas, and the fact that the school is outside the Guarani villages have a great influence on younger Guarani and their language use. Evidence of this can be seen in the presence of non-indigenous habits in their behaviour and Portuguese words in their language choices. As reported in the interviews, younger Guarani already show signs of mixing language which could lead to a shift to Portuguese if the community does not do anything to slow or stop it.

The imposition of Portuguese was part of the colonization process of indigenous peoples in Brazil. On the other hand, the maintenance of the minority language without mastering the official language can also serve to marginalize social groups. Thus, the challenge is to think about language policies that foster bilingualism, in collaboration with indigenous communities, in order to preserve their autonomy, cultural identity and language.

The primary contribution of this chapter is in the identification of factors that have contributed to the maintenance and/or shift of the Guarani language. Moreover, we present the history of the Guarani people in the state of ES relating to their culture and language use. Notwithstanding this important contribution, other studies are called for to better understand the sociolinguistic situation of Guarani especially in relation to the contact with Portuguese in the region, analyzing language contact and use among Guarani children and adolescents. Also, descriptions of existing variations in the Guarani language spoken in Aracruz would be necessary so as to compare with other varieties spoken in other locations in Brazil and in South America.

Results of these research endeavours are important contributions to the maintenance of the Guarani language in what concerns the design of teaching materials and approaches as well as to sociolinguistic situation of these people in regards to their status of indigenous minority population surrounded by a majority non-indigenous language/population.

A final consideration is in hand. We understand that the responsibility for the maintenance of indigenous languages and customs is shared by the indigenous communities and the society at large. It is up to indigenous peoples to decide whether they want to maintain their language and traditions, though it is the responsibility of all to recognize and respect diversity in all its forms finding non-threatening ways of co-existence.

References

ALAI (América Latina en movimiento). 2007. *I Assembleia continental do povo Guarani*. [I Continental assembly of the Guarani people]. https://www.alainet.org/pt/active/16905 (accessed 21 October 2016).

Appel, René & Pieter Muysken. 1996 [1987]. *Bilinguismo y contacto de lenguas* [Language contact and bilingualism]. Barcelona: Editorial Ariel.

Baker, Colin & Sylvia P. Jones. 1998. *Encyclopedia of bilingualism and bilingual education*. Clevedon, UK: Multilingual Matters.

Brandão, Carlos R. 1988. Os Guarani: Índios do sul, religião, resistência e adaptação [The Guarani: Southern indians, religion, resistance and adaptation]. *Estudos Avançados*, 4 (10), 53–90. http://www.scielo.br/pdf/ea/v4n10/v4n10a04.pdf (accessed 20 July 2013).

Calazans, Poliana C. 2014. *Para uma sócio-história da língua guarani no Espírito Santo: Uma análise sob a perspectiva sociolinguística* [For a socio-history of the Guarani language in Espírito Santo: An analysis from the sociolinguistic perspective]. Vitoria-ES: Universidade Federal do Espírito Santo MA thesis.

Coulmas, Florian. 2005. *Sociolinguistics: The study of speakers' choices*. Cambridge: Cambridge University Press.

Couto, Hildo H. 2009. *Linguística, ecologia e ecolinguística: Contato de línguas* [Linguistics, ecology and ecolinguistics: Language contact]. São Paulo: Contexto.

Fasold, Ralph. 1996 [1984]. *La sociolingüística de la sociedad* [The sociolinguistics of society]. Madrid: Visor Libros.

Finardi, Kyria R. 2017. What Brazil can learn from multilingual Switzerland and its use of English as a multilingua franca. *Acta Scientiarium* 39 (2). 219–228. http://periodicos.uem.br/ojs/index.php/ActaSciLangCult/article/view/30529 (accessed 12 May 2020).

Fishman, Joshua A. 1967. Bilingualism with and without diglossia; diglossia with and without bilingualism. *Journal of Social Issues* 23 (2). 29–38.

Grupioni, Luís D. B. 2001. Índios: Passado, presente e futuro [Indians: Past, present and future]. In Luís D. B. Grupioni (ed.), *Índios do Brasil*, 07–29. Brasília: MEC/SEED/SEF.

Heredia, Christine de. 1989. Do bilinguismo ao falar bilíngue [From bilingualism to bilingual speaking]. In Geneviève Vermes & Josiane Boutet (eds.), *Multilinguismo*, 177–220. Campinas: Editora da UNICAMP.

IBGE (Instituto Brasileiro de Geografia e Estatística). 2010. *Censo demográfico 2010. Características gerais dos indígenas*. [2010 Census. General characteristics of indigenous people]. http://indigenas.ibge.gov.br (accessed 05 February 2014).

IPHAN (Instituto do Patrimônio Histórico e Artístico Nacional). 2010. *Inventário Nacional da Diversidade Linguística*. [National Inventory of Linguistic Diversity]. http://portal.iphan.gov.br/uploads/ckfinder/arquivos/Decreto%207387%20-%202010.pdf. (accessed 12 September 2016).

Megale, Antonieta H. 2005. Bilinguismo e educação bilíngue: discutindo conceitos [Bilingualism and bilingual education: discussing concepts]. *Revista Virtual de Estudos da Linguagem* – ReVEL 3 (5). 1–13.

Morello, Rosangela & Ana Paula Seiffert. 2011. Inventário da língua Guarani Mbya – Inventário nacional da diversidade linguística [Guarani Mbya Language Inventory – National Inventory of Linguistic Diversity]. Florianópolis: Ed. Garapuvu.

Peres, Edenize P. 2014. Aspectos sócio-históricos do contato entre o dialeto vêneto e o português no Espírito Santo [Socio-historical aspects of the contact between Veneto dialect and Portuguese in Espírito Santo]. *Revista (Con)textos Linguísticos*. 8 (10). 57–71. http://periodicos.ufes.br/contextoslinguisticos (accessed 02 March 2015).

Peres, Edenize P. 2017. Os contatos entre os dialetos italianos e o português no Espírito Santo [Contacts between Italian dialects and Portuguese in Espírito Santo]. In Luiz F. Beneduzi & Maria Cristina Dadalto (eds*.). Mobilidade humana e circularidade de ideia: Diálogos entre a América Latina e a Europa* [Human mobility and circularity of idea: dialogues between Latin America and Europe], 17–28. Venezia: Edizioni Cà Foscari Digital Publishing.

Revista da Campanha Guarani. 2007. *Povo Guarani, um grande povo: Vida, terra e futuro*. [Guarani people, a great people: Life, land and future]. http://www.djweb.com.br/historia/arquivos/cartilha02.pdf. (accessed 22 August 2013).

Ribeiro, Darcy. 2010. *Falando dos índios* [Speaking about Indians]. Brasília: UnB.

Silva, Diego B. 2009. Extinção, preservação e vitalidade de línguas: Uma proposta brasileira para as línguas minoritárias [Language extinction, preservation and vitality: A Brazilian proposal for minority languages]. *Cadernos do Congresso Nacional de Linguística e Filologia*. 13 (4). 599–610.

Silva, Margareth A. 1999. *Comunidade Guarani: Em busca de subsídios para uma educação socioambiental*. [Guarani community: Seeking subsidies for social and environmental education]. Vitória, ES: Universidade Federal do Espírito Santo MA thesis.

Teao, Kalna M. 2009. As visões dos Guarani Mbya do Espírito Santo sobre a escola [The views of Mbya Guarani from Espirito Santo about the school]. *Tellus*. 9 (16). 105–126. http://www.tellus.ucdb.br/index.php/tellus/article/view/179/209 (accessed 10 March 2015).

UNESCO. 2003. *Language vitality and endangerment*. http://www.unesco.org/new/fileadmin/MULTIMEDIA/HQ/CLT/pdf/Language_vitality_and_endangerment_EN.pdf (accessed 8 November 2019).

Weinreich, Uriel. 1970 [1953]. *Languages in contact: Findings and problems*, 9th. edn. Paris: The Hague Mouton.

Martin Guardado
Chapter 4
"My Gain Would Have Been Their Loss": Key Factors in the Heritage Language Socialization and Policies of a Middle-class Mexican Family in Canada

Abstract: This chapter, part of a larger ethnographic study, examines a Mexican-Canadian family's language ideologies, HL practices, and the children's affective connection to their relatives in Mexico. Drawing on data from participant observation, naturalistic linguistic interactions, and interviews, the chapter analyzes how the parents attempted to socialize their children into particular ideologies and identities, and to inculcate a sense of value for other cultures and languages in the community. Given that the family spent extended time in Mexico every year, parents stated that their children had strong emotional ties to their extended families and that those trips were a source of great excitement for them, which afforded them an opportunity to strengthen the emotional ties among family members, mediated by Spanish. The findings also highlight the subjective and complex nature of the parents' perceptions and perspectives about multilingualism, and support the notion that language socialization is a fluid, unstable and changeable process.

Keywords: heritage language socialization, identity, parental strategies, community language schools, Spanish, Hispanic

1 Introduction

Given that the family has usually been identified as the nucleus of the community interactions that are vital to language socialization (Schieffelin and Ochs 1986, Ochs and Schieffelin 2012), it is not surprising that a clear link between the family and heritage language development (HLD) has been reported (Tannenbaum and Berkovich 2005). Nevertheless, the presence of family alone is insufficient to foster HLD – nor is any one person or group. Indeed, the more domains and groups in

---

Martin Guardado, University of Alberta, Canada, E-mail: guardado@ualberta.ca

https://doi.org/10.1515/9781501514692-004

which the heritage language[1] is spoken by individuals, the more likely it is to be developed and maintained (Fishman 2004). While the role of family in heritage language development might appear in some ways obvious, it is somewhat surprising that scholarly interest in this relationship is relatively recent (Guardado 2002, Schecter and Bayley 2002, Fishman 2004, Tannenbaum 2005, Schwartz and Verschik 2013, Slavkov 2017). Some of the themes addressed by this growing body of work include benefits and consequences of language maintenance, factors surrounding family language policies, psychological motives for pursuing language maintenance, interactional processes within families, among many others. In this chapter, I profile a Spanish-speaking family of Mexican descent, and present key findings related to their heritage language socialization policies, practices, history, and particular circumstances which impacted their family communication dynamics. This is part of a large ethnographic study conducted in Vancouver, Canada over two years. Thus, following a longitudinal approach, the research question addressed in this chapter is: What are the contextual and family factors that impacted the heritage language socialization efforts of a middle-class family of Mexican descent in Vancouver, Canada? To address this question, the chapter first provides some background on heritage language socialization and identity before describing the design of the study and the specific family characteristics. The findings are organized in six themes, each engaging with one key factor that had direct bearing on the heritage language socialization experiences, possibilities, and outcomes of the family. The chapter concludes with limitations and points for consideration in future research.

2 Heritage language and identity

The term heritage language refers to a language spoken by immigrants – and sometimes indigenous groups (Wiley 2001). According to Fishman (2001), HL refers to a language with a special family connection for individuals, which emphasizes the role that identity and affiliation play in relation to HLs. Other definitions draw attention to the speakers' proficiency in the HL. Valdés (2000) defines the HL learner as an individual who is raised in a family where a minority language is spoken and who has some level of proficiency in that language. Thus, in this chapter the term HL is used to refer to a language spoken in the home that is different from the main language of society. This definition of HL is intended to be inclusive, encompassing a broad range of aspects of subjective

---

[1] In this chapter, first language (L1) and heritage language (HL) are used interchangeably.

relevance to families and their children, whether aspirational or enacted. Over the last three decades, the scholarship on heritage language development has intensified in North America, significantly advancing our knowledge of this research area. As a result, our understanding of ethnolinguistic minority families' beliefs and opinions about HL socialization is well established in the research literature (e.g., Kouritzin 1999, Schecter and Bayley 2002).

Being that the ability to maintain the heritage language in a dominant language context enables ethnic minorities to develop a strong cultural identity and sense of self, having a strong cultural identity has been identified as an important factor conducive to language maintenance (e.g., Guardado 2006). However, much about the relationship between cultural identity development and HL development remains unclear. Studies examining this link rarely problematize or account for the inevitable reconstruction of culture that takes place in the diaspora, effectively excluding a potentially rich – if not central – avenue of HL socialization analysis (for exceptions see Zentella 1997, Baquedano-Lopez 2000).

Outside of HL studies, identity and language have been found to be closely related, and as Norton (2000) has argued, social identity can be seen as "how people understand their relationship to the outside world, how that relationship is constructed across time and space, and how people understand their possibilities for the future" (410). Identity, from this perspective, can be understood as situated, fluid, dynamic, and multifaceted (Eckert 2000, Norton 2000, Zilles and King 2005). Indeed, the relationship between identity and HL development is a highly complex phenomenon that plays out at micro and macro levels, both for individuals and communities. In fact, for HL speakers and their families, the significance of the HL in their lives and sense of self may be much deeper than can be captured in scholarly studies. As Anzaldúa (1987: 59) poignantly declared, "I am my language. Until I can take pride in my language, I cannot take pride in myself." This statement connects to several aspects of what a HL means to individuals and families, and suggests that at the very least, the HL is meaningful as a way of linking to ethnic roots, as an emotional connection or means to express emotion, as a way for speakers to be recognized and valued, and as key to fostering a sense of unity and continuity (Guardado 2018).

3 Heritage Language socialization

HL socialization has evolved out of the vast body of research that has documented the language socialization trajectories of individuals. Language socialization refers to the process by which children are socialized both through language and into language use within a community (Ochs and Schieffelin 2008). Although the foundational language socialization work was conducted in first language settings, it quickly inspired work in other settings, including second language contexts where further complicating factors were uncovered. The work of Duff (see e.g., 2012) and others has shown that second language socialization poses many challenges and complexities not found in first language socialization contexts. These factors are further amplified in relation to HL socialization, which includes features of first and second language socialization. For instance, often the features of first language or second language socialization may be more present in some individuals, families, and settings than in others, further complicating the possibility of developing a single approach to HL socialization. Given the increasing acknowledgement of language socialization as a robust and flexible paradigm, however, there is growing acceptance and use of this framework in HL investigations.

A scholarly area to which language socialization research has contributed significantly is the process of identity formation. Indeed, there is now a great deal of research documenting the language socialization process of individuals as they are inducted into cultural communities. This work has examined how novices and other individuals become particular kinds of people and how they gain membership in communities. Having evolved out of this tradition, HL socialization is also deeply concerned about these processes, though additional layers of complexity are involved. In this vein, Ochs and Schieffelin posit that "a twist in the interface of language learning and socialization into identity construction is the phenomenon of heritage language socialization, in which learners are expected to use the heritage code that displays them as suitable moral persons as envisioned by an idealized 'heritage culture'" (2012: 16–17). Indeed, heritage language socialization explains the processes of language development and use while examining the identity development and interactional complexity that are often associated with these processes. Thus, like language socialization, HL socialization is also concerned with how children develop a sense of who they are through the use of their various linguistic repertoires as they engage in daily life (He 2017). In this way, heritage language socialization research is not only enriched by the growing sophistication in the theorization of the language socialization model, but it is also making valuable contributions of its own. Indeed, a growing number of studies have indicated that that HL socialization, development, and maintenance play an important role in cultural identity development.

The study reported on in this chapter attempted to address HL socialization issues, including the ones discussed in this section. This is done through a thematic and discourse analysis of ethnographic data, highlighting issues of language, culture, and identity. I report on the analysis of interview and other interactional data with an eye to documenting, describing, explicating, and understanding the factors affecting the language and literacy development of the children through a language socialization lens. Throughout my analysis two themes persistently emerged: the construction of L1 development as a bridge between their children's past and future, and the purposeful effort on the part of Mrs. Aguirre and Mr. Ramírez to socialize their children as transnational or global citizens.

4 The study

The larger study (Guardado 2008) upon which this chapter is based involved a two-year ethnographic examination of the language socialization ideologies and practices experienced by 34 immigrant Hispanic families and their children in home, school, and community settings in Vancouver, Canada. The families were recruited through convenience and snowballing. I invited participants through three Spanish language radio programs and also contacted individuals whose community or employment roles put them in contact with Hispanic community networks. These individuals identified potential participants and referred them to me for further eligibility screening. I sought potential participating Hispanic families with at least one child of school age, preferably attending elementary school. I hypothesized that the most influential language socialization milieu for immigrant children in terms of HL development or shift outside the home was the school environment. As part of the larger study, this chapter profiles one of three focal families, the Aguirre-Ramírez family, in order to investigate the following question: What are the contextual and family factors that impacted the heritage language socialization efforts of a middle-class family of Mexican descent in Vancouver, Canada? This particular family was chosen for closer examination in this chapter because of their revealing linguistic ideological perspectives, unique HL activities, and for the children's expressed affective connection to their family members in Mexico. Reporting on these issues was deemed of high relevance to this volume as they provide theoretical and empirical insights to scholars, and potentially also practical strategies to families.

The main data collection strategy used was the semi-structured interview, which is a flexible type of interview that allows new questions to be brought up in order to probe themes more deeply or to get the interviewee to elaborate on their responses. I considered this strategy valuable in order to "respond to the situation at hand, to the emerging worldview of the respondent[s], and to new ideas on the topic" (Merriam 1991: 74). I conducted eight interviews with the family over a period of two years in Spanish and digitally-recorded them, totalling about 16 hours. I then transcribed the interviews and translated the examples in this chapter into English. Other forms of data that I collected during ethnographic observations of linguistic interactions included fieldnotes and fieldwork journal entries. Analyses of some of these and other data are not included in this chapter; however, it is prudent to discuss them here, albeit tangentially, since they served to formulate interview questions during the data collection process.

I analyzed and categorized the interview transcripts according to Bogdan and Biklen's (1998) guidelines for analyzing qualitative research data as well as some of the steps suggested by Ryan and Bernard (2003). These procedures served in the development of coding categories and the identification of emergent themes. Data analysis was an ongoing process that began with the collection of data and ended with the writing of the chapter. The data were analyzed keeping in focus the overriding theoretical proposition (Yin 1994) of language socialization, which guided the data collection and analysis. The data were analyzed using the qualitative data analysis software package NVivo, which allows researchers to manage, code, analyze, and report on text data. This computer program was used to help in the coding and identification of emerging themes.

4.1 Family background

Mrs. Aguirre and Mr. Ramírez (all names are pseudonyms) were upper-middle class professionals from Mexico. They had three daughters: Perla, Florencia and Penelope (see Table 4.1 for details). The youngest daughter was born in Vancouver, Canada. In many ways they were a privileged, transnational Hispanic family. Additionally, Mr. Ramírez's mother had lived in Vancouver for several decades, and had been married to an Anglo-Canadian man, Mr. Ramírez's stepfather. Because of this connection to Vancouver, Mr. Ramírez had visited the city many times before immigrating. Having studied in a private bilingual school from kindergarten to grade 12, Mr. Ramírez was already fluent in English when he arrived, which occurred six months ahead of Mrs. Aguirre and the two girls. The family had decided that Mr. Ramírez would precede them in order to find employment and secure suitable accommodation. He found accommodation on the West Side, one of Vancouver's affluent neighbourhoods. Mr. Ramírez started working for the Vancouver branch of a Swiss chain of specialty stores shortly after immigrating, and was soon promoted to an executive position.

Mrs. Aguirre described the initial adaptation experiences of the family as typical to those of other immigrants. They participated in community activities,

Table 4.1: Aguirre-Ramírez Family Profile.

Country of origin: Mexico Length of Residence in Canada: 4 years	
Mrs. Gracia Aguirre – Age: 44 – Years of formal education: 16 (Psychology) – Current occupation: Stay at home mother – English proficiency: Intermediate	Mr. Orlando Ramírez – Age: 46 – Years of formal education: 16 (Architecture) – Current occupation: Sales Manager – English proficiency: Fluent/near-native
Children: 3/female Penelope: 2 Florencia: 5 Perla: 6	

joined weekly support groups, and attended drop-in meetings at community centres and places of that sort, in an attempt to learn the local customs and perhaps also to build a social network.

According to Mr. Ramírez, his own adjustment to life in Vancouver was rather seamless. Their daughters apparently did not face many difficulties adjusting either. Both parents explained that the children struggled with the language for a short time, but otherwise learned it quickly from television and their initial school experiences where they reportedly made friends and found their place in a group of peers without much trouble. However, Mrs. Aguirre reported having struggled tremendously during the first two years in Canada. Coming from a large family, she found it distressing not having her network of extended family and friends. Mr. Ramírez, when referring to this period, stated that the first two years in Canada "were very difficult for her. She cried daily"[2] (Mr. Ramírez, Interview). Additionally, since her English was not very strong, she felt isolated and helpless. She realized at that time that she could have created opportunities for English practice with the children, but chose not to do so. She stated: "The girls are perfectly bilingual. My English is still very limited. I could have benefited from my girls in order to improve my English, but my gain could have been their loss" (Mrs. Aguirre, Interview). She asserted that her gain in English skills would have meant a loss in Spanish proficiency for the

---

[2] All interview quotes and linguistic interactions were originally recorded in Spanish, but due to space constraints, only the English translations are included in the chapter.

girls and she was just not willing to make that trade-off. For Mrs. Aguirre, socializing the children into an appropriate linguistic behavior, which for the family also meant fluency in Spanish, was a far more important goal than increasing her proficiency in English, if that meant her daughters would have less opportunity to develop their Spanish proficiency.

5 Findings

5.1 Language socialization practices at home

The family maintained a Spanish-only rule at home. When their daughters moved to Canada at the ages of two and a half and four they already spoke Spanish well. The family attributed the relative ease with which they learned English to the fact that they already had a solid foundation in L1. Mrs. Aguirre remembered that shortly after their arrival, people started to question their decision to still speak Spanish to the girls, but apparently, they were immovable in their stance: "People can lecture us, but we are going to continue emphasizing they keep speaking Spanish" (Mrs. Aguirre, Interview). The family made a deliberate and firm decision to create and maintain a rich Spanish language socialization milieu in which the children could develop their Spanish language and literacy abilities. The following example is a typical example of the type of language behavior that was expected and demanded from Penelope and the other two girls (Mrs. A=Mrs. Aguirre):

Example 1:
Mrs. A: what is that Flo-Penelope?
Penelope: it's a (0.2) **paper**=
Mrs. A: =it's a WHAT?=
Penelope: =a °**paper**° (xx[x)
Mrs. A: [I don't understand
Penelope: (xxxx)

In this extract, Mrs. Aguirre was making a clear attempt at reinforcing the Spanish-only rule at home. The ways in which the children were being socialized into a particular linguistic behavior varied along an implicit-explicit continuum. Sometimes the mother only modeled the expected behavior and other times she offered cross-code recasts (repeating what the child had said but in Spanish, see Guardado 2013, 2018 for a detailed description and analyses). In this particular interaction, it is clear that the mother was not interested in the content of three-year old Penelope's utterances, but in the code she used. Mrs. Aguirre started the interaction by asking Penelope what it was she had in her hand. In line 2, Penelope seemed to struggle momentarily just before producing *paper*, an indication that she might have been unsuccessfully looking for the word *papel* in Spanish. In line 3 Mrs. Aguirre spoke immediately after Penelope used the English word *paper*, which Mrs. Aguirre did not accept. Instead, she attempted to encourage her to use the right Spanish word, raising her voice in the word *WHAT?*, indicating emphasis. In her reply, Penelope again used the word *paper* and was still talking, possibly explaining what it was she had in her hand. However, as soon as Penelope pronounced *paper*, failing to self-repair, Mrs. Aguirre decided that she had heard enough. She only seemed interested in Penelope's code choice, evidenced in her overlap in line 5. This extract illustrates how in the family, the language socialization process was not straightforward. It was complex and marked by non-conformity, intentional or not, which created tensions and interrupted the natural flow of communication, in this case, between a mother and her three-year old daughter.

The decision to maintain and use Spanish in the family was made from the very beginning, and the parents expressed a strong belief in the advantages of having two languages. As Mrs. Aguirre asserted "if they have three or four [languages] it will be better" (Mrs. Aguirre, Interview). In our interviews and other interactions, it became evident that both Mrs. Aguirre and Mr. Ramírez valued multilingualism. When referring to one of her daughters, Mrs. Aguirre explained: "Perhaps she is not the most brilliant girl in school. She does quite well. However, she is not the star of the school, but this girl is learning two languages. And that is very valuable. She is walking two paths" (Mrs. Aguirre, Interview). According to her, the fact that her daughters were growing up with at least two languages was far more important than whether they excelled in school or not.[3] Elaborating on the reasons for pursuing their goals more specifically, the family also addressed the transferability of skills from one language to another as evidenced in this quote by Mrs. Aguirre: "I think that by creating an avenue for another language, one is broadening the options for other languages" (Mrs. Aguirre, Interview).

In general, the language policy at home was Spanish-only, but this was not enforced at all times. As is the case in many immigrant families, a combination of both languages was the norm. Figure 4.1 illustrates the language use patterns

---

[3] Based on interviews and observations, a more nuanced depiction of the families' goals would highlight the pursuit of a balance between multilingual development and school success.

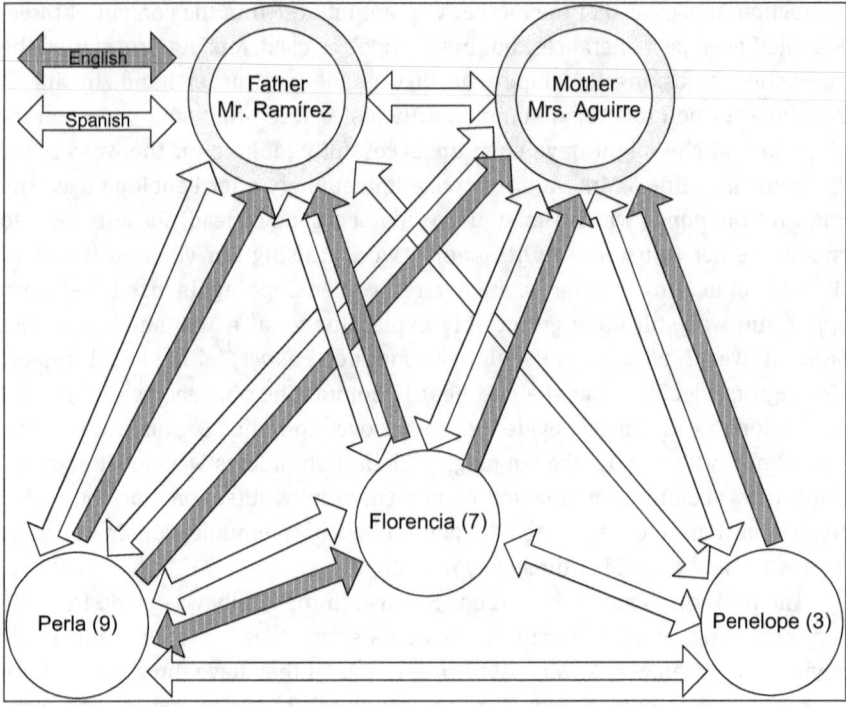

Figure 4.1: Patterns of Language use in the Aguirre-Ramírez Family.

in the home. Mrs. Aguirre and Mr. Ramírez spoke Spanish to the children all the time. The children spoke Spanish to them most of the time. Among themselves, Florencia and Perla tended to use English, especially during play, although they were often reminded to use Spanish. To Penelope, however, the older girls tended to use Spanish because otherwise she did not understand them.

These language patterns were affected by variables such as the time of year, the interactants, and the context, among others. For instance, it was not unusual for them to start speaking in English to Mrs. Aguirre right after they got home from school, because according to her, they still had not "changed the tape in their brains." This was especially so when there had been a significant incident that the children were excited about and wanted to tell their parents quickly.

5.2 Socializing linguistic and cultural awareness

Multilingualism had a high place in the family's value system, but this was part of a larger belief system that included not only a strong interest in raising linguistic and cultural awareness within the family with a strong emphasis on Spanish and Latin American culture, but also on valuing all languages and cultures equally. Mr. Ramírez, for instance, declared that the family was interested in transmitting and reinforcing the notion that there is more to language than just Spanish. They wanted the children to understand "that it is not only Spanish. There are other languages" (Mrs. Aguirre, Interview). Language and cultural awareness seemed intricately tied to their cultural values and belief systems, as well as to their social position, which at the same time influenced the cultural patterns and ways of behaving that the children were socialized into, nurturing and shaping their evolving identities.

It appears that the main thrust in the family was to raise children who were aware of their roots and proud of who they were. At the same time, they wanted them to value the place where they lived, the languages that were spoken and the cultures that were practiced in that milieu. Mrs. Aguirre believed that the children's experiences were enriched

> by all the opportunities they have to coexist with different people from different countries and I think that in some form it always leads them to think about their own [culture], in what we customarily do, in everything we intend to do, no? I think the challenge Orlando [Mr. Ramírez] is referring to, that they maintain ours [our culture] and assimilate the positive aspects of other cultures and learn to respect different [cultures] . . . that is what I think is the base, that is, the theory here in Canada is one that holds that you respect other individuals as they are, their beliefs, their behaviors, as long as you DO NOT interfere in your . . . not in your space, rather that does not harm others, what liberty is, to be free and to do what you . . . where you want to go, but without harming others, so I think that aspect is very, very enriching for them. (Mrs. Aguirre, Interview)

Mrs. Aguirre and Mr. Ramírez's cultural beliefs reflected their understanding of Canadian official multiculturalism, one in which all the different cultures ideally co-habit in the same geographical and socio-politico-cultural space, without interfering with one another's cultural practices. Living in such an environment – a cultural market of sorts – the family members could choose to take what appealed to them and discard the rest. The parents felt that the children would benefit from a socialization that allowed them to value all cultures, but at the same time, to feel proud of their own roots, holistically raising children that they appeared to describe as more emotionally-stable human beings: "All this reinforces that emotional aspect and I think that in the long run it can, I hope, foster human beings that are more secure, stronger and prouder of themselves, but in addition, who are interested in others" (Mrs. Aguirre, Interview). In other words, they felt that the maintenance of their own cultural roots and an appreciation of other cultures was the ideal balance with which to grow up:

> Maybe that is the challenge, no? Because it would indeed be sad if they lost these traditions as a result of absorbing others and not because some are necessarily better than others, no, rather because these traditions stem from their roots, no? So, that is the challenge, perhaps that the girls, uh, maintain that open spirit, no? So they absorb everything they are experiencing in their surroundings, but without losing their roots and the traditions they brought or that we have in Mexico, no? (Mr. Ramírez, Interview)

So as part of that process of awareness raising, culturally and linguistically, in Canada's multicultural context, the children, and to some extent the adults, might have been developing syncretic identities that were, in many ways, unlike those of their counterparts both in Mexico and in Canada.

5.3 HL literacy

The older Aguirre-Ramírez daughters were reportedly somewhat proficient in reading and writing in Spanish. In our interviews, both Mrs. Aguirre and Mr. Ramírez stated that their goal was for the girls to "have the ability to understand and speak it (. . .) and write it. That is the last part and it is possibly the one we will have to pay the most attention to. Right now they speak and understand it, but writing is what requires more work" (Mrs. Aguirre, Interview). For Mr. Ramírez, "It is an ability that is easily lost. Even if you do not speak it, you will always understand it. The second level is that you can also speak it. But the fact that you can speak it does not mean you will be able to write it. Therefore, that is the third ability and we would like for it not to be lost." (Interview)

They made it clear that they wanted their children to understand, speak, and write in Spanish, and that writing was the most challenging. They felt that it was easy to lose writing ability and for that reason, they strongly emphasized it. The family seemed quite confident about the girls' maintenance of the language, but appeared to view literacy as the "final frontier" to conquer. Penelope, the youngest one, was also interested in reading. When she was younger, she would pick up a book and pretend to be reading it in English, when in fact she was mostly inventing the vocabulary.

Although the parents stated that they wanted to see their daughters develop a high level of Spanish literacy, they were aware that it was not realistic in this context and had decided that they were ". . . not going to ask them to have the same level of Spanish writing proficiency as children in Mexico because [they thought] it is very difficult" (Mrs. Aguirre, Interview). They wanted them to develop a high command of English language and literacy, because they will live and study in the

Canadian context. They would like to give them the tools, the basics, in Spanish so they could build on it when they had the opportunity or the need to do so in the future. Because the family spent two months in Mexico every summer, they brought books and other materials when they returned.

5.4 The effect of home culture visits on language socialization

The family's most significant shared activity was their annual visit to Mexico. This was seen as an exceptional situation for the family to spend time with their large extended family in Mexico; it was an opportunity that many other families with similar language socialization goals did not have access to. For this family, it was a regular routine that for several years – almost as long as the girls' lives – they had taken them at the same time, to the same place, to do the same thing: spend time with the family. It was an event that the children anticipated with excitement and it was also by far the most important mechanism for their language socialization process. During an interview with the older children, I asked them about their language practices when they brought up the topic of Mexico (Martin=interviewer):

Example 2:
Martin:	What do you speak most to each other, English or Spanish?
Perla:	English=
Florencia:	=both of them
Martin:	both and do you like Spanish a lot?
Florencia:	[yes
Perla:	[yes
Martin:	and why do you think–do you think that it will be useful when you are older to speak Spanish well?
Perla:	we can go to Canada and to Mexico
Florencia:	Can I tell you why I like Mexico better?=
Martin:	=why?=
Florencia:	=than here?
Martin:	yes
Florencia:	because
Perla:	there
Florencia:	I have my cousins there

In response to my initial question about what language they spoke with each other they replied: "both of them," echoing Zentella's (1997) young participants' replies in New York's *El Barrio*. In line 5, I asked them whether they liked Spanish and both responded affirmatively and in a chorus. What led to their comments about Mexico was my question about why they thought Spanish would be useful in the future. First, they referred to the possibility that Spanish gave them to communicate both in Canada and in Mexico, signaling the internalization of multicultural, transnational identities particularly in association with Spanish. Then in line 11, Florencia offered to reveal why she liked Mexico better, explaining that her cousins lived there. This suggests that the children had a strong connection and affiliation to their family in Mexico, which undoubtedly had a strong influence on their socialization to speak Spanish and display a Latin American cultural identity.

The family members valued the socialization experiences that their trips to Mexico offered, and explained that these trips were the centre of their annual cycle. For them one cycle ended in Mexico at the beginning of the summer vacation and a new one began in Vancouver in September upon their return. The children's Spanish was at its highest when they returned and over the following months it slowly decreased, until they received, in Mrs. Aguirre's words, their next "Spanish injection" the following summer. Mrs. Aguirre described the incentives and interest of the children during their stays in Mexico and the effects of these stays on their Spanish, especially at the end of the cycle when it became a struggle to keep them from switching to English:

> It is as though every year they take an intensive course solely in Spanish because nobody speaks to them in English there, nobody. During the whole year when we are here, or during the ten months we are here, you can see the process through which Spanish gets left behind. Now it is problematic. It is a challenge. "Here, you speak to me in Spanish". I have especially emphasized it to them, in Spanish (. . .) "and I do not understand". And since they know I do not speak well, for them it is real. But, since they see I sometimes speak when we are out they say, "you do understand". So, I say, "yes, yes, I understand, but if you do not speak in Spanish I will only get one ticket to Mexico, not four.[4] Because in Mexico nobody will understand you in English". It is like an incentive, or perhaps a threat (. . .) so that they speak it, do you know what I mean? They love it, they are looking forward to it. They have a great time. They want to do it. (Mrs. Aguirre, Interview)

Toward the end of every summer, the children were already talking to Mrs. Aguirre and asking her questions in English fairly frequently, especially Florencia. She would remind them right away to keep talking, but in Spanish. According to Mrs. Aguirre, even in the first few weeks in Mexico they would talk, and even fight, in English. She recalled an incident soon after their arrival in Mexico that year when Florencia and Perla had gotten into an argument, in English.

---

4 Mr. Ramírez was usually not included as he had to work, but he sometimes joined them in Mexico for part of the time.

She witnessed the whole exchange, but did not understand what had happened. She asked the girls and, still in the excitement of the moment, they tried to tell her what each had said to the other and it proved quite confusing. Perla reacted by turning to Florencia and saying: "We'd better fight again in Spanish" (Mrs. Aguirre, Interview), ending the conflict with her comment. Upon their return in September, they were still having their arguments in Spanish. There was no doubt that the girls had a high level of Spanish proficiency and seemed comfortable switching between Spanish and English. Mr. Ramírez agreed: "they have practically conquered the Spanish language orally" (Mr. Ramírez, Interview).

5.5 The role of school on language socialization

There can be no doubt that the annual stays in Mexico had a strong influence on the girls' proficiency in Spanish, together with the strengthening of their home cultural identity. Conversely, school had a strong influence on the predominance of English and "Canadian" culture in several ways.

Although the family, and more specifically Mrs. Aguirre, would like to engage the girls in home literacy activities more intensively, they felt that they already had many school-related reading and writing activities at home, which did not leave much room for extra literacy work in Spanish. The books that they had brought from Mexico had not been used as much as they would like. Mr. Ramírez explained that they did not want to overload the girls:

> What they are lacking here, Martín, is activities; number one in reading, and number two in writing. That is where they are lacking. And we have not forced them much because the time they spend on those kinds of activities is normally on homework, reading books for school, but we still have to find a way for them to do it without it representing something onerous to them, right? That is why Family Centre serves that function, because although it is only once per week . . .   (Mr. Ramírez, Interview)

However, this does not mean that Spanish literacy was completely precluded in the home. When Perla started pre-school, Mrs. Aguirre decided not to start her on Spanish literacy yet for fear of confusing her, although she was very eager to do it, but fortuitously, one day Perla asked her how to write her own name, then she also wanted to know more about the letters in her name, and answers to other questions. Mrs. Aguirre was happy to teach Perla and Florencia the basics of Spanish writing and reading at that time. Because Mrs. Aguirre's background was in educational psychology and early childhood education, she started doing activities that she used to do with the children she taught in Mexico.

The girls appeared to enjoy school a great deal. They reported that they mostly talked and played in English in school, except when they wanted to tell a secret. Although at home Mrs. Aguirre insisted that they played in Spanish, she had a different attitude about play in school, out of consideration for others: "I do not like the girls to play in Spanish at school. It seems disrespectful" (Mrs. Aguirre, Interview). According to Mr. Ramírez, school was the great homogenizer. He felt that no matter where children came from, through the school's strong socializing force, the children tended to subscribe to a more or less standardized culture and behavior, which was something the family did not resist entirely, and very often the girls brought that culture home to their younger sister. Arguably, the most open exponent of the school culture that was brought home was the language and the parents had to constantly remind the children that they were home where Spanish was the rule.

Although school was a strong assimilative force, the parents felt that it also provided unique opportunities to highlight the home culture. Florencia once had a school project that consisted of preparing and presenting an aspect of family life that showcased their home culture. The project's objective appeared to be to turn students into cultural ambassadors. The project could be related to food, special occasions and activities, dress, or any other aspect that represented the home culture and gave the family cultural pride. Mrs. Aguirre felt that it was a wonderful idea to create such projects which highlighted the children's cultures and showed what contributions the children and their families made to the shaping of a Canadian identity.

Florencia decided to do her project on typical dresses made by a group of Mexican aboriginals, the *Masaguas*. As part of the project, Florencia had to write parts of her script in order to describe what the clothes she would be wearing represented. Perla became interested in the project as well and wanted to do a similar project, but instead, she was invited to participate in Florencia's project by helping with some of the writing and decision-making. Mrs. Aguirre spent a significant amount of time working with them, giving them the necessary information and taking the opportunity to teach the whole family about aspects of Mexican history that had to do with the aboriginal people and their way of life before and after the arrival of Europeans. Penelope got excited about it as well and ended up dressing up and going along with Florencia the day of the presentation. Mrs. Aguirre commented that she appreciated that schools promoted those kinds of projects and activities that helped the children value their cultures and "feel genuinely PROUD of their origins" (Mrs. Aguirre, Interview). Despite the well-founded belief that schools were strong assimilative forces for immigrants, it appears that this particular school project, rather than alienating the children from their own cultures, created opportunities for reinforcing their identities – socializing them into first culture identities – and involving the whole family, providing a powerful school-home connection.

Evidently, the Aguirre-Ramírez family had a strong commitment to the transmission of the language to their children, which could not be separated from their efforts in the maintenance of the culture. Their motivations, objectives, visions, attitudes, and strategies were best summed up by Mr. Ramírez:

> Our final objective is for them to learn Spanish. That they learn to express themselves, they learn to read it, they learn to write it. On the other hand, we do not want them to lose their cultural roots and family. The most important, the most important work we have in order to achieve this is that it not become a conflict. To be subtle in how we pressure them. That they know it is a constant pressure, but without it generating a reaction against it. Not only that they do not lose it, but that they realize at some point that it is important to know two or more languages. (Mr. Ramírez, Interview)

5.6 Language socialization and language dominance

In the family the issue of the girls' dominant language was still open to debate. In order to answer a question about the dominant language of the girls in the initial pre-interview questionnaire, Mr. Ramírez and Mrs. Aguirre engaged in the following exchange, which illustrates this point (Mrs. A=Mrs. Aguirre; Mr. R=Mr. Ramírez):

Example 3:

```
Mr. R:   What is the girls' dominant language?
Mrs. A:  Spanish
Mr. R:   Spanish? Are you sure?
Mrs. A:  I am sure
Mr. R:   Even though they speak it 20% of the time?
Mrs. A:  No, it is still Spanish
Mr. R:   Even though they cannot write it (.) even though they write better
         in English than in Spanish?
Mrs. A:  No, it is still their avenue (.) look, they spend five hours at school=
Mr. R:   =Yes, and they speak only in English
Mrs. A:  And they spend the rest of their day at home=
Mr. R:   =But, but Florencia and Perla speak in English (.) if we do not stop them
Mrs. A:  Yes, but with me they only speak in Spanish, and they are always with me
Mr. R:   There is a very fine line there
Mrs. A:  No, it is still Spanish
```

The above interaction was characterized by competing stances regarding the dominant language of the two older children, Florencia and Perla. In response to Mr. Ramírez's question, all of Mrs. Aguirre's turns focused on asserting the dominance of Spanish in the children's linguistic economy. On the other hand, all of Mr. Ramírez's utterances pointed toward English being the dominant language, countering Mrs. Aguirre's affirmations and assessments and expressing skepticism about her assertions and explanations.

The spoken and written Spanish of the children was very high, as shown in elicited written language samples (not analyzed as part of this chapter). Their Spanish literacy was not age-appropriate, but sufficiently comprehensible. Their oral production was native-like and could suggest their dominant language was indeed Spanish.

6 Discussion and conclusion

The present study sought to examine the contextual and family factors that impacted the heritage language socialization efforts of a middle-class family of Mexican descent in Vancouver, Canada. I found that the parents held various beliefs, values, and attitudes in relation to Spanish language and Latin American culture, which seemed to help shape their language socialization practices. The findings also reported on how they asserted their goal of socializing their children into hybrid transnational identities and a global outlook. It was clear from the analysis that the parents' aims of heritage language socialization were motivated by their beliefs about language in general, and Spanish in particular. They assigned diverse meanings to Spanish maintenance and held expectations of improved well-being in various respects as a result of their children's multilingual development. These expectations pointed to such matters as family cohesion, adaptable identities, and broad worldviews (Guardado 2018). The fact that the present study focused on only one family might be seen as a limitation. Arguably, an approach like this offers one the opportunity to zoom in on issues with a level of detail and integratedness that would not be possible across a large number of families. Indeed, the larger study did provide a broad view of 34 families, so the present chapter enabled me to highlight the issues shaping the experiences of one family. Nevertheless, future research would ideally track multiple families longitudinally, especially if these are families from across ethnolinguistic groups and socio-economic backgrounds. This work could also gather the perspectives of children and youth in conjunction with the perspectives from adults, and perhaps also study the impact of social networks (friendships) in young children's Spanish language development.

Scholars have long held that linguistic minorities' ability to successfully maintain the home language in a dominant language environment gives them a stronger identity and sense of self (Kouritzin 1999, Schecter and Bayley 2002). Pacini-Ketchabaw et al. (2001), for instance, reported that participating Latin American families saw L1 maintenance as a way to foster Latino identity. Schecter and Bayley's (2002) study found that families saw Spanish as "a necessary social resource for maintaining cultural tradition and ethnic identity" (79), which was closely reflected in the present study. The findings also indicated that a strong HL identity supported HL socialization, echoing other research (e.g., He 2008).

Another factor I uncovered in the study was the construction of the HL in relation to the children's emotional well-being. Hence, the participants addressed aspects of their affective domain as a crucial part of their HL socialization goals. The parents assigned a vital role to the HL in the transmission of values by stressing the emotional and moral benefits (Wong Fillmore 1991), and highlighted psychological consequences of not transmitting the language. In this way, they connected the successful continuation of their children's Latin American roots and Spanish language with their affective domain as well as their social, mental, and moral development. Given that the family spent extended time in Mexico every year, both parents stated that their children had strong emotional ties to their extended families and that these trips were always a source of great excitement for them, which afforded them an opportunity to strengthen the emotional ties between the families, mediated by Spanish.

The study found that although the children did not seem to have significant difficulties expressing themselves in Spanish, in writing or orally, English seemed to be the preferred language. This pattern of communication was common when the children had just arrived from school and were eager to relate experiences arising from their school day, especially when their speech was affected by emotion. The interactional data analysis indicated that the children sometimes resisted the socialization into the Spanish-only rule, despite the parents' best intentions.

The study findings echo scholarship that points toward the school environment as playing a significant role in the development of the language use patterns of minority language children (e.g., Mangual Figueroa and Baquedano-López 2017, Wong Fillmore 1991). Thus, although this family perceived the strong assimilative influence of the school on their children's socialization, the parents stated that it also provided unique opportunities to highlight the home culture.

This chapter highlighted the complexity of the goals and practices of HL socialization experienced by the children. There was a variety of ways in which children were socialized into ideologies that valued Spanish, and they reacted in diverse ways by sometimes accommodating and other times resisting such socialization. In addition to socializing their children into Spanish ideologies and Hispanic / Latin American cultural identities, these parents also attempted to inculcate a sense of value for other cultures and languages in the community, including English. In this way they worked to add a hybridized, cosmopolitan layer to their children's identities (Guardado 2010). In their attempts to socialize their children into ideologies of linguistic equality, the parents posed a paradox to their children. In English-speaking contexts, and elsewhere, English is generally a hegemonic force in relation to other languages. Despite the parents' attempts to cast all languages as equal, English may continue to be more powerful than minority languages, and this is a fact that will make the process of socializing children into such ideologies, a struggle, forcing families to have to continuously grapple with this challenge.

Finally, a further layer of HL socialization complexity was revealed in this chapter, which indexed the parents' deep investment in the topic. This layer of complexity underscored their ongoing efforts to analyze their children's linguistic lives, shedding light on their attempts to make sense of their evolving realities. Perhaps it did not even matter whether English or Spanish was their daughters' dominant language at that point. It might even have shifted from one to the other, especially through the effect of their stays in Mexico, or even from moment to moment, as when they returned from school. What seemed to matter the most to the family was that the children were capable of using both languages effectively in the contexts where they lived and interacted. As Mr. Ramírez pointed out, there seemed to be a fine line between their use of the two languages, possibly also blurring the definition of *first language*, *mother tongue* and *second language*, and what it means to be a native speaker of a language. This may index the subjective and complex nature of the parents' perceptions and perspectives about multilingualism, which supports the notion that language socialization is a fluid, unstable, and changeable process.

Appendix – Transcription Conventions (Adapted from Wooffitt 2001)

(.)	A dot enclosed in a bracket indicates a pause in the talk of less than two tenths of a second
(0.5)	The number in brackets indicates a time gap in tenths of a second
(x)	An 'x' enclosed in single parentheses indicates the presence of an unclear word in the recording. The number of 'x's indicates the number of unclear words
[	A left-hand bracket indicates the beginning of overlapping speech, shown for both speakers
Bold	**Bold** typeface indicates the text was originally spoken in English
–	A dash indicates the sharp cut-off of the prior word or sound
=	The 'equals' sign indicates contiguous utterances
CAP	With the exception of proper nouns, capital letters indicate a section of speech noticeably louder than that surrounding it
° °	Degree signs are used to indicate that the talk they encompass is spoken noticeably quieter than the surrounding talk

References

Anzaldúa, Gloria. 1987. *Borderlands/La frontera: The new mestiza*. San Francisco: Aunt Lute Books.

Baquedano-Lopez, Patricia. 2000. Narrating community in doctrina classes. *Narrative Inquiry* 10 (2). 429–452.

Bogdan, Robert & Biklen, Sari Knopp. 1998. *Qualitative research for education: An introduction to theory and methods*. Boston: Allyn and Bacon.

Duff, Patricia A. 2012. Second language socialization. In Alessandro Duranti, Elinor Ochs & Bambi B. Schieffelin (eds.), *The handbook of language socialization*, 564–586. West Sussex, UK: Wiley-Blackwell.

Eckert, Penelope. 2000. *Linguistic variation as social practice*. Oxford, U. K: Blackwell.

Fishman, Joshua. A. 2004. Language maintenance, language shift, and reversing language shift. In Tej K. Bhatia & William C. Ritchie (eds.), *The handbook of bilingualism*, 406–436. Malden, MA: Blackwell.

Fishman, Joshua A. (ed.). 2001. *Can threatened languages be saved?* Clevedon: Multilingual Matters.

Guardado, Martin. 2002. Loss and maintenance of first language skills: Case studies of Hispanic families in Vancouver. *Canadian Modern Language Review* 58 (3). 341–363.

Guardado, Martin. 2006. Engaging language and cultural spaces: Latin American parents' reflections on language loss and maintenance in Vancouver. *Canadian Journal of Applied Linguistics* 9 (1). 51–72.

Guardado, Martin. 2008. *Language socialization in Canadian Hispanic communities: Ideologies and practices*. Vancouver, Canada: University of British Columbia dissertation.

Guardado, Martin. 2010. Heritage language development: Preserving a mythic past or envisioning the future of Canadian identity? *Journal of Language, Identity, and Education* (9)5, 329–346.

Guardado, Martin. 2013. The metapragmatic regimentation of heritage language use in Hispanic Canadian caregiver–child interactions. *International Multilingual Research Journal* 7 (3). 230–247.

Guardado, Martin. 2018. *Discourse, ideology and heritage language socialization: Micro and macro perspectives*. New York & Berlin: De Gruyter Mouton.

He, Agnes W. 2008. Chinese as a heritage language: An introduction. In Agnes Weiyun He & Yun Xiao (eds.), *Chinese as a heritage language: Fostering rooted world citizenry*, 1–12. Honolulu, HI: National Foreign Language Resource Centre.

He Agnes W. 2017. Heritage Language Learning and Socialization. In Patricia A. Duff & Stephen May (eds.), *Language Socialization. Encyclopedia of Language and Education* (3rd ed.), 183–194. Springer, Cham.

Kouritzin, Sandra G. 1999. *Face[t]s of first language loss*. Mahwah, NJ: Lawrence Erlbaum.

Mangual Figueroa, Ariana & Patricia Baquedano-López. 2017. Language socialization and schooling. In Patricia A. Duff & Stephen May (eds.), *Language socialization: Encyclopedia of language and education* (3rd ed.), 141–153. New York: Springer.

Merriam, Sharan B. 1991. *Case study research in education: A qualitative approach*, 2nd edn. San Francisco, CA: Jossey-Bass Publishers.

Norton, Bonny. 2000. *Identity and language learning: Gender, ethnicity, and educational change*. Harlow, England: Pearson Education.

Ochs, Elinor & Bambi B. Schieffelin. 2008. Language socialization: An historical overview. In Patricia A. Duff & Nancy H. Hornberger (eds.), *Encyclopedia of language and education. Vol. 8: Language socialization*, 2nd edn, 3–15. Philadelphia/Heidelberg: Springer.

Ochs, Elinor & Bambi B. Schieffelin. 2012. Language socialization: An historical overview. In Patricia A. Duff & Nancy H. Hornberger (eds.), *Encyclopedia of language and education. Vol. 8: Language socialization*, 2nd edn., 3–15. Philadelphia/Heidelberg: Springer.

Pacini-Ketchabaw, Veronica, Judith K. Bernhard, and Marlinda Freire. 2001. Struggling to preserve home language: The experiences of Latino students and families in the Canadian school system. *Bilingual Research Journal*, 25(1–2), 115–145.

Ryan, Gery W. & H. Russell Bernard. 2003. Techniques to identify themes. *Field Methods* 15 (1). 85–109.

Sakamoto, Mitsuyo. 2001. Exploring societal support for L2 learning and L1 maintenance: A socio-cultural perspective. *ARAL* 24 (2). 43–60.

Schecter, Sandra R. & Robert Bayley. 2002. *Language as cultural practice: Mexicanos en El Norte*. Mahwah, NJ: Lawrence Erlbaum Associates.

Schieffelin, Bambi B. & Elinor Ochs. 1986. Language socialization. *Annual Review of Anthropology* 15. 163–191.

Schwartz, Mila & Anna Verschik. 2013. 'Achieving success in family language policy: Parents, children and educators in interaction.' In Schwartz, M., Verschik, A. (eds), *Successful Family Language Policy: Parents, Children and Educators in Interaction*, 1–20. New York: Springer.

Slavkov, Nicolay. 2017. Family language policy and school language choice: Pathways to bilingualism and multilingualism in a Canadian context. *International Journal of Multilingualism*, 14(4), 378–400. doi: 10.1080/14790718.2016.1229319

Tannenbaum, Michal. 2005. Viewing family relations through a linguistic lens: Symbolic aspects of language maintenance in immigrant families. *Journal of Family Communication* 5 (3). 229–252.

Tannenbaum, Michal & Marina Berkovich. 2005. Family relations and language maintenance: Implications for language educational policies. *Language Policy* 4. 287–309.

Valdés, Guadalupe. 2000. Spanish for native speakers: AATSP professional development series handbook for teachers K-16, Volume 1, 1–20. New York: Harcourt College.

Wong Fillmore, Lily. 1991. When learning a second language means losing the first. *Early Childhood Research Quarterly* 6. 323–346.

Wiley, Terrence. 2001. On defining heritage languages and their speakers. In Joy Kreeft Peyton, Donald A. Ranard & Scott McGinnis (Eds.), *Heritage languages in America: Preserving a national resource*, pp. 29–36. Washington, DC & McHenry, IL: Center for Applied Linguistics & Delta Systems.

Wooffitt, Robin. 2001. Researching psychic practitioners: Conversation analysis. In Wetherell, M., Taylor, S., Yates, S. J. (Eds.), *Discourse as data: A guide for analysis*, 49–92, London, UK: The Open University/Sage.

Yin, Robert K. 1994. *Case study research: Design and methods*, 2nd edn. Thousand Oaks, CA: Sage Publications.

Zentella, Ana Celia. 1997. *Growing up bilingual: Puerto Rican children in New York*. Oxford, UK: Blackwell.

Zilles, Ana M. S. & Kendall King. 2005. Self-presentation in sociolinguistic interviews: Identities and language variation in Panambi, Brazil. *Journal of Sociolinguistics* 9 (1). 74–94.

Hiroki Hanamoto
Chapter 5
Gesture Sequences and Turn-taking Strategies in Communication Settings in the Multilingual Philippines

Abstract: In an English as a lingua franca (ELF) interaction, where participants exhibit different communication behaviors, they might negotiate to overcome these differences and enhance clarity in the course of an interaction by using communication strategies. However, scant research has been conducted to investigate resources other than the verbal language that ELF speakers employ in the process of their negotiation. Thus, the aim of this study is to understand the functions of gesture sequences and turn-taking strategies when pre-empting problems in understanding. Two dyadic interactions, each consisting of a Japanese university student and a Filipina English instructor, form the basis of this study. This research study is based on multimodal analysis using conversation analysis transcription conventions. I discovered that the study participants employed gestures (i.e., iconic, beat, and deictic, see McNeill 2005) for different functions such as filling in details, enhancing explicitness, building rapport, and making correction explicit. These findings indicate that the research participants attempted to employ different interactional communication strategies in turn-taking and close gaps in understanding in verbal interactions through the use of gestures.

Keywords: multimodal analysis, gesture, catchment, ELF, face-to-face interaction

1 Introduction

The aim of this study was to understand the functions of gesture sequences and turn-taking strategies in English as a lingua franca (ELF) communication settings. It is apparent that, in face-to-face interaction, interlocutors employ not only linguistic but also para-linguistic and non-verbal features. These features include gaze, whole body movements, and hand movements such as gestures (Goodwin 2003). In particular, Gullberg (1998) has observed that speakers in ELF contexts employ gestures more often when negotiating to overcome

---
Hiroki Hanamoto, Tokyo Denki University, Japan, E-mail: hiro_warriors@mail.dendai.ac.jp
https://doi.org/10.1515/9781501514692-005

problems in understanding with their use of verbal communicative elements. In fact, several studies have shown that speakers in interactions frequently employ gestures synchronized with speech when overcoming difficulties (e.g., Gullberg 1998), creating a complete meaning (e.g., McNeill & Duncan 2000), searching for words (e.g., McCafferty 2002), and enhancing clarity and alignment (e.g., McNeill 2005). What is important to note is that previous ELF research has been based mostly on audio-recorded data and has not taken any significant account of resources, other than language, that ELF speakers employ in the process of their interaction. This study, therefore, attempts to clarify the process of how, in an ELF setting, a non-native-speaking Filipina English instructor and a Japanese English learner are engaged in interaction, through a multimodal analysis of gesture sequences and turn-taking strategies. In other words, the present study will answer the following research question: How do ELF speakers integrate gestures with speech when pre-empting problems in understanding?

2 Literature review

2.1 Communicating in English as a lingua franca

The environment surrounding English has gradually changed globally, and English is used increasingly among non-native speakers of English (Seidlhofer 2011). According to Crystal (2003), the number of non-native speakers of English has far surpassed that of native speakers of English, with a ratio of three to one. This ratio suggests that a number of English speakers have been exposed to different non-native varieties of English in their education, through their work, or when traveling.

ELF encompasses all English users, including those speaking it as a native language, second language, or foreign language. In other words, we can summarize that ELF is the common means of communication among speakers who are from different lingua-cultural and language backgrounds (e.g., Jenkins 2009; Seidlhofer 2011). Therefore, in an ELF interaction, where participants exhibit different communication behaviors, they might negotiate to overcome these differences and enhance the clarity of meaning in the course of an interaction through the use of communication strategies.

Even if native speakers of English are included in an ELF interaction, they do not necessarily set the linguistic agenda: all the participants have to "make adjustments to our local English variety for the benefit of (. . .) [the] interlocutors" (Jenkins 2009: 201), negotiating meaning for mutual understanding. People communicate using "multiple means of meaning making" (Jewitt, Bezemer, & O'Halloran 2016: 2), which is called *multimodality*. As mentioned above, interlocutors in a conversation use not only linguistic but also para-linguistic and non-verbal features such as gesture, gaze, and back-channeling (Goodwin 2003), namely, multimodal resources in a face-to-face interaction. In particular, many studies (e.g., Hanamoto 2016, 2017; Kaur 2011; Ke & Cahyani 2014; Matsumoto 2015) emphasize the important use and function of gestures to enhance the construction of successful communication in ELF contexts. For instance, Gullberg (1998) acknowledges that ELF speakers utilize some multimodal resources as well as language, when they find it difficult to express their message and need to negotiate to overcome problems.

2.2 Gestures: Types and function

Gesture is one of the most frequently used means of non-verbal communication, mainly or together with verbal communication, between a speaker and a listener (McNeill 1992), although some gestures are not synchronized with speech, such as when relying on visual and mimetic imagery. In particular, gesture – one semiotic resource – plays an important role in intersubjectively constructing meaning between interlocutors. In fact, Kendon (2004) has investigated many aspects of gestures and then defined manual movements as gestures. Additionally, he illustrated four kinds of different gesture use, namely *gesticulation, mime, emblems,* and *sign language*, with regard to the relationship between gestures and speech and also in relation to gesture's degree of conventionalization (for details, see Kendon 2004). However, the present study mainly focuses on gestures synchronized with speech, because the aim of this study is examining gestures in face-to-face interaction.

Co-occurring speech and gestures can create a complete meaning, namely *co-expressivity* (McNeill & Duncan 2000). It is well documented that a speaker conveys her/his message using hand and/or body movements, namely gestures, together with what s/he is willing to express verbally (McNeill 2005). According to McNeill (2005), gestures synchronized with speech are classified into four types: *iconic, metaphoric, deictic,* and *beat* (as will be described in Results and discussion section).

McNeill (2005) also reports that gestures can enhance clarity in interaction, or *catchment*, which is "recognized when one or more gesture features occur in at least two (not necessarily consecutive) gestures" (116). It is apparent that a speaker takes turns and co-creates meaning through the use of resources that they employ in the course of interaction. In an interaction, catchment seems to play a significant role in "achieving alignment" between a speaker and a listener when establishing "a common ground" (McNeill 2005: 164). Thus, we can conclude that gesture has a range of functions and is used pragmatically in interaction.

Gestures often occur simultaneously with other gestures, and also have a range of functions such as "modal, performative, parsing and interactive or interpersonal" (Kendon 2004: 159). In other words, the pragmatic functions of gesture may relate to features of an utterance's meaning and, at the same time, co-create meaning between interlocutors to achieve common ground. Therefore, language analysis that integrates gesture might reveal the orientation of practices of turn-taking (Mondada 2007) and provide a clearer understanding of the process by which participants negotiate meaning for understanding.

Based on the above discussion, in what follows, I illustrate a research gap related to this study and make clear the thinking behind this interactional approach. Previous ELF interaction research has been centered primarily on linguistic interactional behaviors and the verbal strategies that ELF speakers utilize when interacting (e.g., Cogo 2010; Jenkins 2000; Seidlhofer 2004). Participants in ELF interactions employ gestures interpersonally with speech; therefore, studies that integrate gesture into analysis are necessary. This study considers gesture as one part of the whole complex of multimodal interactional resources. The following research question was formulated for the present study: How do ELF speakers integrate gestures with speech when pre-empting problems in understanding?

3 Method

3.1 Research aims

As described previously, the goal of this study is to understand the functions of gesture sequences and turn-taking strategies when pre-empting problems in understanding. The data analyzed for this study are based on two video-recorded ELF conversational interactions between a Japanese university student and an English-language Filipina instructor in one-on-one classrooms.

3.2 Participants

The participants were two female Japanese learners of English who participated in the language programs in the Philippines and two female Filipina English instructors in a language school in the Philippines. Two native speakers of

Japanese (Sakura and Mizu), majoring in English and Communications in their university in Japan, and two Filipina English instructors (Jasmin and Sophia) participated voluntarily in this study (the names are pseudonyms to protect the privacy of the participants). The two instructors were selected because they were very popular among students there, and recommended by the language school. The course they taught was "speaking" in a one-on-one class and the two students attended most of the weeks. The participants' attributes, such as gender and first language (L1), as well as other details like duration of recording, and type of instruction are shown in Table 5.1. Sakura's and Mizu's primary motivation to learn English in the Philippines was to interact with and learn English from non-native English speakers. They stayed in the Philippines for about a month and attended an average of eight English classes a day.

Table 5.1: Participants in the Recorded Interactions.

Dyad	Name	Gender	Nationality	L1	Duration of recording (min:sec)	Instruction
1	Sakura	Female	Japanese	Japanese	49:30	One-on-one
	Jasmin	Female	Filipina	Hiligaynon		
2	Mizu	Female	Japanese	Japanese	49:28	One-on-one
	Sophia	Female	Filipina	Hiligaynon		

3.3 Procedure

Two videos of face-to-face interaction between a Japanese university student and an English-language Filipina instructor form the basis of this study. The data recording was undertaken in August 2016, upon receiving informed consent forms and obtaining permission from the participants to video record their conversational interactions in a one-on-one class and to use their images in publications. The length of one lesson was 50 minutes. The study participants were asked to record themselves to help the interaction occur more naturally and to avoid the influence of the researchers on the study setting (Maxwell 1996). The Japanese students were assigned discussion topics by the instructors prior to the session, based on the question "Why do you think people marry?" The topics, however, were ultimately agreed upon through the interaction between the student and the instructor. Then, they were encouraged to explore possible topics and talk freely in English about whatever topic they chose.

3.4 Data analysis

I took a locally situated, emic approach to data analysis, employing *ELAN* open-source annotation software for multimodal analysis, and using conversation analysis transcription conventions (see Appendix for transcription conventions) in order to explicate the detailed process of interaction. The analysis provides us with simultaneous visibility of participants in the course of their interaction and their actions beyond speech. It should be noted, again, that this study aimed to focus on non-verbal communication strategies and multimodal interactional resources, namely gestures using hand and body movements, which are employed in interaction.

Based on previous studies (e.g., Schegloff et al. 2002), I employed sequential analysis in order to clarify the process of coming to understanding. Sequential analysis explicates the detailed process of making unintelligible utterances clear as participants make progress toward understanding. I attempted to address instances where difficulty in understanding was displayed overtly and explicitly through multimodal repair sequences (Olsher 2008). I transcribed and analyzed the dyadic face-to-face interactions using Jefferson's (1984) conversation analytic conventions and McNeill's (2005) conventions for non-verbal elements (see Appendix for transcription conventions). Through these inspired conventions, it is possible to establish common principles in their turn-taking and meaning making (Jewitt et al. 2016). More specifically, I used multi-layered annotation software, ELAN, to analyze what initiates gestures and how gestures are produced in an interaction to identify gesture "*strokes*" (McNeill 2005).

4 Results and discussion

Fine-grained multimodal and sequential analysis reveal that the study participants employed multimodal interactional resources such as language, paralinguistic features (such as silence, speech volume, and overlapping speech), and non-verbal actions (such as body and hand movements), often in combination. However, by paying careful attention to sequence organization, I found that participants often employed repetition as part of the repair work with gestures and that they used gestures for different functions: filling in details, enhancing explicitness, building rapport, and making correction explicit. In what follows, we will look at three cases relating to each of these functions. Background information, such as the gender and nationality of the participants, is also provided at the beginning of each example.

Chapter 5 Gesture Sequences and Turn-taking Strategies in Communication — 69

4.1 Sakura and Jasmin's interaction

The first example consists of a conversation between Sakura (S) and Jasmin (J). Example 1 is part of a conversation, in which they discuss the latest fashions in Japan. A multi-layered ELAN transcript is provided in Figure 5.8. In the sequence below, the Japanese student, Sakura, is trying to answer Jasmin's question by employing gestures with speech.

Example 1: "Camisole"
S (f) = Japanese; J (f) = Filipina

```
 1.  J: uhn:: what's the latest fashion: now in Japan
 2.  S: uhn:::: (.)
 3.  J: the latest (.) TRENDS
 4.  S: trends
 5.  J: uhn: ((back-channeling))
→6.  S: (.) uhn:cami-so{le=
→7.             {((iconic-both hands moving expressing clothes))
→8.  J: =what-it-that
→9.  S: cami-{camisole↑
→10.        {((iconic-both hands moving expressing clothes more widely))
 11. J: cami-sole?
 12. S: (.) ye-ah.
 13. J: wh[at
 14. S:    [no:sleeve?
 15. J: OH::
```

Figure 5.1: Lines: 6–7 (1).

Figure 5.2: Lines: 6–7 (2).

Figure 5.3: Lines: 6–7 (3).

Figure 5.4: Lines: 9–10 (1).

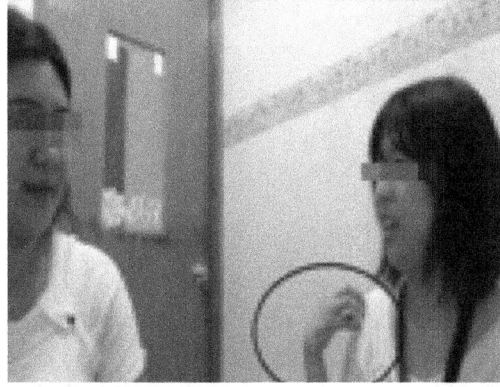

Figure 5.5: Lines: 9–10 (2).

Figure 5.6: Lines: 9–10 (3).

Figure 5.7: Lines: 9–10 (4).

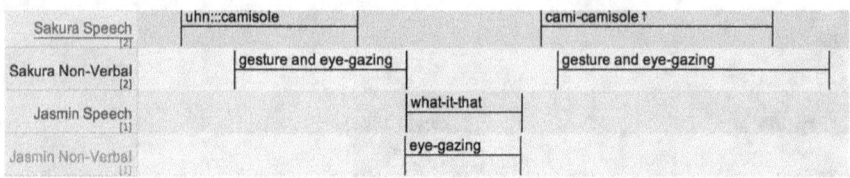

Figure 5.8: Multi-layered transcript: Lines 6–10.

In the sequence above, Sakura is struggling to express that the camisole is the latest fashion in Japan in lines 6–7, after exhibiting what might be her thinking process through nonverbal vocalization ("*uhn*") (Figures 5.1–5.3). Here, most of Sakura's gestures function merely to add emphasis to her speech; that is, her series of iconic gestures, which resemble aspects of the actual events and display "picturable aspects of semantic content" (McNeill 2005: 39). These can become an effective visual cue in addition to the co-occurring speech, namely "*camisole*," which makes the meaning of the message clearer and facilitates comprehensibility. In lines 9–10, Sakura employs the same iconic gestures, along with a cut-off (Figures 5.4–5.7), but more emphatically than when compared to lines 6–7. In other words, the gestural size that Sakura employed here is larger and clearer than those in Figures 5.1–5.3, which enhances the clarity of her gestures to Jasmin.

Employing larger and clearer gestures constitutes a gestural catchment. In other words, one possible reason Sakura re-employs the gestures described above is that her use of gestures leads to making her meaning richer, because Jasmin expresses her non-understanding to Sakura (line 8). According to McNeill (2005), catchment seems to play an important role in establishing a common ground and co-creating meanings between gesture and speech. Here, Sakura's iconic gestures appear to demonstrate and explain the fashion trend "camisole" to Jasmin, through constructing gestural catchments. It can be argued that Sakura employs iconic gestures repeatedly to make up for missing verbal components and to enhance explicitness by providing visualizing objects. Therefore, the series of iconic gestural catchment employed by Sakura might be considered as a strategy of enhanced explicitness and also as functioning to maintain coherent turn-taking.

4.2 Mizu and Sophia's interaction

When gestures are employed, their function seems to be to build or maintain rapport in the interaction, in order to confirm whether speech is linguistically correct. Example 2, below, is from the conversation between the Japanese student Mizu (M) and the Filipina instructor Sophia (S), talking about Mizu's favorite song and the song's meaning.

Example 2: "Song meaning?"
M (f) = Japanese; S (f) = Filipina

```
 1. M: ah:: ((nodding repeatedly)) I::{I learn: I learn:
 2.                                  {((beating- right hand moving and
 3.                                  leaning back in her chair))
 4. S: OK: lear[n:
 5. M:         [I learn::
 6. S: O:K:
→7. M: (.) uhn:: song meaning↑ ((beating- both hands moving))
→8. S: ah:: $OK$: song's {MEANING=
→9.                      {((beating-both hands moving slowly))
10. M: =song's meaning ((nodding repeatedly))
11. S: yeah-oh. what kind of song
```

Figure 5.9: Line: 7 (1).

Figure 5.10: Line: 7 (2).

Figure 5.11: Line: 7 (3).

Figure 5.12: Line: 7 (4).

Chapter 5 Gesture Sequences and Turn-taking Strategies in Communication — 75

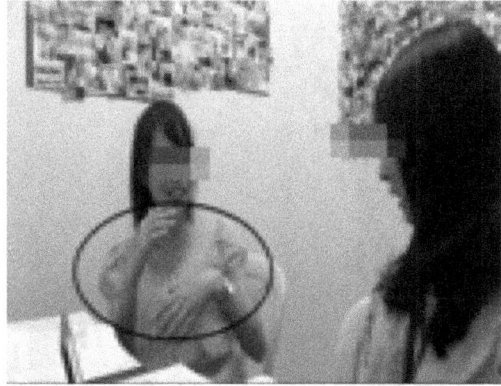

Figure 5.13: Lines: 8–9 (1).

Figure 5.14: Lines: 8–9 (2).

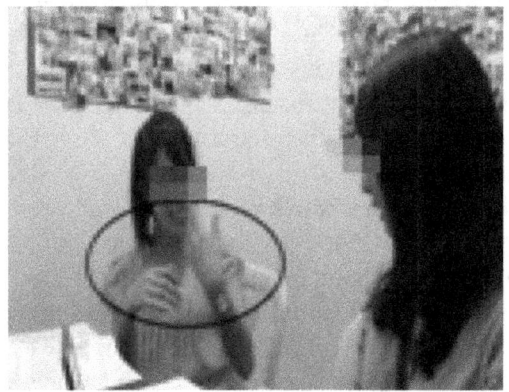

Figure 5.15: Lines: 8–9 (3).

Figure 5.16: Lines: 8–9 (4).

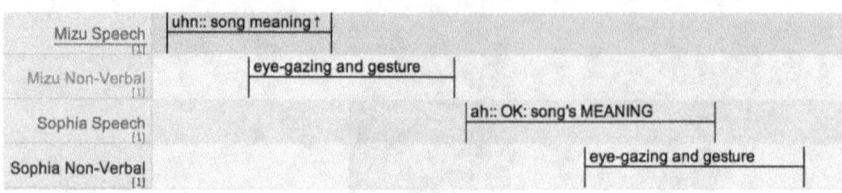

Figure 5.17: Multi-layered transcript: Lines 7–9.

The sequence of speech above reveals that the Filipina instructor, Sophia, makes use of various communication strategies simultaneously to try and correct Mizu's linguistic error through non-verbal means. First, after Mizu's utterance with the beat gesture (line 7) (Figures 5.9–5.12), Sophia utters "*ah*," implying there is a "role in interaction which is almost purely sequential" (Heritage 1989: 29), then she shows her acknowledgement with the topic shift marker "*OK*" (Beach 1993). She is going to take her turn (line 8). This clearly exhibits that Sophia acknowledges Mizu's previous turn. Sophia's movement here produces a change in the interactional flow and signals that, now, she is going to become involved in resolving Mizu's linguistic error (line 7), correcting "*song meaning*" to "*song's meaning*."

In this interaction, Sophia uses beat gestures with speech "*song's MEANING*" (lines 8–9 and Figures 5.13–5.16). McNeill (2005) explains that beat gestures mean "flicks of the hand(s) up and down or back and forth that seem to 'beat' time along with the rhythm of speech" (40). It is said that beat gestures bring attention to speech and monitor speech production and flow, but do not have a semantic relationship with speech (McNeill 2005). The beating rhythm employed by Sophia here, however, was much more slowly exhibited, compared to that gestured by Mizu in line 7, in order to negotiate the modification of the linguistic error explicitly. The beat gestures employed here by Sophia seem to illustrate a communicative strategy for repair initiation. In other words, this sequence indicates that speech concurrent with gesture builds or maintains rapport between the participants in the interaction when involved in resolving problems.

On the other hand, Sophia initiates a repair sequence by employing another kind of gesture, deictic, with speech in the next example. In this example, Mizu is telling Sophia that her boyfriend sings a song for her.

Example 3: "S-sing↑"
M (f) = Japanese; S (f) = Filipina

1. M: uhn:: my boyfriend::
2. S: ah:uhn:yes:
→3. M: ((beating- both hands moving)) (.) s-sing↑((eye-gazing))
→4. S: OK: a. s-SANG↑ ((deictic- left hand moving expressing emphasis))
→5. M: sang↑
6. S: sang. OK:
7. M: sang this song for me

Figure 5.18: Line: 4 (1).

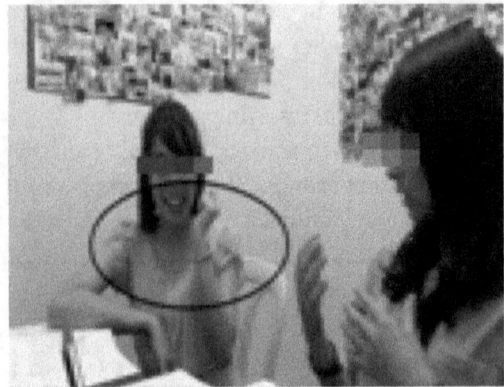

Figure 5.19: Line: 4 (2).

Figure 5.20: Line: 4 (3).

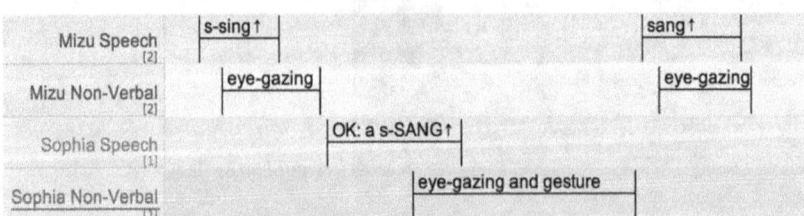

Figure 5.21: Multi-layered transcript: Lines 3–5.

Mizu attempts to confirm with Sophia whether her use of tense is correct in line 3 "*s-sing↑*". Mizu's self-confirmation check is displayed to Sophia with non-verbal resources, namely a combination of beat gesture, cut-off, marked rising intonation and gaze, to see "if the partner can follow the speaker"

(Jamshidnejad 2011: 3762). Then, Sophia, in line 4, says "*OK*" to acknowledge Mizu's previous turn (as explained in a similar exchange in Example 2) and then continues, saying, "*s-SANG↑*" with a change in her speech volume. Simultaneously, Sophia extends her left hand and lifts it to her face (Figures 5.18–5.20). This gesture can be interpreted as a pointing gesture, or deictic, which is one that serves "a metaphorical function by referring to abstract entities" (McNeill 2005: 39–40). However, this particular pointing gesture is not devoted to a specific deictical reference (Mondada 2007), but rather highlights the interactional practices in repair settings. Thus, this negotiation of meaning, through both verbal and gestural modes, contributes to Mizu's understanding of the accurate use of tense, in line 5. In short, Sophia's deictic pointing gesture was instrumental in terms of achieving joint attention and making the correction explicit and comprehensible to Mizu.

5 Conclusion

This study aimed to understand the functions of gesture sequences and turn-taking strategies in ELF communication settings, by using a multimodal analysis of both verbal and non-verbal cues. Although preliminary, based on a multimodal analysis using conversation analysis transcription conventions, I found that the study participants employed gestures with speech for different functions, such as filling in details, enhancing explicitness, building rapport, and making correction explicit. This finding indicates that they attempted to take turns and close the understanding gaps by using gesture with speech. In fact, the participants employed a range of gestures that could be classified as iconic, beat, and deictic, depending on specific purposes at each interactional turn-taking. In employing a range of gestures during their verbal interaction, they enhanced explicitness, built or maintained rapport before repair sequences, and made corrections explicit for clarity. Therefore, the series of gestural catchment employed by the interlocutors in their interaction might be considered as a strategy of engaging in the interaction and having a function of maintaining coherence when turn-taking. Moreover, the beating and pointing gestures employed by participants in this study do not appear to have a direct relationship with speech, but rather, offer different opportunities for overt repair practices.

These findings have significant implications for ELF and other areas of communication. It seems that gestures function by co-constructing meanings beyond or with speech and enhancing explicitness relating to speech. Moreover, the literature shows that gesture facilitates the thinking process (e.g., McNeill & Duncan

2000) and enables interlocutors to interact, think conceptually, and express conceptual understanding. In other words, gestures seem to be useful not only when highlighting problems in understanding, with or without speech, when dealing with difficulties, but also for facilitating speech production. Gestures benefit listeners' meaning making and speaker's own "mental representation" (McNeill 1997: 190). The findings of this study suggest the importance of incorporating multimodal interactional resources in an interaction. They also point to the significant role of gesture, together with speech, in constructing meaning to form multimodal turn and sequence organization for a successful interaction.

In spite of those obvious findings and implications, it is clear that the current study has some limitations. One concerns the limited inclusion of just three analyzed data examples, and thus the findings presented in the above conclusion cannot simply be generalized and applied to the whole phenomenon of gestural use in interaction. Similarly, another limitation is that this study analyzed the interactions in one-on-one based classrooms between an instructor and a student; therefore, research which includes interactions from large classrooms or between ELF students would be needed to uncover the details of their use of gesture as a multimodal resource, knowledge that would contribute significantly to an understanding of multilingual situations in general, including in the context of ELF.

Acknowledgements
This study is supported by a Japanese Government Grant-in-Aid for Scientific Research (No. 15K02767). The author, first and foremost, is grateful to Dr. Yuriko Kite who spared time out of her busy schedule to share her valuable inside perspectives with him. This study would also have been impossible without the help offered by the four participants in this study.

Notes

An earlier version of this paper was presented at the MELDC17 Conference, Slovenia on September 30, 2017.

Appendix Transcription conventions

(Adapted from Jefferson 1984 and McNeill 2005)

[	overlapping utterances
=	latched utterances
{	overlapping utterances with non-verbal actions
.	fall in intonation
:	extended sound or syllable
(.)	short pause of less than 1 second
-	cut-off by the current speaker
MEANING	speech much louder than surrounding talk
$	smile voice
(( ))	non-verbal action
→	feature of interest to analyze

References

Beach, Wayne A. 1993. Transitional regularities for 'casual' "Okay" usages. *Journal of Pragmatics* 19 (4). 325–352. doi:10.1016/0378-2166(93)90092-4

Cogo, Alessia. 2010. Strategic use and perceptions of English as a lingua franca. *Poznań Studies in Contemporary Linguistics* 46 (3). 295–312. doi:10.2478/v10010-010-0013-7

Crystal, David. 2003. *English as a global language* (2nd edn). Cambridge: Cambridge University Press.

Goodwin, Charles. 2003. Pointing as situated practice. In Sotaro Kita (ed.), *Pointing: Where language, culture, and cognition meet*, 217–241. Mahwah, NJ: Lawrence Erlbaum Associates Publishers.

Gullberg, Marianne. 1998. *Gesture as a communication strategy in second language discourse: A study of learners of French and Swedish.* Lund, Sweden: Lund University Press.

Hanamoto, Hiroki. 2016. How participants in English as a lingua franca (ELF) employ communication strategies: Multiple realities in minimal response in ELF. *Asian Englishes* 18 (3). 181–196. doi:10.1080/13488678.2016.1229832

Hanamoto, Hiroki. 2017. Negotiation of meaning in ELF (English as a lingua franca) interaction: Multimodal approach focusing on body movements including gestures. *Journal of Multimodal Communication Studies* 4 (1–2). 23–28.

Heritage, John. 1989. Current developments in conversation analysis. In Derek Roger & Peter Bull (eds.), *Conversation: An interdisciplinary perspective*, 21–47. Clevedon: Multilingual Matters.

Jamshidnejad, Alireza. 2011. Functional approach to communication strategies: An analysis of language learners' performance in interactional discourse. *Journal of Pragmatics* 43 (15). 3757–3769. doi:10.1016/j.pragma.2011.09.017

Jefferson, Gail. 1984. On the organization of laughter in talk about troubles. In J. Maxwell Atkinson & John Heritage (eds.), *Structures of social action: Studies in conversation analysis*, 346–369. Cambridge: Cambridge University Press.

Jenkins, Jennifer. 2000. *The phonology of English as an international language*. Oxford: Oxford University Press.

Jenkins, Jennifer. 2009. English as a lingua franca: Interpretations and attitudes. *World Englishes* 28 (2). 200–207. doi:10.1111/j.1467-971X.2009.01582.x

Jewitt, Carey, Jeff Bezemer & Kay O'Halloran. 2016. Navigating a diverse field. In Carey Jewitt, Jeff Bezemer & Kay O'Halloran (eds.), *Introducing multimodality*, 1–13. Oxon & New York: Routledge.

Kaur, Jagdish. 2011. Raising explicitness through self-repair in English as a lingua franca. *Journal of Pragmatics* 43 (11). 2704–2715. doi:10.1016/j.pragma.2011.04.012

Ke, I-Chung & Hilda Cahyani. 2014. Learning to become users of English as a lingua franca (ELF): How ELF online communication affects Taiwanese learners' beliefs of English. *System* 46. 28–38. doi:10.1016/j.system.2014.07.008

Kendon, Adam. 2004. *Gesture: Visible action as utterance*. Cambridge: Cambridge University Press.

Matsumoto, Yumi. 2015. *Multimodal communicative strategies for resolving miscommunication in multilingual writing classrooms*. Pennsylvania: The Pennsylvania State University dissertation.

Maxwell, Joseph A. 1996. *Qualitative research design: An interactive approach*. Newbury Park, CA: Sage.

McCafferty, Steven G. 2002. Gesture and creating zones or proximal development for second language learning. *The Modern Language Journal* 86 (2). 192–203. doi:10.1111/1540-4781.00144

McNeill, David. 1992. *Hand and mind: What gestures reveal about thought*. Chicago, IL: University of Chicago Press.

McNeill, David. 1997. Growth points cross-linguistically. In Jan Nuyts & Eric Pederson (eds.), *Language and conceptualization*, 190–212. New York, NY: Cambridge University Press.

McNeill, David. 2005. *Gesture and thought*. Chicago, IL: University of Chicago Press.

McNeill, David & Duncan Susan D. 2000. Growth points in thinking-for-speaking. In David McNeill (ed.), *Language and gesture*, 141–161. New York, NY: Cambridge University Press.

Mondada, Lorenza. 2007. Multimodal resources for turn-taking: Pointing and the emergence of possible next speakers. *Discourse Studies* 9 (2). 194–225. doi:10.1177/1461445607075346

Olsher, David. 2008. Gesturally-enhanced repeats in the repair turn: Communication strategy or cognitive language-learning tool? In Steven G. McCafferty & Gale Stam (eds.), *Gesture: Second language acquisition and classroom research*, 109–130. London: Routledge.

Schegloff, Emanuel, Irene Koshik, Sally Jacoby & David Olsher. 2002. Conversation analysis and applied linguistics. *Annual Review of Applied Linguistics* 22. 3–31. doi:10.1017/S0267190502000016

Seidlhofer, Barbara. 2004. Research perspectives on teaching English as a lingua franca. *Annual Review of Applied Linguistics* 24. 209–239. doi:10.1017/S0267190504000145

Seidlhofer, Barbara. 2011. *Understanding English as a lingua franca*. Oxford: Oxford University Press.

Anna Khalizova
Chapter 6
The Phenomenon of Code Alternation by Multilingual Speakers

Abstract: *Code alternation* belongs to an area of research with a long and intensive tradition. In contrast to the numerous papers on language change dealing with bilingual speakers there is little work on this phenomenon with multi- and plurilingual speakers. Due to globalization, such speakers are no longer an exception today. This chapter focuses on the phenomenon of language change in institutional multilingual communication. To achieve common understanding in this complex framework participants must bridge knowledge divergences of an institutional, interlingual and intercultural nature. Different methods and procedures are used by interlocutors to achieve the main goal of the communication. In this chapter, I present how the phenomenon of code alternation (code-switching and transfer) is used primarily as a resource in the process of understanding in an enrollment consultation between German and English lingua franca speakers. The phenomenon of language change is primarily examined using conversation analysis perspective (Auer 1984). In line with Auer (1984) I can firstly differentiate between code switching and transfer, secondly between participant-related and discourse-related code alternation. Participant-related code-switching is the most common type of language change in the data corpus. Different types of language change are caused by different factors, for instance, better competence of the speaker in another foreign language or change of situation. They serve in the dataset different purposes, for example, to secure understanding or to negotiate understanding or in the function of bridging a (current) word gap. Overall, this process can be classified as successful in organizing understandings. The chapter answers the following questions: In which situations during the enrollment consultation does the language change occur? Which factors cause the language change? Which purposes does the language change serve in the dataset serve? And: How successful is the language change as a strategy in the process of organizing understanding? The phenomenon of language change is primarily examined using conversation analysis.

Anna Khalizova, Goethe University Frankfurt, Germany, E-mail: Khalizova@em.uni-frankfurt.de

https://doi.org/10.1515/9781501514692-006

Keywords: institutional communication, enrollment consultation, conversation analysis, language change, codeswitching, transfer, multilingualism, lingua franca speakers, the process of understanding

1 Introduction

Regardless of whether one is in contact with government authorities for the first time, or has contacted them in the past, communication is rarely smooth. Rosenberg (2014: 1) notes: "Communication with government authorities is often difficult. It often fails even with the same mother tongue, the same cultural background and the best will". Communication with authorities has long been intensively and thoroughly studied. In contrast to the numerous papers dealing with administrative texts, there is little known work on conversations occurring with the administration (Becker-Mrotzek 1999: 1398).

In the context of oral administrative communication, Becker-Mrotzek (1999, 2001) distinguishes between three different discourses: data collection interviews (Germ. *Datenerhebungsgespräche*), counseling discourse (Germ. *Beratungsdiskurse*) and discourse of objection (Germ. *Widerspruchsgespräche*). The focus of this chapter is on the interviews in the enrollment counselling, which ranked according to the categorization of Becker-Mrotzek (1999: 1399, 2001: 1514–1518) to the data collection interviews. Becker-Mrotzek, Konrad and Fickermann (1992: 245) define data collection interviews as "those in which the counselor collects personal data from the client, for example, for an application." As early as 1980, Grosse (1980: 19) documented that many authorities have their own advisors whose only task is to assist with filling in the forms or correcting errors within completed forms. Data collection interviews are a type of interaction characterized by a shift from written to oral administrative communication, as the written content of the form, which forms the basis of the interaction, is "voiced over" by the counselor (Becker-Mrotzek 2001: 1514). On one hand, data collection interviews support citizens in carrying out this activity (Lüdenbach and Herrlitz 1981) and "in transforming their life world into institutional circumstances" (Becker-Mrotzek 2001: 1514). On the other hand, they allow a direct check for the completeness of the information and the supporting documents (Becker-Mrotzek 2001: 1514). The data collection interview is a type of conversation strongly influenced by the omnipresence of a form. Thus, the form constitutes the indispensable object of the interaction or the "significant object" (Deppermann and Schmitt 2007: 111). Thereby the form constructs the interaction and becomes the coordinative center and reference point that regulates the entire course of the communication from the beginning. The conversation is initiated by the consultant according to the questionnaire on the form, and questions and answers become the central activity (Becker-Mrotzek 2001: 1514). Over and above that, it is an interactive situation in which the participants are engaged in verbal interaction with the realization of a practical activity, namely the completion of the form. Thus, the activity of filling in becomes an integral part of the interaction process. The interaction makes the complete filling in of the form possible. The blank form builds the content of the interaction, while the completed form represents the purpose of the interaction.

2 Data

This investigation is based on a dataset of approximately 55 hours of audio and video of form-based data collection interviews in an enrollment office, which were a part of the enrollment procedure for international students at the University of Freiburg. 150 interviews were documented in total. The observation of interviews and the making of audio and video recordings began in March 2014 and ended in April 2016. In total, the fieldwork spanned a period of three years. Access to the research site took place in three stages: first, obtaining permission from the head of the Service Center Study Freiburg; second, obtaining the permission of consultants to be recorded and to present at the data collection interviews; and third, obtaining the permission of students to be present at the data collection interviews and to record them. The data are characterized by strong cultural diversity. Students and consultants from 49 countries participated in the study. The spectrum includes countries from five continents, although German and English dominated the interviews. Further analysis only included conversations in German or English as lingua franca. Thus, a total of 114 audio and 24 video conversations were used in the analysis.

Although predominantly German and English are used as the main languages of communication, a wide range of languages is represented in the dataset. Overall, the dataset contains a variety of code alternations, so not only are German and English exchanged, but also other languages, whose dominance is suspected, such as French, Spanish, Chinese, Hindi, Swedish. The change between several languages within a conversation is a special feature of this type of conversation.

3 Literature review

3.1 A conversation analytic approach to code-switching

I took a conversation analytic (CA) approach to examining the phenomenon of code alternation in the enrolment consultation as a resource in the process of organizing understanding. The CA approach to code-switching was proposed by Auer (1984) in his publication, *Bilingual Conversations*, and was further developed in his later publications (1988, 1995, 1998). Others who have used conversation analysis in their research have been Wei (1994), Alfonzetti (1998), Sebba/Wootton (1998), Guardado (2009, 2018) and Khalizova (2019). The CA approach examines the conversational structure of language change independently of the macro-social structure. From this perspective, code-switching is seen as a *contextualization cue*, that is, as a resource for organizing the ongoing conversation (Cashman 2005: 304). Auer (1984) sees code-switching as an interactional activity that requires a method of analysis that focuses on the sequential principle of conversation. When used in this type of analysis, CA examines the strategies that participants in the interaction use to achieve mutual understanding. Auer (1995) points out the sequential embeddedness of the code-switching in interaction and emphasizes the necessity of analyzing the sequential environment by investigating the code-switching phenomenon, because its meaning is determined by this sequential environment (Auer 1995: 116). Auer (1988: 210) emphasizes that code-switching in conversation does not necessarily have a metaphorical function in the sense of Gumperz (1972). Auer's (1998) objections eventually led to the abandonment of the distinction between "situational" and "metaphorical" code-switching and introduced "conversational" code-switching. Though his analysis is based on Gumperz's (e.g., 1972, 1982) basic assumptions, Auer opposes his view that a specific situation in the conversation is given a priority. He assumes that the situation in which bilingual speakers change to another language emerges during the course of the conversation. According to Auer the strategy of code change contributes to the meaningfulness of a certain statement and thus serves to organize the conversation.

In my study, I use Auer's (1984) classification system: by code alternation he differentiates between two other important phenomena, namely code-switching and transfer. If code-switching means "any language change at a certain point in the conversation without structurally (and thus predictable) return to the first language," transfer is "any language change for a particular unit with a structurally provided point for the return to the first language with the completion of that unit" (Auer 1984: 26). In both code-switching and transfer, Auer differentiates between discourse- and preference-related forms. Another difference relates to the object of the signaling process: when it comes to an aspect of the conversation, then it is about the discourse-related language change, if it is a property of the participants themselves, then it is the participant-related language change (Auer 1984: 94).

In the following sections I demonstrate how the phenomenon of code alternation (code-switching and transfer) is used primarily as a resource in the process of understanding in the enrollment consultation between lingua franca speakers of English and German. The following questions guide my analysis: In which situations during the enrollment consultation does the language change occur? Which factors cause the language change? Which purposes does the language change in the dataset serve? How successful is the language change as a tactic in the process of organizing understanding? The basic model for my investigation is the model of Auer (1984), who examined this phenomenon in bilingual speakers.

3.2 Code alteration

The term *codeswitching* was first proposed by Vogt (1954) in his review of Weinreich (1953) and not, as is often assumed, by Haugen (1956) (quoted in Auer 1998: 27; Stell and Yakpo 2015: 1f.). Although the first scientific work on the phenomenon of code-switching already existed in the 1950s and 1960s, little attention was paid to codeswitching in research at that time. Only with the emergence of sociolinguistics as an independent research discipline did code-switching become a subject of research interest (Treffers-Daller 2005: 1470; Stell and Yakpo 2015: 2). In particular, the works of Blom and Gumperz (1972), Poplack (1980), and Gumperz (1982) motivated further investigations of this phenomenon in the context of syntax research as well as in sociolinguistics and psycholinguistics (Biegel 1996: 7; Cantone 2007: 54; Treffers-Daller 2005: 1470). Due to the fact that code-switching has been investigated from very different perspectives, there is no consensus in research on its terminology or its definition (Özdil 2010: 41; Stell and Yakpo 2015: 2). In this paper I am using the definition by Auer (1984, 1995) who analyzed this phenomenon from a conversational perspective. Auer (1995) uses the term 'code-alternation' as hyperonym for both code-switching and transfer. He (1995: 116) defines it as follows:

> Code-alternation (used here as a cover tern, i.e. hyperonym, for code-switching and transfer) is defined as a relationship of contiguous juxtaposition of semiotic systems, such that the appropriate recipients of the resulting complex sign are in a position to interpret this juxtaposition as such.

Most studies on codeswitching deal primarily with bilingual speakers. There is very little work on the phenomenon of codeswitching by multi- and plurilingual speakers. Notable are the studies of Poulisse (1997), Poulisse and Bongaerts (1994), Khalizova (2019) who analyzed code-switching by L2-learners. This can probably be explained by the fact that speaking two or three foreign languages in Germany and some other European countries used to be a rarity. As a result of globalization, such speakers are no longer an exception today. Significant is the work of Lüdi (2004), in which he deals with the question whether L2-learners can codeswitch. He points out that the use of their L1 or other language is a commonly used communication strategy of non-native speakers to prevent certain communicative difficulties, a phenomenon Lüdi (2004) calls "translinguistic wording." He emphasizes that even balanced bilingual speakers use this communication strategy, as they also have certain lexical gaps. Lüdi (2004: 347) emphasizes that a broad definition of multilingualism blurs the boundaries between "code-switching" and "translinguistic wording". Referring to Wode (1990: 37), Lüdi (2004) writes: "[code-switching] is not limited to a particular level of competence or a particular stage of development of languages being switched between, these languages are so far developed, so that the speaker has two linguistic codes" (348). He concludes that L2-speakers can also codeswitch.

4 Code alternation as a resource in the process of organizing understanding

4.1 Code-Switching

4.1.1 Participant-related code-switching

Participant-related code-switching not only represents the first type of code-switching, as mentioned above, but also the most common type of language alternation within the dataset. Within this type of code-switching we can distinguish (with reference to Auer, 1984) competence-related (code-switching related to the linguistic competence of a speaker) from preference-related code-switching. The latter is conditioned by a speaker's preference for a particular other language (Auer 1984: 21).

4.1.2 Competence-related code-switching

Competence-related code-switching is due to insufficient competence in the first foreign language. It serves both to negotiate and to secure understanding.

Example 1: ((16.04.2014/ Student from UK/ Counselor from Togo/ Form field, "Information on previous studies at German institutions of higher education"/ German/ 04:50–4:56 sec.)) {0:06} Counselor (B), Student (S)

	01	B:	haben sie schon in DEUTSCHland studiert?
			(have you ever studied in Germany before?)
	02	S:	NEIN.
			(no)
	03		(0.5)
→	04	B:	**is the FIRST time?**
			(ist es das erste mal?)
	05		zum ERSTmal?
			(for the first time?)
	06		(0.5)
	07	S:	uHU.

The participants are a consultant from Togo (mother tongue: French) and a student from the UK (mother tongue: English). The interaction is in German. In this sequence, the counselor and the student are filling in the form field "Information on previous studies at German institutions of higher education." After the student appears to have answered (l. 02) the question of the counselor (l. 01), and after a short break (l. 03) the counselor reformulates the question in English (l. 04), which is the mother tongue of the student. Thus, there was *competence-related code-switching*. The counselor wanted to be sure that the student had understood the question correctly and that the form field was filled in correctly. In the following turn, he repeats the question in German (l. 05). After a short pause (l. 06), the student answers the question again (l. 07). The fact that the counselor repeats the question in their following turn despite what might be a clear answer can be seen as a tactic for securing understanding and forms a special feature of this type of conversation.

Based on this example, we can see that the understanding in the interaction must be constantly secured in order to achieve the main goal of the communication, namely the correct filling in of the form. This is done not only by verbatim repetition of what has been said, but also by reformulating it in another language via *competence-related code-switching*. It is used either to secure or to negotiate understanding.

Another typical case of competence-related code-switching can be seen in situations where counselors work with multiple students at the same time, or as they quickly respond to another student's question, switching to another language and sometimes not immediately back to the first language of communication. In such cases, code-switching serves the purpose of enabling understanding.

4.1.3 Preference-related code-switching

Preference-related code-switching signals the speaker's preference for one language over another; altogether it occurs rarely (Auer 1984). It is mainly inserted for the negotiation of the main language of communication. Auer (1984: 22) emphasizes that bilingual speakers' preferences for a definitive language can be explained through the factor of language competence or behavior. As I analyzed the interaction between the lingua franca speakers, I was looking to see whether there might be exceptions to Auer's model (1984).

The next example offers a very interesting case of *preference-related code-switching*. In this example, I observe how both interlocutors try to use their preferred language as the main communication language. The student, who was born in Germany, but grew up in Turkey (mother tongue: Turkish), stated that English is her preferred language. According to her, she feels safer discussing official matters in English than in German. Thus, the cause of the preference might be greater linguistic competence in English. The consultant, on the other hand, found German easier than English, even though he speaks English well. It is important to mention that at the beginning of the conversation, the counselor asked the student why she does not want to speak German, because she speaks it well. She remarked that the counselor could continue to speak German, but that she would rather speak English. It is interesting that both interlocutors tried to accommodate each other's language preferences. But after each topic change, both tried to use the preferred language.

Example (2): ((14.04.2015/ Student from Turkey/ Counselor form Togo/ Form field, "Information on university entrance qualification" and, "Information on health insurance"/ German and English / 04:50–06:15 sec.)) {01:25} Counselor (B), Student (S)

35	B:	DAtum von (.) diesem diplom weißt du?
		(do you khow the date of this diploma?)
		(do you khow the date of this diploma?)
36	S:	(1.2)
37		HM?

38		(1.0)
39	B:	HIER (.) schreibst du einfach mal (.)-
		(here you just write)
40		geNAU.
		(exactly)
41	S:	HIER?
		(here?)
42	B:	JA.
		(yes)
43		das JAHR.
		(the year)
44	S:	das JA:HR.
		(the year)
45	B:	uHU.
46		(1.6)
47	B:	WANN war das?
		(when was it?)
48	S:	(0.4)
49		JA (.).
		(yes)
50		moMENT.
		(just a moment)
51		zweitausend elf
		(two thousand eleven)
52		(1.0)
53	B:	ACHT?
		(eight?)
54	S:	ZWEI (.) zwei tausend –
		(two two thousand)
55		SIEbn.
		(seven)
56	B:	SIEben,
		(seven)
57		(2.0)
58		HIER (.)-
		(here)
59		AUSlands;
		(abroad)
60	S:	ah entSCHULdigung.
		(sorry)
61		(26.28)
→ 62	S:	äh (.) i have a PRIvate insurance [so its],
63	B:	[do you have] (.) pr PRIvate insuarance?

64	S:	yYES.
65	B:	CAN I see?
66	S:	YES.
67	B:	(20.7)
68		okAY,
→ 69		**was KOStet das pro (.) monat?**
		(what does it cost per month?)
70	S:	äh (.) einundACHTzig euro;
		(eighty one euros)
71	B:	(0.9)
72		EIN (-)und-
		(one and)
73		ACHTzig euro.
		(eighty euros)

The conversation begins with a discussion of the form field "Information on university" question of the consultant concerning the student's high school year (after the meaning of the German term "Abitur" has been clarified). The counselor asks the student about the high school year (l. 47). After a filled break (l. 48, 49) and a delay (l. 50) she says the year (l. 51) and the counselor repeats it (l. 53) after a short pause (l. 52). The student does not confirm the consultant's year, but names another year (l. 54, 55). The counselor repeats the high school year again (l. 56) and after a short pause (l. 57) gives the instruction to complete the field (l. 58), which is formulated here only with the help of the local deictic *hier* 'here'. Through a linguistic specification (l. 59), he explains to the student in which box exactly she should fill in the information. The student apologizes (l. 60), as she probably started to fill in the wrong box. This is followed by a long pause (l. 61), in which the student fills in the field. In the following turn (l. 62) she goes over to the next question in the form concerning "Information on health insurance." She changes from German to English (*preference-related code-switching*). This change marks the change of subject or the transition to the next form field, but it can also be interpreted as the student's preference for another language. In this context, the new form field functions as a "transition point" (Auer 1984: 16). The counselor adapts himself linguistically to the student and then also changes to English (l. 63). He asks her for permission to look at her health insurance certificate (l. 65). After a long pause (l. 67), in which the consultant presumably looks at the documents, he switches back to German for the question (*preference-related code-switching*), because, as already mentioned, German is easier for him than English. Thus, the preference for one of two linguas franca was based on greater competence. In addition, the consultant knows that the language competence of the student in German is sufficient for completing the form. The student adapts the language and switches to German (l. 70). The ensuing conversation is characterized by constant language change, since both interlocutors had preferences for certain languages, which were conditioned by greater competence. Interestingly, the constant change of language did not affect the process of understanding between the interactants – on the contrary – it served to secure understanding.

Each of the interactants in this example had a clear preference for a particular language, which can be explained by better language proficiency. For the student, it was English; for the counselor, German. Interestingly, both interlocutors adapted to each other's preferences, but nevertheless tried, on occasion, to switch to their own preferred language. In some instances, while speaking to different students the counselors simultaneously forgot to switch to the expected language (German or English) for the interaction.

4.1.4 Discourse-related code-switching

The analyzed data also include examples of *discourse-related code-switching*. Structurally discourse-related code-switching marks a change of the conversational context and thus a new activity. Discourse-related code-switching occurs in situations where students switch to their native language to discuss answers with friends or acquaintances, or when counselors discuss specific information relevant to students with each other. Thus, this type of code-switching is used to negotiate or to secure understanding, as in the following examples:

Example (3): ((16.04.2014/ Student from Great Britain/ Student from Great Britain/ Counselor from Togo/ Form field, "Studies in other countries or in your native country"/ German/ 06: 19–06:40 sec.)) {00:21} Counselor (B), Student 1 (S1), Student 2 (S2)

```
    01   B:    wie lange hast du in INgland studiert?
                (how long have you studied in england)
    02   S1:   (1.0)
    03         hm (1.0)
    04         (2.0)
    05         in meinem LEben?
                (in my life?)
    06         äh::
→   07         how many YEARS?
```

→	08	S2:	**this is ähm two (.) TWO years of study.**
	09	S1:	AH studiert,
			(studied)
	10	B:	JA studiert.
			(yes studied)
	11	S:	ZWEI.
			(two)
	12	B:	(1.0)
	13		ZWEI jahre?
			(two years)
	14	S1:	(2.0)
	15		ich habe gedacht (.) in in die SCHUle.
			(i thought at school)

In this excerpt, a consultant from Togo (native language: French) and a student from the UK (native language: English) fill in the form field "Studies in other countries or in your native country". The conversation begins with the question concerning the duration of the study (l. 01). In this context, the consultant uses the verb *studieren*. After a filled pause (l. 02, 03, 04), a demand (l. 05), and a short delay (l. 06), the student finally changes to English (l. 07). The difficulties in understanding require *discourse-related code-switching*. The student asks her acquaintance, who is also from the UK, the number of her previous years of study. After he has answered her in English (l. 08), the student changes back to German. She shows her understanding by using the interjection "ah" and by the repetition of the verb "studieren". The cause of the problem of understanding in this example lies in the phonetic similarity of the German *studieren* and the English *study*. If the verb studieren in this context is limited only to the university, the verb *to study* means the entire learning process. Thus, this sequence provides an example of *interlanguage interference*, in which the student transfers certain linguistic structures from her mother tongue, English, to the foreign language, German. After she has understood that this is about university studies, the consultant, who was probably not aware that the student is thinking about the entire study, also verifies this (l. 10). The student answers the question (l. 11) and the consultant repeats (l. 13) for confirmation, her answer after a short pause (l. 12). The student does not reply. Presumably, understanding becomes multimodal, for example realized by a nod. After a short pause, she explains to the counselor the reason for the misunderstanding (l. 14, 15).

Chapter 6 The Phenomenon of Code Alternation by Multilingual Speakers — 97

The student in the foregoing example changed languages to answer a question. Code-switching thus helped to negotiate the understanding. In the next example the student changes languages after she has already answered the question. As we will see, in this case, the code-switching serves to secure and to revise the understanding.

Example (4): ((24.04.2014/ Two students from India/ Counselor from China/ Form field, "Information on university entrance qualification"/ English/ 05:52–07:02 sec.)) {01:10} Counselor (B), Student 1 (S1), Student 2 (S2)

01	B:	so in which year did you FInish your HIGH school?
02	S1:	ah HIGH school?
03	B:	aHA;
04	S1:	two thousa::nd (.) SIX.
05	B:	two thousand SIX.
06		(5.0)
07		in INdia?
08	S1:	in INdia?
09	B:	(8.0)
10		so m(.)may i have you:r HEALTH insuarance?
11		(1.0)
12		THANK you.
13		(8.0)
14	S1:	**HIGH school matlab tenth grade ya twelfth grade?**
		(Bedeutet high school tenth grade oder twelfth grade?)
→ 15	S2:	**paTA nahi.**
		(Ich bin mir nicht sicher.)
→ 16		**SHAYad tenth?**
		(Vielleicht tenth grade?)
17	S1:	ah one MInute,
18		exCUse me?
19		by HIGH school do you mean the tenth grade or twelfth grade?
20	B:	(1.0) ah i DONT quite understand you.
21		the year you have FInished the high school.
22	S1:	YES high school.
23		RIGHT?
24		ja oKAY two thousand six.
25	B:	oKAY.

In this sequence, a consultant from China (native language: Chinese) asks a student from India (native language: Hindi) the year in which she graduated (l. 01). The student repeats "high school" with rising intonation (l. 02), as she may not have expected such information to be requested for enrolling at the university. The counselor assures her with an affirmative "aha" that she has understood the question correctly (l. 03). Subsequently, the student answers the question of the consultant (l. 04), who now repeats her answer to ensure mutual understanding (l. 05). After a short pause (l. 06), the counselor inquires whether the student has completed her high school diploma in her home country (l. 07) and she replies affirmatively to this question (l. 08). As the conversation continues, the transition to the next field "Information on health insurance" takes place (l. 09, 10, 11, 12, 13). During the pause (l. 13), in which the counselor reads the documents, the student turns to her friend, who is also from India and is also filling in the form, and asks for the exact definition of "high school". For this the student changes to Hindi (l. 14). After the meaning of high school has been clarified (l. 15, 16), a revision of the understanding by a demand follows (l. 17, 18, 19). After a short break, the consultant thematizes his lack of understanding (l. 20) and reformulates the question in the following turn (l. 21). The student confirms the understanding of the question (l. 22, 23) and the correctness of the answer (l. 24). Her answer is ratified by the counselor (l. 25).

4.2 Transfer

According to Auer (1984), the term *transfer* refers to "any change of language for a particular unit with a structurally provided point for the return to the first language with the completion of that unit" (Auer 1984: 26). Similar to code-switching, transfer can be further subdivided into participant-related and discourse-related transfer. The first transfer type refers to the language competence of the interlocutor, and the second signals the change of topic. In the following I deal with the two transfer types in more detail.

4.2.1 Participant-related transfer

Participant-related transfer is a common occurrence in my dataset. In interaction, transfer is one of the strategies used to organize understanding. This strategy is used for a variety of purposes and is used by both students and consultants. It serves to both secure and negotiate understanding. It is also used to close the (current) word gap. Although transfer is generally considered to be successful, there are examples in the dataset that are unsuccessful. In these cases, understanding is achieved, but not as smoothly as desired by the speaker. One implementation of transfer is the use of synonyms. In examining the data collection interviews, I found that the students had the greatest difficulty understanding the German word *Name* in its language-specific meaning and the German word *Abitur*. In the conversations, the pair forms Vorname/name and Nachname/family name are normally used. Semantically, the German lexeme "Name" and the English lexeme "name" are cognates. The difference in meaning leads to difficulties for many applicants, as in the following example:

Example (5): ((16.04.2014/ Student from Italy/ Counselor from USA/ Form field, "Application for Unicard"/ German/ 13:41–14:02 sec.)) {00:21} Counselor (B), Student (S)

	01	B:	und (.) ä:hm VORname (.) nachname unterschrift (.) und ein passfoto müssen wir da: kleben.
	02	S:	(3.0)
→	03		so vorNAme ist **the::** (.) **NAme** ja?
			(Vorname)
	04	B:	ä::h n ne nach (.) so deine ERSTname.
	05		so das WÄ:re-
→	06	S:	**the** NAme.
→	07	B:	JA your **first name**.
			(Vorname)
	08	S:	oKAY.
	09	B:	JA.

In this excerpt a student from Italy (native language: Italian) must fill in the last form field "Application for Unicard" on the last page of the form. The counselor from the USA (native language: English) explains to the student that he should fill in his name and first name as well as paste a photo in the appropriate form field (l. 01). After a short pause (l. 02), the student asks the counselor for the meaning of the German word *Vorname*, using the English synonym *name (participant-related transfer)* (l. 03). After a short delay, the counselor explains to the student that this is his first name (l. 04). Notably, after the delay, the counselor uses the word *Erstname*, which she presumably translates directly from the English *first name*. This suggests that the counselor probably did not intend to change to English but wanted to continue speaking German. She likely wanted to explain to the student the meaning of the term by using a corresponding German synonym. In order to make this more understandable for the student, she also tries to find the first name of the student in the documents in the following turn (l. 05). Without waiting for the counselor to find his first name in the documents, the student completes the sentence (l. 06) again using the English synonym *name*, thereby demonstrating that he understands the counselor (l. 06). In contrast to the first attempt of the student (l. 03), this time the counselor agrees with him immediately (l. 07). In her answer, she uses not only the confirmation particle *ja* (yes), but also the English *first name*. This firstly confirms my hypothesis that she has already thought of this term in line 1. 04 and, secondly, it shows a cultural difference: In British English, *name* and *surname* are mostly used, however in American English, *first name* and *last name* are more common forms. As the counselor originally comes from the USA, she might be more inclined to use the term "first name" to the term "name" and because of that may have responded to the student's question (l. 03) with a delay (l. 04). The student, who has learned English as a foreign language, uses "name" and may or may not be aware of these cultural differences. After the counselor has answered his question, mutual understanding is reaffirmed (l. 08, 09). This example shows that a seemingly simple question to do with one's names can not only cause brief confusion, but sometimes significant understanding problems as well.

In the dataset, another major source of difficulty can be found with the use of the German word *Abitur*. *Abitur* corresponds to the acquisition of the general university entrance qualification. Every applicant wishing to enroll at the University of Freiburg must have obtained the university entrance qualification in their home country and should bring it in the form of a diploma. The term for *diploma* varies from country to country. While *Abitur* is common in Germany, in other countries other names are common, such as *Matura* (Austria), *Matura/Matur* (Switzerland), *Diploma di Maturá/Esame di Maturità* (Italy), *el bachillerato* (Spain), *Baccalauréat* (France), *high school diploma* (USA), *Ammecmam (Attestat)* (Russia), Gaozhong (China), A-Level (India), *Examen* (Sweden), *Maturité* (Belgium) or *αποφοίτησηαπότολύκειο*(Greece). Due to the different names of the university entrance qualification in different cultures it is not surprising that the question of the counselors concerning Abitur often causes confusion. Selting (1987) describes misunderstandings in institutional communication arising from the different use of the same term by clients and agents as local problems (in German, *lokale Probleme)* – a description that applies also to my research findings.

To achieve mutual understanding, the consultants resort in part to similar strategies used to clarify the German *Name*. The first tactic here is also transfer. *Abitur* is explained through the English synonym *high school*, and although the high school (and Abitur) is a culturally specific education system concept, it is generally better known and thus helps applicants to understand more quickly what is meant by the German *Abitur*. The transfer in this context is also used either to secure or to negotiate understanding.

Chapter 6 The Phenomenon of Code Alternation by Multilingual Speakers — 101

In Example 6, I can see that the student, despite having answered the question quickly and correctly, seems uncertain about the meaning of *Abitur*. In order to ensure understanding, the consultant therefore uses *high school*.

Example (6): ((30.03.2016/ Student from Greece/ Counselor from China/ Form field, "Information on university entrance qualification"/ German/ 01:45–02:03 sec.)) {00:18} Counselor (B), Student (S)

	01	B:	u:::nd WANN hast du dein abitur gemacht?
			(and when did you finish your high school?)
	02	S:	zweitausendELF.
			(two thousand eleven)
	03	B:	(0.3) ELF.
			(eleven)
	04		hier (.) zweitausendELF bitte.
			(here two thousand eleven please)
	05	S:	(2.0)
	06		also wir haben kein abiTUR aber sowas in der art.
			(so we do not high school/abitur but something like that)
→	07	B:	hm so end von dem (1.0) **HIGH school oder?**
	08	S:	JA (.) griechisches abitur ja.
			(yes greek higk school yes)
	09	B:	uHU.

In this example, a consultant from China (native language: Chinese) and a student from Greece (native language: Greek) are filling in the form field "Information on university entrance qualification." The student answers the counselor's question immediately (l. 02) about graduation year (l. 01). The counselor repeats the student's answer (l. 03) and gives instructions to complete the field (l. 04). In the following verbal pause (l. 05), the student fills in the appropriate form field. Afterwards he mentions that *Abitur* doesn't exist in Greek, but there is a similar term (l. 06). In Greece, the university entrance qualification is αποφοίτησηαπότολύκειο. The counselor explains the meaning of the question and uses for this purpose high school (l. 07) to help the student better understand the concept. The student agrees (l. 08) and the counselor confirms her understanding (l. 09).

In addition to the functions of securing and negotiating understanding, the transfer also bridges a current word gap. It fulfills a word replacing function such as in the case of names of courses, cities, universities, and institutions. For example, Auer (1984: 57) writes that participant-related transfer is predominantly used in the case of current word loss or a current word accessibility problem. Chlopek (2007: 35) points out that lexical transfer (as well as other transfer forms) is typical for both production and reception in an insufficiently controlled target language and is a kind of "rescue tactic" of the learner, mostly used unconsciously.

The following example refers to filling in the form field "Information on fields of study". In this example, the student immediately translates the program into German but only after the consultant has already expressed his understanding.

Example (7): ((14.04.2015/ Student from Sweden/ Counselor from Burkina Faso/ Form field, "Information on fields of study"/ German/ 07:11–07:30 sec.)) {00:19} Counselor (B), Student (S)

	01	B:	ja schreibst du dein FACH.
			(here you write your subject)
	02	S:	mein FACH?
			(my subject?)
	03	B:	geNAU (.) was du studieren wirst.
			(exactly what are you going to study here)
	04		was WILLST du studieren?
			(what do you want to study here?)
→	05	S:	**BUSsiness administration.**
	06		=beTRIEBSwirtschaftslehre
	07	B:	geNAU ja genau-
			(exactly yes exactly)
	08		SCHREIBST das.
			(write this)
	09	S:	oKAY.
			(ok)
	10	B:	das ist hier (.) VOLKSwissenschaftlehre.
			(this is here national econimics)
			beTRIEBSwissenschaftlehre.
			(business administration)
	11	S:	so beTRIEBSwirtschaftslehre?
			(so business administartion?)
	12	B:	YES.
	13	S:	oKAY.

The consultant from Togo (native language: French) asks the student from Sweden (native language: Swedish) the name of the degree program in which he is going to enroll (l. 01, 03, 04). The student mentions the program first in English (l. 05) and then repeats it in German (l. 06). The counselor gives the instruction to complete the field (l. 07, 08) and the student shows his understanding (l. 09). Following this, the counselor explains what the program is officially called (l. 10). After having entered the name of the program, the student asks whether it is correct (l. 11). The counselor confirms this (l. 12), the student signals his understanding by using the confirmation particle "okay" (l. 13).

In some cases in the dataset, the speaker's speech deficiency is repaired by translating into the original communication language, while in other examples the use of the original term may cause a momentary confusion. Maintaining the original terms could be explained by the fact that students are trying to provide as much information as they can, even though they cannot always correctly assess the relevance of the information for a particular question.

5 Conclusion

In summary, my analysis showed that language change, with its two forms, code-switching and transfer, is one of the most popular tactics in organizing the process of understanding in multilingual encounters in the context under study. It was used frequently by both counselors and students in my research. Following Auer (1984), I distinguish firstly between the participant-related and discourse-related language change and secondly between code-switching and transfer. In contrast to the most previous studies, which have mainly examined this phenomenon using the example of bilingual speakers, this study presents the use of code alternation by multilingual (respectively lingua franca) speakers. Furthermore, this study deals with two linguas francas, i.a. German opposite to the most studies on English as lingua franca.

Participant-related code-switching represents the most common type of language change in the dataset and can be further classified into competence-related and preference-related code-switching. Competence-related code-switching is mainly used for currently insufficient competence in the first foreign language. In particular, competence-related code-switching is used with the clarification of terms. It is used either to negotiate or to secure understanding. Another typical case of competence-related code-switching can be seen in situations where counselors work with multiple students at the same time, or as they quickly respond to another student's question, switching in the course of this to another language and afterwards sometimes switching not immediately back to the first language of communication. In such cases, code-switching serves the purpose of enabling understanding.

Preference-related code-switching signals the speaker's preference for one language over another and is primarily due to the speaker's better competence in a foreign language or better activation of that foreign language compared to another. All in all, preference-related code-switching does not occur as often in my dataset and is used primarily to negotiate the main communication language and the process of understanding. In some instances, the counselors forget to switch to the expected language while speaking to different students, so this type of code-switching takes place.

Discourse-related code-switching is also present in the dataset. Structurally, it marks the change of the conversational context and thus a new activity. It occurs in situations where students change to their native language to discuss the answer to a question with their friends or acquaintances or when counselors discuss specific information with each other that is relevant to students. Thus, it serves either to negotiate or to secure understanding.

Participant-related transfer is a common phenomenon in my dataset. In the interaction process, transfer functions as one of the tactics to organize the process of understanding, which is used for different purposes, namely to secure or to negotiate understanding or in the function of bridging a (current) word gap. Discourse-related transfer occurs in the dataset very rarely and is used to signal a topic change. Unlike code-switching, the transfer is mainly used to clarify terms. Code-switching emerges in other communicative contexts, such as clarification of the main communication language.

All in all, the language change can be considered as successful in the process of organizing understanding. However, there are also some examples in the dataset in which the opposite effect is achieved, often by the use of categories "name/Name" and the term "Abitur". It should be mentioned that such examples are not often at data corpus. In these cases, mutual understanding is achieved, but this process of understanding is not as smooth as it is desired.

This study examines the use of code alternation by multilingual speakers in intuitional university context. It can be interesting to do further research in another institutional contexts to compare the results. Quantitative analysis of all the subcategories across the corpora can be another interesting perspective of research.

References

Alfonzetti, Giovanna. 1998. The conversational dimension in code-switching between Italian and dialect in Sicily. In Peter Auer (ed.), *Code-Switching in Conversation: Language, Interaction and Identity*, 180–214. London: Routledge.
Auer, Peter. 1984. *Bilingual conversation*. Amsterdam: Benjamins.
Auer, Peter.1988. A Conversation Analytic Approach to Code-switching and Transfer. In Monica Heller, *Codeswitching: anthropological and sociolinguistic Perspectives*, 187–213. Berlin [u.a.]: Mouton de Gruyter.
Auer, Peter. 1995. The pragmatics of code-switching: A sequential approach. In Lesley Milroy & Pieter Muysken (eds.), *One speaker, two languages: Cross-disciplinary perspectives on code-switching*, 115–135. Cambridge: Cambridge University Press.

Auer, Peter. 1998. *From code-switching via language mixing to fused lects: Toward a dynamic typology of bilingual speech.* Universität Konstanz, Philosophische Fakultät, Fachgruppe Sprachwissenschaft. http://kops.uni-konstanz.de/handle/123456789/3677 (accessed 31 Oktober 2019).

Becker-Mrotzek, Michael, Ehlich Konrad & Ingeborg Fickermann. 1992. Bürger-Verwaltungs-Diskurse. In Reinhard Fiehler & Wolfgang Sucharowski (eds.), *Kommunikationsberatung und Kommunikationstraining. Anwendungsfelder der Diskursforschung*, 234–253. Opladen: Westdeutscher Verlag.

Becker-Mrotzek, Michael. 1999. Die Sprache der Verwaltung als Institutionensprache. In Ludger Hoffmann, Martin Kalverkämper & Ernst Wiegand (eds.), *Fachsprachen, Handbücher zur Sprach- und Kommunikationswissenschaft*. Band 14.2., 1391–1401. Berlin: de Gruyter.

Becker-Mrotzek, Michael. 2001. Gespräche in Ämtern und Behörden. In Klaus Brinker, Gerd Antos, Wolfgang Heinemann & Sven F. Sager (eds.), *Text- und Gesprächslinguistik*. 2. Halbband, 1505–1525. Berlin: de Gruyter.

Biegel, Thomas. 1996. *Sprachverhalten bei deutsch-französischer Mehrsprachigkeit: soziolinguistische Untersuchungen mündlicher Kommunikation in der lothringischen Gemeinde Walscheid.* Frankfurt am Main [u.a]: Lang.

Blom, Jan-Petter & John J. Gumperz. 1972. Social meaning in linguistic structures. Code switching in Northern Norway. In John J. Gumperz & Dell H. Hymes (eds.), *Directions in Sociolinguistics. The Ethnography of Communication*, 407–434. New York: Holt, Rinehart and Winston.

Cantone, Katja F. 2007. *Code-switching in bilingual children.* The Netherlands: Springer.

Cashman, Holly R. 2005. Identities at play: Language preference and group membership in bilingual talk in interaction. In Li Wei (ed.), *Conversational code-switching*, 301–316. Amsterdam: Elsevier.

Chlopek, Zofia. 2007. *Der zwischensprachliche Transfer beim Drittsprachenerwerb – Einstellungen der DeutschlehrerInnen zum Transfer aus dem Englischen ins Deutsche.* Glottodidactica 42 (1). http://pressto.amu.edu.pl/index.php/gl/article/view/4143 (accessed 31 October 2019)

Deppermann, Arnulf & Reinhold Schmitt. 2007. Koordination. Zur Begründung eines neuen Forschungsgegenstandes. In Reinhold Schmitt (ed.), *Koordination. Analysen zur multimodalen Interaktion*, 15–54. Tübingen: Narr.

Grosse, Siegfried. 1980. Allgemeine Überlegungen zur sprachlichen Fassung von Vordrucken und Formularen. In Siegfried Grosse & Wolfgang Mentrup (eds.), *Bürger – Formulare – Behörde. Wissenschaftliche Arbeitstagung zum Kommunikationsmittel ‚Formular'. Mannheim, Oktober 1979*, 11–24.Tübingen: Gunter Narr Verlag (Forschungsberichte des Instituts für Deutsche Sprache Mannheim 51).

Guardado, Martin. 2009. Speaking Spanish like a boy scout: Language socialization, resistance and reproduction in a heritage language Scout troop. *The Canadian Modern Language Review* 66 (1). 101–129.

Guardado, Martin. 2018. *Discourse, ideology and heritage language socialization: Micro and macro perspectives.* New York & Berlin: De Gruyter Mouton.

Gumperz, John J. 1982. *Discourse strategies.* Cambridge: Cambridge University Press.

Khalizova, Anna. 2019. *Formularbasierte studentische Lingua-Franca-Immatrikulationsberatung. Multimodale Konversationsanalysen von hochschulischen*

Datenerhebungsgesprächen, Baden-Baden: Tectum Verlag, Reihe „Dynamiken der Vermittlung: Koblenzer Studien", Band 5 dissertation.

Lüdenbach, Norbert & Wolfgang Herrlitz. 1981. Zur Verständlichkeit von Formularen: Ein handlungstheoretischer Versuch. In Ingulf Radtke (ed.), *Der öffentliche Sprachgebrauch, 2: Die Sprache des Rechts und der Verwaltung*, 305–321. Stuttgart: Klett-Cotta.

Lüdi, Georges. 2004. Code-Switching/Sprachwechsel. In Ulrich Ammon, Norbert Dittmar, Klaus J. Mattheier & Peter Trudgill (eds.), *Sociolinguistics: An international handbook of the science of language and society/ Soziolinguistik. Ein internationales Handbuch zur Wissenschaft von Sprache und Gesellschaft*. HSK 3.1, 341–350. Berlin/New York: de Gruyter.

Özdil, Erkan. 2010. *Code-Switching im zweitsprachlichen Handeln. Sprachpsychologische Aspekte verbalen Planens in türkisch-deutscher Kommunikation*. Münster [u.a.]: Waxmann.

Poplack, Shana. 1980. Sometimes I'll start a sentence in Spanish Y TERMINO EN ESPAÑOL: Toward a typology of code-switching. *Linguistics 18 (7–8)*. 581–618.

Poulisse, Nanda. 1997. Language production in bilinguals. In Anette M.B. de Groot & Judith F. Kroll (eds.), *Tutorials in bilingualism: Psycholinguistic perspectives*, 201–224. Mahwah: Lawrence Erlbaum Associates Publishers.

Poulisse, Nanda & Theo Bongaerts. 1994. First language use in second language production. *Applied Linguistics* 15 (1). 36–57.

Rosenberg, Katharina. 2014. *Interkulturelle Behördenkommunikation. Eine Gesprächsanalytische Untersuchung zu Verständigungsproblemen zwischen Migranten und Behördenmitarbeitern in Berlin und Buenos Aires*. Berlin [u.a.]: De Gruyter dissertation.

Sebba, Mark & Tony Wootton. 1998. We, they and identity: Sequential versus identity related explanation in code-switching. In Peter Auer (ed.), *Code-Switching in Conversation: Language, Interaction and Identity*, 262–286. London [u.a.]: Routledge.

Stell, Gerald & Kofi Yakpo. (eds.). 2015. *Code-switching between structural and sociolinguistic perspectives*. Berlin: de Gruyter.

Treffers-Daller, Jeanine 2005. Code-switching. In Ulrich Ammon (ed.), *Handbücher zur Sprach- und Kommunikationswissenschaft*, 1469–1482. Berlin: de Gruyter.

Wei, Li. 1994. *Three generations, two languages, one family: Language choice and language shift in a Chinese community in Britain*. Clevedon: Multilingual Matters.

Weinreich, Uriel. 1953. *Languages in contact*. The Hague: Mouton.

Part II: **Pedagogical Aspects of Multilingualism**

Asunción Martínez-Arbelaiz, Isabel Pereira
Chapter 7
Identity and Language Proficiency in Study Abroad: A Case Study of Four Multilingual and Multicultural Students

Abstract: One of the challenges in gauging the impact of study abroad (SA) is to understand how identity, personal development, and second language proficiency are interrelated. Indeed, most studies have researched identity and proficiency gains as separate constructs. Following Benson, Barkhuizen, Bodycott, and Brown (2012) the present study focuses on the links between identity and second language proficiency, paying attention to both the form and the content of student narratives produced while studying abroad. Four US university students enrolled in intermediate and advanced Spanish courses in a 15-week SA program in Madrid completed two written tasks. The first task was a narrative in Spanish describing crucial events for language learning, and the second task was to write a reaction paper in English about their overall experience. We analyzed the relationship between the content of both the English and Spanish essays and the students' proficiency in their written Spanish, in terms of complexity, accuracy, and fluency (Pallotti 2009). The results point to a higher cultural integration in the two students with higher Spanish attainments.

Keywords: Second language identity, study abroad, second language proficiency, personal narratives, third space, investment

1 Introduction: Identity and second language learning

In the last decade, identity has become a major topic of research not only in the field of applied linguistics but also in the social sciences in general. The reason behind the popularity of this construct is mainly that identity-related research can provide a more holistic and humanized view of what learning a

---
Asunción Martínez-Arbelaiz, University Studies Abroad Consortium, Spain,
E-mail: asuncion.martinez@usac.edu
Isabel Pereira, NYU Madrid, Spain, E-mail: ip15@nyu.edu

new language and culture entails for individuals. In this chapter, we adopt Bucholtz and Hall's (2005) definition of identity, in which they draw on a number of different social theories to conceptualize identity as "the social positioning of self and others" (586). Crucially, these positionings take place in local interactional contexts. In this sense, research in second language acquisition (SLA) has started to observe the nature of the different social contexts where these identity performances take place, entailing a change in focus that has been termed "the social turn in SLA" (Block 2003).

It is precisely this author, Block (2007), who offers one of the most thorough and compelling arguments for the need to pay attention to identity transformations when learning a new language. He writes that:

> when individuals move across geographical and psychological borders, immersing themselves in new sociocultural environments, they find that their sense of identity is destabilized and they enter a period of struggle to reach a balance. At this stage, it is easy to conceive of identity as contested in nature because the new and varied input provided to the individual serves to upset taken-for-granted points of reference. (Block 2007: 864)

This struggle is not adding the new to the old, nor is it creating a half-and-half individual. Rather, Block (2007) proposes that what emerges can be considered a "third space," a concept originally proposed by Bhabha (1994) and applied by Block to situations where individuals encounter a new language and culture.

It has been claimed that the study abroad (SA) experience increases intercultural sensitivity, but it may also trigger identity conflicts (Block 2003, 2007; Kinginger 2008, 2009, 2013, 2015, among others). Only a few studies have investigated changes in the social positioning of the self and others using qualitative data, and particularly how identity changes and language proficiency are related (Menard-Warwick and Palmer 2012). That is, we need further investigation to determine how learners' investment in the target language relates to their identity (Norton Peirce 1995; Norton and McKinney 2011) and vice versa.

In this chapter, we continue this line of research and explore the following research question: How does second language (L2) proficiency and identity affect each other in a SA context? In order to answer this question, we first reviewed previous studies that link SA with language and identity development. We then adopted a narrative approach to analyze four cases of college students who spent a semester in Madrid in order to improve their Spanish and familiarize themselves with the local culture.

We coded and interpreted an English and a Spanish written narrative whose topic was related to L2 identity development, linking what the students said regarding their experiences in the target community in English and Spanish compositions with their degree of *complexity, accuracy, and fluency* (CAF) (Pallotti 2009) reflected in the Spanish compositions. We found that differences in their degree of involvement with the target-language community went hand-in-hand with differences in language proficiency. Finally, we concluded that the two constructs, namely, L2 proficiency and identity, are shaken by the SA experience and that the study of the two in combination can be a very revealing research endeavor.

2 Identity and study abroad

The phenomenon of SA, namely, when students travel and live in a different country for study, can be a source of identity destabilization and conflict. According to Kinginger (2013, 2015), the new practices students encounter inside and outside academia have to be negotiated. This usually creates feelings of ambivalence among the students, which Kinginger has referred to as "negotiation of difference" (2013: 341).

In general, researchers believe that local social networks can help students to move away from ethnocentrism and toward greater intercultural sensitivity (Kinginger 2008). What remains to be determined is whether such networks can help students acquire the target language. Although the literature on students' experiences abroad is growing, few studies report students' voices directly. For language acquisition researchers and SA practitioners, it is important to not only collect quantitative information using tools such as the Language Contact Profile (Freed, Dewey, Segalowitz, and Halter 2004) but also to find out about the nature of students' encounters with, feelings about, and evaluations of the target language and cultures.

According to Oxford, Pacheco Acuña, Solis Hernandez, and Smith (2015), narratives written by SA students are contextualized data that describe stories of language learning, and, more importantly, "describe the strategies they used to handle specific learning challenges and needs, and explain how they felt in various episodes and instances" (101). Following the trajectories of six bilingual individuals learning English, the authors claim that "if we want to understand what stirs learners' hearts and minds and what lights inner fires, we need more studies involving learner histories, which let learners speak in their own voices" (108). Thus, the personal narratives of SA students recounting their experiences can be a valuable tool for SLA research.

Following a narrative approach, Benson, Barkhuizen, Bodycott, and Brown (2012) investigated L2 identity development during SA based on the experiences of nine Hong Kongese pre-service teacher education students. These students were enrolled in six- and 13-week language immersion programs in Australia,

Canada, and the United Kingdom. Benson and his colleagues suggested that SA led to the students' identity-related development in three domains: 1. Identity related to L2 proficiency; that is, pragmatic competence, 2. Linguistic self-concept, including self-confidence, self-esteem, willingness to communicate, motivation, etc. and, 3. L2-mediated personal development or the ability to do things for themselves and become more independent.

In relation to identity and the domain of language proficiency, Benson et al. (2012) did not detect significant changes in the students' proficiency in the pre- and post-tests. However, most of the students thought that they had improved their listening and oral abilities in English. Only two of the nine students reported that their enhanced language competence related to their ability to express their desired identities. Their narratives conveyed not only an improvement in their English skills but also in their capacity to express "identities that would lead English speakers to want to interact and make friends with them" (184). With respect to the domain of linguistic self-concept, this study found that, with the exception of one, all students had become more confident. For these authors, SA clearly had an important impact on students' sense of self as learners and users of English.

The results for the third domain, L2-mediated personal development, showed that this group of students, with the exception of one, reported feeling more independent because they were able to do things in English by themselves. They also said that they had become more tolerant and open-minded. In this study, students with a high level of English had strong feelings about these changes. However, the authors concluded that there were individual differences among the students regarding their expectations of SA and investment in the experience, as we will also note for our own student cohort.

As Norton Peirce (1995) explains, the notion of investment portrays the language learner as having a complex social identity and multiple desires: "when language learners speak, they are not only exchanging information with target language speakers but they are constantly organizing and reorganizing a sense of who they are and how they relate to the social world. The investment in the target language is also an investment in learners' own identity, which is continuously changing across time and space" (19). Norton and McKinney (2011) elaborate on this idea and propose that identity is an ongoing process, and "learners often have differential investments in the language practices of their classrooms and communities" (89). The authors also adopt the concept of imagined communities (Anderson 1991), which language learners envision when they acquire a new language. A focus on imagined communities in L2 acquisition enables us to explore how learners' connection with these communities might affect their learning trajectories since these imagined communities are no less real than the ones that learners engage with daily and that that might have an even stronger impact on their identities and investments.

Du (2015) followed 29 US students in China and noticed that "they fully took advantage of their foreigner identity and used their language skills to get things done" (263). That is, Du also found support for the impact of SA on most of her students' L2-mediated personal development. These students felt that Chinese native speakers valued their efforts to communicate, which empowered them. Despite their obvious otherness, the students "were able to actively take advantage of and even create opportunities to use the language and, as a result, make critical discoveries about their identity, develop a more sophisticated national and global perspective, and further validate their sense of self" (262).

Thus, the students felt that they had developed a new global perspective that changed their American view of China. However, seven students reported that they did not get accustomed to life in China and their love for their own country increased every day, falling into what Kinginger (2013: 340) calls the discourse of American superiority. Du's (2015) study, however, does not report on the students' linguistic improvement.

In two previous studies, we investigated how 27 US university learners of Spanish spending a semester abroad in Madrid made use of the context. In Martínez-Arbelaiz and Pereira (2015), the data collection tools were a questionnaire to measure the degree to which students integrated into the host culture, a composition in Spanish that described their learning experience, and an essay in English (L1) that addressed how their image of the target culture had changed. Results showed that some participants developed deep and significant relationships with members of the community beyond mere service encounters. These students experienced the development of new L2-mediated identities, as also reported in Benson et al. (2012). Through the students' introspection of and reflection on their own cultural identity, we could explore the destabilization that they were experiencing. After a period of struggle, the students began to build a third space, where they became people with translingual and transcultural skills.

In a closer observation of the students' narratives, Martínez-Arbelaiz and Pereira (2018) found that frequent tensions emerged between the participants' identity and the local identity. These tensions caused identity destabilization that often entailed challenging stereotypes about the target culture. However, some students reinforced their preconceptions and retreated to a sense of their own community's superiority (Block 2007). Therefore, each individual's identity seems to have an effect on the way in which students approach the new culture. In this chapter, we demonstrate the extent to which students' different SA experiences relate to different levels of language proficiency.

To the best of our knowledge, Menard-Warwick and Palmer (2012) is the only study that has connected the narratives of students abroad with specific features of their linguistic development. They analyzed the journals of three English L1 students and prospective teachers from a university in Texas during their one-month SA experience in Mexico studying Spanish. Two of the students, Jessica and Kate, were of Latino heritage although they reported that they spoke English at home. The third student, Surjit, came from an Indian immigrant family and spoke some Gujarati in addition to English. Jessica and Surjit showed linguistic development by making ample use of the imperfect tense in Spanish, but the third student, Kate, "who had the most cultural difficulties, showed no obvious linguistic progress in her journals" (Menard-Warwick and Palmer 2012: 407). In this sense, it is relevant to not only describe the experiences, emotions, and feelings that students refer to in their narratives but to also try to link them to actual linguistic features that may or may not emerge in the students' evolving L2. Menard-Warwick and Palmer (2012) focused on the difference between the preterite and imperfect in Spanish, a distinction that is difficult for English speakers to acquire, and showed that of the three cases, Kate was the one who expressed discomfort. She constructed a strongly negative attitude toward life in Mexico, which could have affected her language development. In fact, Kate was the only student who used very few cases of the imperfect to provide background in her narratives.

In addition, Menard-Warwick and Palmer (2012), drawing on Kinginger (2008, 2009), contend that "there are few studies that both measure language acquisition and also attend to learner experiences or identities; more socially-oriented research often lacks documentation of linguistic outcomes" (Menard-Warwick and Palmer 2012: 387). Therefore, we need further investigation into how individual identities and SA experiences influence linguistic gains. As they recommend, a case study design based on personal narratives might be a useful tool for exploring the complexities of language learning abroad. The following research question guides the analysis of our students' narratives: How do students' proficiency gains and their identity positionings relate to each other?

3 Study design

We designed our research as a multiple case study. Out of a larger pool of students (Martínez-Arbelaiz and Pereira 2015, 2018), we analyzed written data from four US students studying in Madrid, Spain, who were enrolled in either an intermediate or advanced Spanish course. We followed "purposive sampling," which, according to Polkinghorne (2005), entails "select[ing] fertile exemplars of the experience for study" (140). Thus, "the purposive selection of data sources involves choosing people or documents from which the researcher can learn about the experience" (Polkinghorne 2005:140). Since our aim was to investigate the relationship between language proficiency and identity, for each Spanish course, we chose the students with the highest and lowest scores on fluency, complexity, and grammatical accuracy, giving us a continuum among intermediate and advanced students.

The students took a required language course. In addition to this course, one of the advanced learners took three more elective courses in Spanish and the other advanced learner took only one more. None of the intermediate students took an elective course. The four students composed a 250–300-word narrative describing crucial events for language learning. They received the following instructions: "Explain what critical facts, incidents or crucial people have had an impact on your learning process of the Spanish language and culture during this semester". This composition was a pen-and-paper task accomplished in 30 minutes during their regular Spanish language class. Also, the students wrote a reaction paper in English about their overall SA experience. The reaction paper was prompted by the reading of *Practical Orientalism: Bodies, Everyday Life and the Construction of Otherness* by Haldrup, Koefoed, and Simonsen (2006), which addresses the concept of *the other* and *the internal other* in modern European societies. The students wrote it at home and sent it by email to the Program Director. Finally, the students filled out an online questionnaire about their personal background, and about what they had done during their stay to immerse themselves in Spanish culture and language.

In undertaking the content analysis, we followed Benson et al. (2012:181) who provide a model to classify SA experiences regarding students' identity work. We examined the English and Spanish essays by means of systematic reading, in which we coded and interpreted aspects of the students' narratives related to L2 identity development. We contrasted the content outcomes with the degree of Spanish proficiency reflected in their compositions in terms of *complexity, accuracy, and fluency* (CAF) (Pallotti 2009). As Pallotti (2009) argues, these notions are used as dependent variables to assess language performance and need to be operationalized in order to determine what they measure. Moreover, CAF measures the properties of language as a product, in contrast to measures of language development, which refer to the properties of the language as a process in terms of route and rate. We operationalized fluency as the number of word tokens the learners produced in a 30-minute essay. In other words, we defined fluency as speed fluency (Tavakoli and Skehan 2005), since speech rate is a frequent measure in SLA research. We operationalized accuracy as students' use of Spanish verbs relative to target-like use, focusing in particular on the past tense. We chose the past tense since its correct use reflects higher degrees of language development (Breiner-Sanders, Swender, and Terry 2002). However, as Pallotti (2009) has remarked, accuracy and development are different constructs, so we tallied all verb tenses equally since language development was not a construct of this study. Finally, complexity was operationalized as the capacity to produce language that is more advanced and was calculated through two different measures: lexical richness, defined as the number of word types, and the number of discourse markers used.

4 Case studies

4.1 Clark, an intermediate student who judged himself as a "stupid American"

Clark was a junior, majoring in sociology. He was a US citizen born in Israel. In his questionnaire, he reported that he had tried to be proactive about learning Spanish in class, as well as in different activities, such as meeting with a conversation partner, going to the gym, doing volunteer work, reading newspapers, and traveling around Spain. Thus, it seems that Clark tried to invest in the target language, in terms of Norton and McKinney (2011), although he also recognized that he could have tried harder.

Clark showed poor results in his proficiency in the text written in Spanish. His narrative was too short (103 word tokens) and not very complex (73 word types). In terms of accuracy, he wrote 11 verbs, seven in the past tense, five in the present perfect; three of the 11 verbs were incorrect (two present tense and one past tense). He used a present tense instead of the preterite in one case, and he confused the verb *hacer* 'to do' for *haber* 'to have' in one sentence. He used three different discourse markers: *además* 'besides,' *cuando* 'when,' and two instances of *como resultado* 'as a result,' which seems to be used as a formulaic utterance. However, Clark showed enthusiasm in his narrative about his Spanish learning experience: "hacia muchas veces cuando hablaba con personas en taxis, restaurantes, estadios y otros edificios y todas esas experiencias ayuda a reinforcar diferente cosas". [There were many times in which I talked with people in taxis, restaurants, stadiums and other buildings and all these experiences helped to reinforce other things].

Perhaps Clark's limited linguistic proficiency could be explained by his sense of having a foreigner identity ascribed to him by locals. This echoes Kinginger's

(2013: 348) assertion that the negotiation of difference in SA "is constrained not only by students' own interpretive framing of their host culture in terms of their own national identity but also by 'foreigner' identities imposed on students within host communities". In his English essay, Clark said that "one of his fears in coming to Madrid was the possibility of being looked at as one of the others". In Clark's experience, he was treated in a different way in different areas of Madrid. In popular neighborhoods, which actively attract tourists, the Spaniards embraced diversity and international presence. He found the same attitude in other tourist destinations throughout his travels in Spain. However, in other areas of Madrid, such as Chamberí, an upper-middle-class neighborhood, Clark felt rejected: "Walking around these streets I feel like I receive more awkward glances, and when I order food at a café or ask for directions (even when I try to do so in my best Spanish) I feel like I am being judged, and all of the "Stupid American" stereotypes are at the forefront of the person's mind". Therefore, Clark's disappointment between what he imagined and what he encountered about living in Spain might have affected his investment in learning Spanish. When Clark felt that local people positioned him as a foreigner with no access to his imagined community, he was distressed and discouraged from trying to be involved in this community (Norton and McKinney 2011). On the occasions when Clark felt safer and more comfortable, like with teachers, waiters, cab drivers, locals, etc., he tried to use common cultural norms and expressions that helped his interaction with his interlocutors: "Learning how to properly introduce myself or exchange pleasantries with a worker has helped me come off in a more positive light to locals. I've learned restaurant, school-place, and workplace etiquette over time, and this has made me seem like less of a foreigner and, in turn, feel like less of an outsider".

4.2 Mary, an intermediate student determined to feel like a Madrileño

Mary was of Latino ethnicity, with a low level of Spanish as a heritage language. She was a junior, majoring in food cultures and lived in an apartment with classmates in Madrid. She reported in the background questionnaire that she was proactive during her stay in Madrid, doing different activities such as watching Spanish movies, reading newspapers, and doing volunteer work, although she thought that she could have learned more Spanish if she had chosen to live in a homestay. She also wrote that she would have liked to do more activities outside her Spanish class.

Mary had the highest number of word tokens in the intermediate group, 264, and she produced 115 word types. She also used the most verbs, 44 and made five errors out of 29 past tense verbs. Four of those were morphological errors but the tense used was correct. Her Spanish essay was also well organized through discourse markers, such as *primero, poco a poco, cuando, también, entonces, siempre,* and *a veces* 'first, little by little, when, also, then, always, and sometimes'.

In her narrative, she explained how much Spanish she had learned thanks to her instructor and to the family of the girl to whom she was teaching English. She enjoyed walking throughout the city and learning more about the culture, especially on the trips with her Spanish class. Mary remarked that her learning process was not a matter of learning more words but learning how to use them. She was also proud of being helpful to others when people in the metro or in the street asked her for directions. In relation to identity and language proficiency, Mary was able to express an identity that would lead her to interact and make friends with Spaniards (Benson et al. 2012).

Mary's first reflection about Spain in her English essay was about the identification of the other: "When I initially arrived in Spain, I felt like the Spaniards were the internal others, but after a couple of days I realized I was the internal other". She began to feel that she was invading the space of the Madrileños, and she was determined to feel like one: "I tried to learn about what types of foods they ate, places where locals like to hang out, and types of activities the locals like to participate in". From the very beginning, Mary was moving to the third space (Bhabha 1994, Block 2007), since she always tried to negotiate the differences. Although she had difficulties, she worked with her past knowledge of and her present experience with Spanish culture. For example, Mary commented on two pieces of information that she received before coming to Spain: First, Spaniards like to stare, and second, it would be quite difficult to follow a vegetarian diet in Spain. Although Mary recognized that when people stared at her it bothered her a lot, she decided not to worry about it too much. Mary also found that it was possible to follow a vegetarian diet in Spain but "American vegetarians would have to adapt and assimilate somewhat in order to satisfy their diets". Therefore, Mary made the effort to assimilate to the new environment without renouncing her own identity as she said: "One must balance absorbing another culture and staying true to who they are". She concluded that despite the differences: "Spaniards and Americans are both human beings and have similar ideas about life, love, family, and happiness. Now that my time in Spain is coming to an end, hopefully, I have learned what it means to be a Madrileño; therefore, I now consider neither myself nor the Spaniards as the 'others' because we are all one". Thus, it seems that Mary has moved away from ethnocentrism, as she wrote in her narrative: "[i]t took me a while to actually realize that I was in Europe and no longer in America," developing greater intercultural sensitivity (Kinginger 2008). For Mary, her L2 has mediated her personal development (Benson et al. 2012) and she has become more tolerant and open-minded during her stay in Madrid. Returning to the learners discussed in Menard-Warwick and Palmer (2012), Mary's cultural and personal development was similar to Jessica's but the opposite of Kate's. In contrast, Clark did not move to the third space (Bhabha 1994, Block 2007) like Mary did; Clark only invested in his Spanish within his comfort zone and he resented being treated as a foreigner in non-tourist areas.

4.3 Keiko, the Japanese-American advanced student

Keiko chose to live with a host family. However, in the online questionnaire, she commented that she could have been more proactive with her Spanish if she had "started going to volunteering earlier and if I actually had dinner with my *señora* and her family instead of just with my housemates". In Norton and McKinney's (2011) terms, she could have been more invested in using her Spanish.

Keiko's Spanish composition had the lowest fluency of the two advanced students: she wrote 119 words. Her verb accuracy was also very low: Out of 17 verbs, 15 were past tenses and for six of those, she chose the wrong tense and used the wrong verb forms. She also seemed to have problems with the non-finite forms of the verbs, using a gerund instead of an infinitive; she also used a conjugated verb that should have been an infinitive. In general, Keiko had problems distinguishing non-finite and finite forms of the verbs. Regarding complexity, she only wrote 61 word types and did not use any discourse markers other than *que* 'that'.

In her English essay, she mentioned that her host mother (*la señora de la casa*) is a source of frustration and misunderstanding. Nevertheless, in her Spanish composition, she wrote that the fact that she could not communicate with her host mother was a positive aspect because it forced her to learn the language: "Me gustó que mi señora no podía entender más inglés y pensé que realmente me obligó a aprender".[I liked that my host mother could not understand more English and that forced me to learn]. In her reflection paper, however, she emphasized the fact that the sounds of the foreign language were uncomfortable to the point of giving her a headache:

> During my first week in Madrid, I was constantly bombarded with Spanish; a language I had only learned within the classrooms intermingled with English. Suddenly, it was constantly swirling around me in different tones, pitches, and different contexts. (. . .) In my opinion, nothing makes a person feel more like an outsider than being unable to communicate. (. . .) With all the unfamiliar sounds, my head was aching within the hour. I hated

that I couldn't understand what people were saying and was so disappointed when the fact that I was a foreigner registered in their eyes.

Keiko displayed a struggling or contradictory positioning regarding her interaction with her host mother, her main source of input and local information outside of class. Furthermore, Keiko clearly positioned herself as a foreigner and she mentioned a number of situations where she felt like the other, identifying a number of embodied experiences of otherness. Like Mary, she reported receiving stares in the metro and noticed a difference in clothing, since Spaniards tended to wear more pieces of clothing, even in situations where it is hot, like in the metro. To add to these feelings of discomfort and alienation, she felt the food was a little unhealthy: "After a few weeks, I began to crave vegetables that were fresh and meats that weren't 'lomo' and 'pollo'. I think in this sense, I perceived the Spanish as the internal other because they were different from what I was used to: a variety of cultural cuisine and more healthy cuisine". Although she described the food she had in Spain as "delicious," she thought it was unhealthy and she craved other types of food. All these aspects of Keiko's daily life acted as indexes of otherness and not belonging and showed her struggle to come to terms with her new life. This illustrates the stage of destabilization described in Block (2007). However, after Keiko's strong embodied feelings eased and the negative evaluations of her experience diminished, in the end, Madrid felt like home for her: "While I still sometimes feel like a foreigner in Madrid, I found myself thinking of Madrid as 'home' during my spring break".

4.4 John, the advanced New Yorker living in the heart of Spain

John stood at the other end of the continuum formed by the two advanced students. He identified himself as a New Yorker. John was a Spanish and linguistics major, very proactive about learning Spanish, and chose to live with a host family. This student made optimal use of the elective class offerings, taking three of them. He wrote that there was not a single class where he did not have to speak and that the classes complemented what was happening outside the classroom.

John displayed high fluency, using 250 word tokens. His grammatical accuracy was 100%, using 34 verbs correctly. John also used the present perfect to evaluate his whole experience in the opening of the composition and he skillfully mixed preterite and imperfect. Regarding complexity, John used 126 word types and a variety of discourse markers. These organizing expressions are *en suma* 'in sum,' *sobre todo* 'especially' and the causal connective *como* 'as'. Despite these high CAF measures, in the questionnaire, he acknowledged that he could have been more proactive in seeking situations to practice his Spanish.

John mentioned that feeling comfortable was a requirement for him to speak Spanish. He wrote in the English essay that, at times, he avoided contact with Spanish-speaking people because of "fear or something like that". When he felt unwilling to practice outside the classroom, his teachers were the ones that forced him into practice. Therefore, the anxiety that speaking a foreign language normally entails was also present in John's essay and in that sense, both the teachers and the family acted as a comfortable context where he could practice and get valuable help. On the occasions that he felt daring (*atrevido*) he would speak with people from other social circles:

> En suma, Siempre había una mezcla entre mis clases, mi familia, y los Madrileños que me ha ayudado. En clase siempre tenía que hablar en español y encontré las frases que quería usar en mi discurso. Como José siempre mandaba que yo hablara en español la familia, la practica allí ha sido algo habitual. Sobre todo, cuando estaba muy atrevido, hablé con los Madrileños.
>
> [In sum, there was always a mix between my classes, my family, and the locals who helped me. In class, I always needed to speak in Spanish and I found the sentences that I wanted to use in my speech. As José always asked that I spoke in Spanish to the family, practice there has been a commonplace. Above all, when I was very daring, I spoke with locals].

In his essay, John remarked on his different behavior with respect to the daily life of people in Madrid. However, far from being a problem, he saw these differences as evidence that "the two cultures have embraced one another". His comment below echoes Bhabha's (1994) concept of third space reformulated by Block (2007):

> I have been the internal other: A New Yorker living in the heart of Spain, Madrid. With most interactions, the residents of this country realize each of my differences. My accent has been called out, they have commented on my unusual diet, and even my dance moves are a symbol of my foreign nature. Conversely, I have noticed several of their broad cultural differences. Despite the fact that this might seem like a nightmare, the two cultures have embraced one another.

John positions himself as a foreigner in his English narrative, and as the one who happens to be the source of laughter among Spaniards. However, that allows him to be critical of some Spanish behaviors he observes, such as throwing napkins on the floor in bars. Nevertheless, there is an acceptance of the differences of the host culture and John mentions human beings' ability to adapt, using a Darwinian metaphor: "Perhaps there is some aspect of their culture that you prefer over your own and, as the adaptable species and varied species we are, you will always have the option of enjoying bits and pieces of each rich culture that is allowed to exist freely".

As opposed to Keiko, John, using irony and sarcasm, enjoyed and fully welcomed the differences, displaying a more nuanced, flexible identity. While both intermediate students resorted to a sense of American superiority (Kinginger 2008, 2009) at times, neither of the two advanced students seemed to do so. In the case of Keiko, she positioned herself as the foreigner and the one that physically suffers and makes the effort to communicate. John, however, could integrate this foreignness into the identity he struggled to create using irony and humor. He enjoyed these differences and used a biological metaphor to say that anyone can enjoy different parts of the cultures that coexist. Much like the SA students in China described in Du (2015), John emphasized his enjoyment of the differences rather than craving the familiar and his comfort zone, as Keiko did. Both John and Mary took advantage of their L2-mediated identity and used their language skills to get things done in the local community.

5 Summary of the case study findings

Our four students reported feeling linguistic and cultural discomfort on some occasions, like the students in Menard-Warwick and Palmer (2012), but the extent and quality of their uncomfortable experiences varied. While Mary and John showed that their SA experience had an impact on their L2-mediated personal development, the third domain of L2 identity in Benson et al.'s (2012) terms, Clark and Keiko had relatively little investment in the language practices of the community where they were living for four months. In fact, Clark did not move beyond the self-ascribed tourist identity. He acknowledged that he only felt comfortable with simple transactions in the Sol area of Madrid. Keiko, on the other hand, emphasized her foreignness, mainly in her English essay. In her contested identity, she felt like a foreigner, but at the same time, Madrid was home for Keiko. In sum, despite the differences that arose, the four students claimed that they had invested in their linguistic, cultural, and social integration.

Mary and John, who used the semester to remake and refashion themselves in terms of their subjectivity, showed high language proficiency in their Spanish L2-writing. They found the third space, which was not the one they started with or the one they observed (Block 2007). For both students, their intercultural flexibility, together with a high level of investment (Norton Peirce 1995), afforded them the opportunity to acquire a new language, as gauged by the CAF measurements. That is, Mary and John showed an identity related to language proficiency development, following Benson et al.'s (2012) first domain, identity related to L2 proficiency; that is, pragmatic competence.

6 Conclusions, limitations, and future directions

In this study, we investigated the interaction between identity and L2 proficiency in the English and Spanish narratives of four US students at the end of a semester abroad. Although results from four students are not generalizable to other groups in other SA contexts, our in-depth analysis of the experiences of these language learners in Spain leads us to the conclusion that the individual differences regarding students' identity modifications toward new and past experiences were linked to their linguistic achievements. We do not propose a causal relationship, rather it can be bidirectional: language proficiency can impact identity development and identity changes, in turn, can affect language proficiency. In this sense, the two students that we have identified as the higher proficiency students, John, from the advanced group, and Mary, from the intermediate group, showed themselves to be better able to adapt to the new culture and to be immersed in the local community in a much deeper way than the other two. As a result, John and Mary moved toward a more flexible and transcultural identity. Future research will have to add to this line of investigation, which seeks to find links between L2-identity development and language proficiency. Nevertheless, this study has several limitations. We acknowledge that our findings remain tentative due to the fact that we did not make any observations at the beginning of the SA program. Future research that examines longitudinal data is needed to determine the developmental relation between identity changes and the emergence of specific linguistic features related to CAF. In addition, we only focused on verb forms, text connectors and raw number of word types, but future studies can analyze other features in the output of the students.

In addition, we can state that our study was exploratory. That is, further research should collect data on different occasions throughout the semester to observe students´ temporal evolution of linguistic proficiency as well as their possible identity changes. Oral data from short interviews would also be very helpful to round our knowledge of the students´ outcomes from SA experiences.

Although quantitative research based on learners' self-reports regarding the amount of time using the target language has not found any correlation with language development (e.g., Mitchell, McManus and Tracy-Ventura 2015), it is still desirable more nuanced and in-depth research on the experiences, feelings, and impressions of students abroad. In this sense, qualitative case studies can illuminate the complexities and individual paths toward multilingualism and multiculturalism.

In addition, we adopted an innovative methodological stance, first proposed by Menard-Warwick and Palmer (2012), which provided examples of students' use of their interlanguage to communicate their experiences. As Kinginger (2009) cautions, studies should not be limited to students' impressions, memories, or feelings about what they tell us they had learned while abroad. It is important to connect student identity with language outcomes, considering observable measurements of CAF.

As SA language teachers, we may also include ways for negotiating our own cultural discourse with the students' discourses about their SA experiences in our classrooms in order to engage the students in their new cultural spaces. We should be aware of what happens outside the classroom, using class time to talk about learners' experiences, feelings, and difficulties when engaged in conversations with members of the local community. For this, it is desirable to design activities that crucially involve interaction with local people and require the development of communication strategies to negotiate not only meaning but also L2-mediated identities.

References

Anderson, Benedict R. O. 1991. *Imagined communities: Reflections on the origin and spread of nationalism*. New York, NY: Verso.

Breiner-Sanders, Karen E., Elvira Swender & Robert M. Terry. 2002. Preliminary Proficiency Guidelines. Writing. Revised 2001. *Foreign Language Annals* 35 (1). 9–15.

Benson, Phil, Gary Barkhuizen, Peter Bodycott & Jill Brown. 2012. Study abroad and the development of second language identities. *Applied Linguistics Review* 3 (1). 173–193.

Bhabha, Homi K. 1994. *The location of culture*. New York: Random House.

Block, David. 2003. *The social turn in second language acquisition*. Washington, DC: Georgetown University Press.

Block, David. 2007. The rise of identity in SLA research, post Firth and Wagner 1997. *The Modern Language Journal* 91. 863–876.

Bucholtz, Mary & Kira Hall. 2005. Identity and interaction: A sociocultural linguistic approach. *Discourse Studies* 7 (4). 585–614.

Du, Hang. 2015. American college students studying abroad in China: Language, identity, and self-presentation. *Foreign Language Annals* 48 (2). 250–266.

Freed, Barbara F., Dan P. Dewey, Norman Segalowitz & Randall Halter. 2004. The language contact profile. *Studies in Second Language Acquisition* 26 (2). 349–356.

Haldrup, Michael, Lasse Koefoed & Kirsten Simonsen. 2006. Practical orientalism: Bodies, everyday life and the construction of otherness. *Geografiska Annaler: Series B, Human Geography* 88 (2). 173–184.

Kinginger, Celeste. 2008. Language learning in study abroad: Case studies of Americans in France. *The Modern Language Journal* 92 (s1). 1–124.

Kinginger, Celeste. 2009. *Language learning and study abroad: A critical reading of research.* New York: Palgrave Macmillan.

Kinginger, Celeste. 2013. Identity and language learning in study abroad. *Foreign Language Annals* 46 (3). 339–358.

Kinginger, Celeste. 2015. Student mobility and identity-related language learning. *Intercultural Education* 26 (1). 6–15.

Martínez-Arbelaiz, Asunción & Isabel Pereira. 2015. Socialización de alumnos de ELE en la cultura meta. *E-AESLA* 1. https://cvc.cervantes.es/lengua/eaesla/eaesla_01.htm (accessed 23 October 2019).

Martínez-Arbelaiz, Asunción & Isabel Pereira. 2018. Parando la acción: Transformaciones identitarias en las narrativas en L1 y L2 de alumnos estadounidenses durante su estancia en el extranjero. *E-AESLA* 4. 77–84. https://cvc.cervantes.es/lengua/eaesla/eaesla_04.htm. (accessed 23 October 2019).

Menard-Warwick, Julia & Deborah K. Palmer. 2012. Bilingual development in study-abroad journal narratives: Three case studies from a short-term program in Mexico. *Multilingua* 31. 381–412.

Mitchell, Rosamond, Kevin McManus & Nicole Tracy-Ventura. 2015. Placement type and language learning during residence abroad. In Rosamond Mitchell, Nicole Tracy-Ventura & Kevin McManus (eds.), *Social interaction, identity and language learning during residence abroad*, 115–137. Amsterdam: The European Second Language Association.

Norton Peirce, Bonny. 1995. Social identity, investment, and language learning. *TESOL Quarterly* 29 (1). 9–31.

Norton, Bonny & Carolyn McKinney. 2011. An identity approach to second language acquisition. In Dwight Atkinson (ed.), *Alternative approaches to second language acquisition*, 73–94. New York: Routledge.

Oxford, Rebecca L., Gilda Pacheco Acuña, Mayra Solís Hernández & Andrew L. Smith. 2015. "A language is a mentality": A narrative, positive-psychological view of six learners' development of bilingualism. *System* 55. 100–110.

Pallotti, Gabriele. 2009. CAF: Defining, refining, and differentiating constructs. *Applied Linguistics* 30 (4). 590–601.

Polkinghorne, Donald E. 2005. Language and meaning: Data collection in qualitative research. *Journal of Counseling Psychology* 52 (2). 137–145.

Tavakoli, Parvaneh & Peter Skehan. 2005. Strategic planning, task structure, and performance testing. In Rod Ellis (ed.), *Planning and task performance in a second language*, 247–287. Amsterdam: John Benjamins.

Anna Szczepaniak-Kozak
Chapter 8
The Influence of the Mother Tongue and L3 on Learning Pragmatics in EFL among Poles

Abstract: There are definite advantages of multilingualism for the development of pragmatic competence, especially with regard to metapragmatic awareness and sociolinguistic sensitivity. Most often, it is assumed that the direction of cross-linguistic influence and its scope is dependent on the perceived proximity/distance between particular languages (psychotypology). Furthermore, previous research on the effect of learning more than one language at a time indicates that more advanced learners are less prone to interference effects. On these theoretical assumptions, this paper focuses on pragmatic features that are transferred into English as a foreign language (EFL) from my study participants' mother tongue (Polish) and third language L3 (German), based on responses provided in a discourse completion task. In doing so, I attempt to answer the question of whether the magnitude and scope of these processes are comparable. One of the conclusions of this research is that interference errors are grounded in Polish and German, but they are predominantly driven by the students' mother tongue and not their L3. Scant instances of L3 transfer in the corpus may support Ringbom's (2007a: 87) conclusions concerning procedural (system) transfer, i.e., that multilinguals are prone to transfer more frequently from the language in which they are more proficient (here Polish).

Keywords: multilingual Poles, pragmatic competence, transfer and overgeneralization in pragmatics, pragmatic accent

1 Introduction

IL processes in the domain of pragmatics, especially represented by multilingual learners, are still far from being fully understood, and working out their theoretical underpinnings is crucial. The existing research on PC development in

---

Anna Szczepaniak-Kozak, Adam Mickiewicz University in Poznań, Poland,
E-mail: annkozak@amu.edu.pl

multilinguals continues to be scattered across different subareas of pragmatics and is mostly generated on the basis of case studies or cross-sectional research. Furthermore, there is a considerable need for research on how Poles develop PC in a second or third language. To illustrate this, the state-of-the-art literature reviews on ILPC put together by Bardovi-Harlig (2010: 223, 227) and Li (2016) do not mention developmental studies of Polish learners of EFL. The scant interlanguage research existing on Polish EFL learners (Herbert 1991; Jaworski 1994; Szczepaniak-Kozak 2018) seems to corroborate the hypothesis that rendering pragmalinguistic nuances poses a more considerable challenge for them than understanding the sociopragmatic background of a given context. Consequently, this group of bi- and multilingual learners can be considered un- or under-represented in the literature.

To address this gap, this study seeks to answer two research questions: (1) of whether the magnitude and scope of language acquisitional processes in multilingual Poles (mother tongue Polish, L3 German) are comparable in the area of pragmatic competence, and (2) to establish whether we can find a common ground for such interlanguage features and patterns observed. The analytic focus here is on the pragmatic features found in requestive and apologetic output of Poles learning advanced English and German, as exhibited in a discourse completion task.

The chapter begins with the presentation of the theoretical underpinnings of the interlanguage study conducted, after which its methodological setup is briefly outlined. These sections are followed by the analysis of the pragmatic data collected and its findings. In the last section, I present the conclusions to the research undertaken and some implications of this type of work.

2 Pragmatic competence from an interlanguage perspective

Research in interlanguage (IL) pragmatics has centered predominantly on pragmatic socialization in second language settings (Barron 2003; Blum-Kulka 1990; Halenko and Jones 2011; Schauer 2009; cf. Li 2016) or pragmatic teaching and learning from a cross-linguistic perspective (Glaser 2014; Majer and Salski 2004; Ogiermann 2009a, 2009b; cf. Kasper and Rose 2002; Taguchi 2017). Additionally, the existing body of empirical studies continues to draw more attention to exploring pragmatic failures as consequences of the transfer of pragmatic norms of one language into another, observed in bilingual speakers (cf. Kecskes 2015). The value of such investigations should not be underestimated, though.

They enable us to understand that, first of all, interlanguage pragmatic competence (ILPC) is an approximative dialect which is unstable and changeable across time. This complex system profits from and bears a resemblance to the learner's native language (L1), target language (TL) or other languages they know, are learning, or have learnt (L3, L4, etc.). However, ILPC differs systematically from these (Tarone 1998: 391). Secondly, with reference to pragmatics, negative pragmatic transfer is frequently caused by learners' lack of awareness that, for example, politeness or speech acts cannot be conveyed by simply translating phrases from their native language into a particular TL. Furthermore, the role of mother tongue in learning another language has been recently revisited (Arabski and Wojtaszek 2016; Odlin 2012, 2016), and is now widely perceived to be facilitative, the argument being that "it provides an important cognitive basis for L2 [second language] learning" or "a foundation upon which new linguistic knowledge can be constructed" (Wach 2018: 210), especially conceptual and metalinguistic knowledge. To illustrate this, Odlin (2012) explored the acquisition of English in Finland by students whose native languages are Finnish and Swedish, and tried to explain why the former experience much more difficulty with English articles and prepositions. On the basis of the data collected by Jarvis (1998), Odlin (2012: 85) posits that L1 Finnish speakers have a tendency to omit prepositions and articles due to the fact that the Finnish language relies much more on nominal case inflections and postpositions. In contrast, he suggests that transfer is not always helpful in understanding why both Finns and Swedes face difficulty in supplying obligatory articles in English. Transfer is not the sole factor which hinders the approximation to the TL norm. Instead, Odlin (2012: 88) remarks, the "L2 Swedish influence thus seems especially helpful with prepositions (at least in avoiding zero prepositions), while any analogous influence is much more subject to individual variation in the case of articles".

Acknowledging that learning a language that is related to our stronger or dominant languages requires less time and effort (Szczepaniak-Kozak 2018: 57), researchers have rightly posited that those who learn a foreign language "seek to establish similarities to prior knowledge, in order to facilitate the learning process" (Ringbom 2007b: 185). Ringbom (2007a: 57) claims that "the extent to which these assumptions actually work determines whether the effect is positive or negative". Therefore, what early IL research called negative transfer is now interpreted as the absence of positive transfer stemming from "wrong assumptions about cross-linguistic similarities" (Ringbom 2007b: 189), while positive transfer is "the application of at least partially correct perceptions or assumptions of cross-linguistic similarity".

Assuming the linguistic similarity orientation allowed Ringbom (2007a, 2007b) to interpret linguistic transfer at a different angle and to postulate that two types of transfer are observed in learning a foreign language: item transfer and procedural (system) transfer. The former refers to a simplified cross-linguistic and concretely perceived "similarity of form combined with an associated assumed similarity of function or meaning" between a given source language item and a TL-one that a foreign language learner establishes in order to lower their learning workload (Ringbom 2007b: 188). In the latter, procedural transfer, "abstract principles of organizing information in [the] L1 are transferred" (Ringbom 2007b: 188), for instance, grammatical rules or semantic properties. According to Ringbom (2007a: 56), procedural transfer is almost always from the learner's mother tongue, "or possibly another source language the learner knows very well" because the rules or properties "must be well internalized, preferably automatized, in order to be transferred".

3 Multilingual students' pragmatic competence

Empirical evidence enabling a deeper and more nuanced understanding of learning TL pragmatic competence (PC) by multilingual students is still in short supply (Kecskes 2015). Studies that have looked into L2 acquisition by multilingual speakers are, for instance, Cenoz and Jessner (2009), Herraiz Martínez and Sánchez Hernández (2019), Safont-Jordà (2012), Sypiańska (2017) and Włosowicz (2011). The majority of studies in this area have traced multilinguals' language acquisition or language learning using case study methodology (Achiba 2002; Ellis 1992; Faerch and Kasper 1986; Sopata 2009). For example, Faerch and Kasper (1986) followed a Danish learner of two languages (advanced English and German) in her older adolescence. On the basis of think-aloud protocols and pragmatic production data, the researchers concluded that there appeared a difference in the speed at which a particular target language started to be produced and the type of knowledge she relied on when speaking. To illustrate this, the learner "processed her English IL more automatically than her German IL, in a situation that allowed for highly controlled processing" (Faerch and Kasper 1986: 224). More specifically, she relied on implicit and intuitive knowledge in English even in those areas for which she knew explicit rules. In contrast, she depended extensively on explicit and metalinguistic rules when she translated from Dutch into German (Faerch and Kasper 1986: 223). Another case study, Safont-Jordà (2012) examined request mitigation devices in a pre-literate successive trilingual boy (L1 Catalan, L2 Spanish, L3 English) during a one-year period. The data collected during play time, including mother-child interaction, led the researcher to conclude that "the three languages interact and seem to modify one another" (Safont-Jordà 2012: 112). Interestingly, the boy assumed different politeness orientations in each of his three languages. He used very similar modifiers in Catalan and Spanish, but exhibited quite a different pattern in English.

On the other extreme, some studies have taken a more holistic approach to exploring multilinguals' PC, trying to establish group tendencies. My longitudinal research into the ILPC of 206 Polish English as a Foreign Language (EFL) speakers falls into this group of studies (Szczepaniak-Kozak 2018). I found that their pragmatic system, operationalized as rendering requests, underwent moderate changes over the period of 32 months. Although cases of pragmatic attainment could be found in the corpus of almost 1500 utterances (e.g., a limited use of direct strategies, a decrease in verbosity), some students appeared to be resistant to formal and non-formal teaching and their PC remained fossilized (Szczepaniak-Kozak 2018: 329). Furthermore, when speaking English, these Poles showed a predilection for certain all-purpose pragmatic features, which, in the majority of cases, stem from pragmatic features in their L1. They also used such features regardless of context. Items which were typically ranked highly across the board are: rendering requestive head acts by means of the query preparatory, overuse of *maybe* for suggestory formulas, unembedded position of *please* and treating *please* as a token of pragmatic force (Szczepaniak-Kozak 2018: 330). Another important conclusion from the data collected in this study was that not all learners were capable of demonstrating their PC in its full under constraints of real-time language use. Apparently, because of cognitive processing limitations and/or fossilization due to the existence of generative entrenchment (Schank and Wimsatt 1986) in their grammatical competence, my study participants could not transfer their knowledge and awareness directly into onsite impromptu production to make their output linguistically correct and situationally appropriate. This applies to even those of the study participants who (1) showed awareness of sociopragmatic differences between their native language and the TL during class discussions, and those who (2) had knowledge of pragmalinguistic features to express socio-contextual nuances, as indicated by their practical grammar test results, (Szczepaniak-Kozak 2018: 54–55). Finally, and notably, the requests collected from my study participants constituted an evident support for Pienemann's (1998, 2015) processability theory. This conception assumes that "the effect of teaching intervention is constrained by the learner's current state of development" (Pienemann 2015: 137). In consequence, the learner must be in an appropriate stage of linguistic development, especially grammatical competence, to acquire certain pragmatic knowledge or skill.

In general, there are definite advantages of multilingualism for the development of pragmatic competence, especially with regard to metapragmatic awareness and sociolinguistic sensitivity. Jessner (2008: 362) has written about the cumulative and dynamic effect that multilingualism may have on the learner, especially due to cross-linguistic influences. Furthermore, Selinker and Lakshmanan (1992: 198) predict that "when language transfer works in tandem with one or more second language processes there is a greater tendency for the associated interlanguage structures to stabilize". These scholars call this phenomenon the Multiple Effect Principle. The same principle can be applied to metapragmatic awareness and sociolinguistic sensitivity, which enables speakers to make a proper choice of topic, register, speech acts with reference to the age, sex, socio-economic status of interlocutors and contexts in which they communicate (Chłopek 2011: 109). However, Arabski (2006: 13), Chłopek (2011: 21) and Ringbom (2006: 44) postulate that any language can constitute a potential source of cross-linguistic interference, especially when the target and non-target (third) language are typologically close. Indeed, there was evidence of the Multiple Effect Principle among my study participants (Szczepaniak-Kozak 2018). Polish students of English and German are prone to make requests more directly, and sometimes aggravate requests more than English NSs do, because both Polish and German are more direct languages when it comes to rendering this speech act (cf. Kasper 1983: 71). However, in certain areas (e.g., grammatical gender categories), Chłopek (2010: 54) has advocated for the primacy of "one's most proficient language (typically the mother tongue)" in unbalanced bi-/multilinguals. Other definite advantages of multilingualism for PC development are mentioned by Safont-Jordà (2005, 2008), especially with regard to interactional competence.

4 Method

4.1 Participants and interventional settings

My study participants were multilingual philology students who learnt German, English, and one more foreign language (Russian, Spanish, or French) to become translators and/or teachers at a university located in Western Poland. Over the course of their BA program, the participants took part in a mixture of explicit and implicit pedagogical interventions, based both on deduction and induction (Modalities A–D, Decoo 1996: 96–98), which was assumed to facilitate their acquisition of PC. Pragmatic training and metapragmatic information regarding pragmatic features of the TL were provided during feedback sessions after testing English practical and descriptive grammar, and after the general linguistics classes in which the students were enrolled. The overall aim of explicit teaching and feedback was always to guide the students toward appropriate language use and less so toward correctness. Their target/expected competence in English and German was C1 (Council of Europe 2001) although not all of them became competent in these two languages to the same level by the end of the study program. Their proficiency level in the fourth language differed even more, and in the majority of cases it was not higher than B2. Despite the uneven levels of their proficiency in these languages, I prefer to call them multilingual speakers of English and German because they used these languages in daily interactions, including classroom and service contexts, due to, for example, their extra-curricular activities (part-time jobs, foreign studies placements, etc.).

At the end of the first year (the end of Phase I), the cohort consisted of 57 participants (48 women and nine men: S1–S57). In the second year (Phase II), there were 40 students (32 women, eight men), and in the third year (Phase III) the cohort comprised 38 students (30 women, eight men).

4.2 Data collection, analysis procedure and analytical categories

Pragmatic competence is operationalized in this study as the students' ability to produce requests and apologies in L2 English. The present investigation of ILPC is based on the data collected by means of a discourse completion task (DCT) distributed to the same group of advanced learners over the period of three years (32 months). There were three data collection points: October 2012, May 2014, May 2015. This research was a part of a longitudinal mixed-methods study, which I conducted to explore the existence of "pragmatic accent" in pragmatic output of Poles learning EFL (see Szczepaniak-Kozak 2018 and the section concluding this chapter).

The DCT was an adapted version of a task originally devised by Liu (2006, 2007). It comprised 15 situations designed to elicit requests (in ten scenarios, R1–R10) and apologies (in five scenarios A1–A5). The situational descriptions were given in English and the students were asked to provide appropriate speech acts. All tasks were conducted with a set time limit of up to 30 minutes.

In total, the findings presented in the subsequent section rely on a qualitative analysis of IL processes in the corpus which included 1248 requests and 1248 apologies. In Phase I, there were 495 requests and apologies collected. At the end of Phase II, the sample included 386 utterances representing each of the speech acts and at the final stage there were 367 requests and apologies. The utterances were annotated following Blum-Kulka et al.'s (1989) typology of requests and apologies.

The data analysis involved looking for instances of (negative and positive) transfer from the learners' mother tongue (Polish) and the third language they were learning (German), overgeneralized forms originating in English, or forms which never/infrequently appeared. Notably, the analysis process entailed not only extracting patterns of change in the corpus and providing reasons for them but also juxtaposing Polish IL data with native speaker (NS) output. In particular, some of the conclusions were supported by comparing the IL data gathered with 1) results of searches within two corpora of NS English (*Corpus of Contemporary American English*/COCA and *Birmingham Young University – British National Corpus*/BYU–BNC), and 2) NS responses to the DCT as generated by Liu (2006, 2007). No corrections were introduced to the original data provided by the study participants.

5 Discussion and findings

5.1 General findings

In general, pragmalinguistic errors appeared at each data collection period, but, on average, the scale and range of pragmatic inappropriateness decreased among the study participants over time. Some students were able to produce very appropriate speech acts by the end of their BA program. A good piece of evidence in favor of this assessment is the utterance in (1), which is an apology to a person who was accidentally hit by another student:

(1) Whoa! So, so sorry. Come on, let's get you a tissue and some ice-cream.
    (Phase I A5 S54).

The analysis of the requests and apologies collected also indicates that at the end of Phase III the majority of students reached the threshold of language competence necessary for them to be able to transfer non-linguistic skills from their L1 and L3 into their L2. This performance limitation is called "linguistic ceiling" (Carrell 1991). In my study participants, this is visible in their evaluation and pragmalinguistic realizations of sociopragmatic variables involved in the DCT scenarios. Two examples will elucidate this argument. Firstly, they judged the sociopragmatic background of a particular DCT scenario correctly and displayed a considerable awareness of transferability constraints at the pragmatic level (cf. Blum-Kulka, House, and Kasper 1989: 26–27). Therefore, pragmalinguistic resources used in the responses vary according to the age of the interlocutors, their position in the power hierarchy, as well as the extent of the acquaintanceship and relations between them. Secondly, some of the speech acts the students created constitute evidence of their progression toward the TL PC but some others indicate what they still need to learn. To illustrate this, the verbosity effect is observable among not only requests but apologies too. On average, the students' PC in English lags far behind their PC in the mother tongue (Polish).

With reference to interference errors, they appear more frequently in requests, and not in apologies. This finding supports Olshtain's (1989: 171) argument that apologies are less varied in terms of pragmalinguistic forms than requests, and that the former are standardly more formulaic. When interference errors are present, in the majority of cases they are motivated by the students' mother tongue (Polish) rather than by German. This would contradict Chłopek and Małgorzewicz (2009: 3), who advance that such learners' errors are frequently caused by interference between German and English, rather than between English and Polish, due to considerable language proximity between the former pair (Polish being a member of the Slavic languages family).

5.2 Interference errors caused by the mother tongue

There are six major categories of negative pragmalinguistic transfer from the participants' mother tongue in the corpus, usually representing inappropriate use of a pragmalinguistic form: intensifiers, see (2), grammatical constructions and tenses, see (3), idioms and collocations, see (4), prepositions, see (5), word choice, see (6) and other (e.g., word order, use of pronouns, diminutives), see (7). In a sense, the examples could be classified as item transfers of the lexical or syntactic type but because they exert a negative pragmatic effect, I treat them as representative of pragmatic transfer, as well.

(2) a. I *very apologize*, I didn't want to hurt you. (Phase II A5 S56)
 b. I have *a great request* for you. (Phase II R9 S31)

(3) a. You're right. I *did a mistake*. (Phase III A3 S56)
 b. *Would you mind to interview* me on Thursday. (Phase III R5 S8)

(4) a. I *would be pleasured* if you would *to* study with me for the upcoming test. (Phase II R7 S35)
 b. Sorry for that, dude. I *took care about myself*. That is very selfish. I have no idea *how could* I help you now (Phase I A4 S53)
 c. Oh, sorry. *I should watch out*. (Phase III A1 S57)

(5) a. I don't deal with it *less you*. (Phase III R6 S25)
    b. I *apologize you*. (Phase II A1 S36)
    c. I'm sorry that you *lost chance to get job*. Don't be *angry on me*. (Phase I A4 S15)

(6) a. That was my mistake, my fault and I can't do *nothing* to fix it. But *I hardly apologize*. (Phase I A4 S14)
    b. Could you *shift a little*? (Phase III R4 S34)

(7) a. I'm sorry, *mine mistake*. Here you are – 1$ back. I'm really tired, that *happened* sometimes, sorry (Phase I A3 S44)
    b. I would like to *borrow me* a little sheet of paper? (Phase II R10 S29)

When the participants needed to formulate a request and they wanted to do this by means of a suggestion (a suggestory formula), they began the head act with the downgrader *maybe*, see (8), followed by *you* (meaning *do you mind*). It is a characteristic feature of Poles learning EFL who prefer this downgrader to the form *how/what about*, which is more typical of NS English. This can be explained on the grounds of negative transfer from Polish. In it, *how/what about* is not conventionalized as a request in a form resembling its literal translation from English. Instead, it is formulated as a question in the future analytic tense with *może* and the understood subject *ty* (Eng. *maybe you*). The same IL process is observed in a few mitigated apologetic head acts, in post-acts (9). This is a case of negative transfer from the students' mother language and German (L3) as well. In Polish and German, suggestory formulas often begin with the equivalent of *maybe* (Pol.: *może*, Ger. *vielleicht*).

(8) I know that you are very busy but *maybe could you* spare one or two hours for interview with me? (Phase I R9 S52)

(9) a. I'm very sorry. It was not special. *Maybe could you* go to doctor? (Phase I A4 S20)
    b. *Maybe you can* call the company and apologize. (Phase III A5 S5)

There are also examples of rendering apologies by means of the word *would* (a case of a literal translation from Polish), which is an inappropriate form in English, see (10), in some contexts:

(10) *I would apologize* to you because I forgot to do an assignment for your historical grammar course. (Phase I A1 51)

These IL forms, in general, corroborate the conclusions Li (2016) drew in her synthesis study of ILPC research. In it, she posited that semantic strategies, but not the exact pragmalinguistic forms applied to convey these strategies, are often shared between two cultures. Therefore, "the acquisition of semantic strategies used to construct a speech act is relatively faster than that of exact pragmalinguistic forms used in a speech act" (Li 2016: 600).

Another interesting feature of the IL English of these multilingual Poles is the location of the politeness marker *please* in the sentence. First of all, for these multilingual students not only is *please* the primary internal mitigator but also they place it outside the head act more frequently than NSs due to negative pragmalinguistic and sociopragmatic transfer from Polish and German, see (11).

(11) Come on, I'm watching this game! Don't block my view, please. (Phase II R4 31).

The wider use of *please* in an unembedded position in my data can be accounted for on a few grounds. In Polish and German, the equivalent to *please* functions as a verb (in the first person singular: Pol. *proszę*, Ger. *ich bitte*). Additionally, while in English *please* is most often classified as an internal modifier, in Polish, it is always external to the head act because Polish *proszę* is a performative verb in itself (see Ogiermann 2009a: 203–204). Another explanation could be what Kasper and Rose (2002: 142) suggest. Perhaps, in the early stages of PC development *please* is not a true mitigator but rather a requestive marker standing on its own. On the contrary, English NSs tend to use *please* across different sociocultural contexts as a customarily polite word, regardless of sociopragmatic factors involved.

With regard to the frequencies of *please* in this corpus of IL requests and apologies, there are 57 instances of *please* in the embedded position and 146 in the unembedded one. In contrast, the embedded position of *please* in combination with four basic modal verbs used to render a request in English (*could*, *can*, *will*, and *would*) turned out 607 matching phrases in the NS corpora of spoken English for the spoken macro/register (COCA and BYU–BNC combined), whereas *please* positioned outside the same phrases is very rare (29 items).

The high percentage of using *please* outside head act in the present dataset seems to corroborate Ogiermann's (2009a: 203–204) tenet that this preference among Polish non-native speakers of English is a negative transfer from Polish, further strengthened by their IL competence in the third language (German). Relatedly, the first two utterances in (12) also show that some students treat *please* as a verb, which is a negative pragmalinguistic transfer both from their mother tongue and German. It also seems that *please* in a non-embedded position is sometimes intended to exert a particular pragmatic effect – it becomes a vehicle of urgency and/or of supplication on the part of the speaker, see (12d). Such usage also appears in NS English but it expresses decisiveness, a reprimand or even annoyance (see Liu 2007).

(12) a. *May I please* you to stay after store hours? (Phase I R6 S45)
 b. I want *to please* you to schedule my interview to 4 o'clock. (Phase III R5 S6)
 c. Good morning. Sorry that I interrupted, but I have *a big please to you*. (Phase I9 R5 S36)
 d. I'm so, so sorry. It's a stupid situation. I promise, I'll find a job for you. Believe me, *please*. (Phase I A4 S22)

All in all, the downtoner *please* has a special significance to Poles. They seem to attach a high pragmatic value to it; *please* bears affective or evaluative qualities for them because its equivalent in Polish is more frequent in nonroutinized forms when the imposition or misconduct is greater. They also consider it a means of increasing the directness of a particular request or a clear marker of the speaker's supplicatory behavior (Szczepaniak-Kozak 2018: 324).

5.3 Interference errors caused by the third language

Among the participants, the negative transfer of German (L3) into the English IL is definitely less frequent than is transfer from Polish. In the majority of cases, it is present as an item transfer of the orthographic, lexical, or syntactic type, all of which may exert a negative pragmatic effect. More importantly, scant instances of L3 transfer in the corpus may support Ringbom's (2007a: 87) conclusions concerning procedural (system) transfer, namely, that multilinguals are prone to transfer more frequently from the language in which they are more proficient (here Polish). As to examples of the transferred forms, the most frequent occurrence was incorrect use of the preposition *by* in combinations which are typical of the assumed German equivalent *bei* (13) with some collocation errors as the second most frequent type:

(13) a. *By me* I did pizza and after we can go out or watch film. (Phase I R6 S31)
 b. Oh, sorry. You *have a right*, Sir. (Phase I A3 S6)

c. Oh, I made a mistake and I want to apologize for it. Here's your *right change*. (Phase I A3 S3)

There were also a few instances of wrong word order, especially the placement of the verb at the end of a sentence, which is characteristic of the German language (14). Furthermore, some students used the -s ending in the genitive/possessive case in the way it is done in German, see (15). Finally, a few instances of lexical transfer occurred (16). The response included in (16) is particularly interesting because the student, under the influence of both Polish and German, uses the adverb *hardly* (in Polish: *mocno*, in German: *hart*) in the meaning of *sincere*. Negative pragmalinguistic transfer is also noticeable in the use of the word *rest* (Pol. *reszta*, Ger. *Rest*) to denote change, see (17).

(14) a. *Could you please it paraphrase?* (Phase I R2 S31)
 b. I have to do my homework for tomorrow *but something wrong with my computer happens*. (Phase I R8 S50)

(15) a. I'm applying for a job in *yours company*? (Phase I R5 S13)
 b. Sorry, can you change *yours place*? (Phase II R4 S39)

(16) I can't do nothing to fix it. But I *hardly apologize*. (Phase I A5 S6).

(17) I'm so sorry it's my fault. Here's the *rest* of your change. (Phase II A3 S10).

5.4 Sociopragmatic transfer

With reference to sociopragmatic features, the students seem to be greatly influenced by the negative sociopragmatic transfer from Polish in their interpretation of the impact of power distance and social distance on linguistic interactions in EFL. The participants seem to be more competent in identifying the impact of the former but they attach a greater value to the latter. To illustrate this, in the DCT scenarios where the speaker is higher in hierarchy, some of the apologies provided can be perceived as disagreeable or self-righteous, rather than apologetic and featuring a remedial role. At the same time, social distance is particularly useful for the justification of the pragmalinguistic choices used, because it overrides the other dimensions, especially imposition in requests. For instance, when students apologize in scenarios of notable social distance (e.g., in exchanges between strangers), they become elaborately polite (use formal address forms and supplicatory expressions), see (18):

(18) a. Sir, I'm ashamed of myself, that I just forgot about the assignment and want to apologize (Phase I A1 S56).
b. Sorry for that, dude. I took care about myself. That is very selfish. I have no idea how could I help you now. It would better if do not say anything more. (Phase I A5 S36)

Interestingly, among the requests collected a surprising pattern appeared. In two situations characterised by the same parameters of power distance, social distance and imposition, the responses were noticeably different in terms of the pragmalinguistic features used. Both involved strangers communicating: one in a dormitory and the other at a basketball stadium. Yet, the participants provided markedly different responses, depending on whether there is a chance for the interlocutors to become acquaintances or not. This sociopragmatic variable, which I tentatively call "the estimation of future social distance" (Szczepaniak-Kozak 2018: 278), seems to explain the differences relatively plausibly but demands further investigation. All in all, it needs to be underscored that in this stage of their advancement in English, the cohort relies more on their overall (mother-tongue-rooted) sociopragmatic competence and prefer to express sociopragmatic nuances by means of pragmalinguistic features typical of their first language, such as honorific titles, and/or adjectives elevating the rank of the hearer.

6 Conclusions, limitations, and pedagogical implications

By way of conclusion, although the IL pragmatic data investigated in the present paper indicate differences in the pragmatic output of individual learners, the results also reveal particular strategies and patterns to be common across learners with the same mother tongue. The transitional pragmatic competence of multilingual Poles learning English and German is a complex construct which is characterized by forms approximating the NS English baseline, including examples of positive transfer from the L1, fossilized overgeneralizations originating in English, or forms that can be explained on the grounds of negative transfer from both the L1 and the L3. It is important to note that overgeneralization is as frequent in their ILPC as transfer is. Learners regularly hold on to TL pragmalinguistic features or combinations of these which are universal, or are able to serve multiple functions and, thus, can be applied in various contexts of use. Furthermore, the familiar seems to play an enormous role in learning the pragmatics of a foreign language even among advanced learners.

Notably, Polish multilinguals in this study prefer certain pragmatic features to others and therefore they never completely overcome their "pragmatic accent" in EFL. By "pragmatic accent" I understand a hybrid system relying on transfer and generalization which Poles have developed as their "third way" between the pragmatic systems of English and Polish (for more on "pragmatic accent" see Szczepaniak-Kozak 2018).

Although interference errors are grounded in both languages, they are more frequently driven by the students' mother tongue (Polish) and not by German. Relative underrepresentation of L3 transfer in the corpus may constitute another piece of evidence supporting the tenet that that multilinguals more frequently transfer from the language which they know better (here Polish) (see Ringbom 2007a: 87). Furthermore, although seeking and establishing similarity by L2 speakers occurs frequently, especially in the area of sociopragmatics, the language-specific pragmatic features and strategies slow down the development of pragmatic competence. Sources of such interference in my corpus include the rules for positioning *please* in an utterance or the pragmalinguistic forms used to express suggestions. At the same time, requests pose a greater challenge for Polish EFL speakers than apologies, most probably due to the latter being characterized by a greater formulaicity and reduced sensitivity to sociopragmatic nuances.

This study revealed some interesting facts about ILPC of Poles learning at least two additional European languages, which in turn revealed some important areas for future research. It would be insightful, for example, to explore the ILs of the particular study participants individually or to establish what relations there are between all three languages. Additionally, due to the limitations characteristic of DCT, the present research has focused too narrowly on utterance-level strategies (pragmalinguistic forms). Therefore, more research on the ILs manifest in on-going interactions would be useful. Finally, a clear limitation of the current study is that it explored only two speech acts. Future research in this area could benefit from covering other speech acts/pragmatic features, or adopting a more macropragmatic perspective (e.g. to analyze speech events).

References

Achiba, Machiko. 2002. *Learning to request in a second language*. Clevedon: Multilingual Matters.
Arabski, Jerzy. 2006. Language transfer in language learning and language contact. In Jerzy Arabski (ed.), *Cross-linguistic influences in the second language lexicon*, 12–21. Bristol: Multilingual Matters.

Arabski, Jerzy & Adam Wojtaszek. 2016. Contemporary perspectives on crosslinguistic influence. In Rosa Alonso Alonso (ed.), *Crosslinguistic influence in second language acquisition*, 215–224. Bristol: Multilingual Matters.
Bardovi-Harlig, Kathleen. 2010. Exploring the pragmatics of interlanguage pragmatics: Definition by design. In Anna Trosborg (ed.), *Pragmatics across languages and cultures*, vol. 7, 219–259. Berlin: Mouton de Gruyter.
Barron, Anna. 2003. *Acquisition in interlanguage pragmatics. Learning how to do things with words in a study abroad context*. Amsterdam: John Benjamins.
Blum-Kulka, Soshanna. 1990. You don't touch lettuce with your fingers: Parental politeness in family discourse. *Journal of Politeness* 14 (2). 259–288.
Blum-Kulka, Soshanna, Juliane House & Gabriele Kasper (eds.) 1989. *Cross-cultural pragmatics: Requests and apologies*. Norwood, NJ: Ablex.
BYU–BNC. *Birmingham Young University–British National Corpus*. http://corpus.byu.edu/bnc/ (accessed 01 March 2017).
Carrell, Patricia L. 1991. Second language reading: Reading ability or language proficiency. *AppliedLinguistics* 12. 159–179.
Council of Europe. 2001. *Common European Framework of Reference for Languages*. 2001. Cambridge: Cambridge University Press.
Cenoz, Jasone & Ulrike Jessner. 2009. The study of multilingualism in educational contexts. In Larissa Aronin & Britta Hufeisen (eds.), *The exploration of multilingualism*, 121–138. Amsterdam: John Benjamins.
Chłopek, Zofia. 2010. Bi-/multilingualism and the perceptions of the gender of objects. *Glottodidactica* 36. 45–56.
Chłopek, Zofia. 2011. *Nabywanie języków trzecich i kolejnych oraz wielojęzyczność. Aspekty psycholingwistyczne (i inne)*. [Third and additional appropriation and multilingualism. Psycholiguistic (and other) aspects]. Wrocław: Wydawnictwo Uniwersytetu Wrocławskiego.
Chłopek, Zofia & Anna Małgorzewicz. 2009. *Niebezpieczne podobieństwa angielsko-niemieckie. Gramatyka angielsko-niemiecka w ćwiczeniach*. [Dangerous similarities between English and German. English-German grammar with exercises]. Warszawa: REA.
COCA. *Corpus of Contemporary American English*. http://corpus.byu.edu/coca/ (accessed 05 March 2017).
Decoo, Wilfried. 1996. The induction-deduction opposition: Ambiguities and complexities of the didactic reality. *International Review of Applied Linguistics in Language Teaching* 34. 95–118.
Ellis, Rod. 1992. Learning to communicate in the classroom: A study of two language learners. *Studies in Second Language Acquisition* 14 (1). 1–23.
Faerch, Claus & Gabriele Kasper. 1986. One learner – two languages: Investigating types of interlanguage knowledge. In Juliane House & Shoshanna Blum-Kulka (ed.), *Interlingual and intercultural communication*, 211–228. Tuebingen: Narr.
Glaser, Karen. 2014. *Inductive or deductive? The impact of method of instruction on the acquisition of pragmatic competence in EFL*. Newcastle upon Tyne: Cambridge Scholars Publishing.
Halenko, Nicola & Christian Jones. 2011. Teaching pragmatic awareness of spoken requests to Chinese EAP learners in the UK: Is explicit instruction effective? *System* 39. 240–250.
Herbert, Robert K. 1991. The sociology of compliment work: The enthocontrastive study of Polish and English compliments. *Multilingua* 10 (4). 381–402.

Jarvis, Scott. 1998. *Conceptual transfer in the interlanguage lexicon*. Bloomington, IN: IULC Publications.
Jaworski, Adam. 1994. Pragmatic failure in a second language: Greeting responses in English by Polish students. *IRAL* 1. 41–55.
Jessner, Ulrike. 2008. Language awareness in multilinguals: Theoretical trends. In Jasone Cenoz & Nancy H. Hornberger (eds.), *Encyclopedia of language and education*, 2nd edn., vol. 6, 357–369. Heidelberg: Springer.
Kasper, Gabriele. 1983. Communicative competence in foreign language teaching: A project report. In Kari Sajavaara (ed.), *Cross-language analysis and second language acquisition*, vol. 1, 65–80. Jyväskylä: University Publishers.
Kasper, Gabriele & Kenneth R. Rose. 2002. *Pragmatic development in a second language*. Oxford: Blackwell.
Kecskes, Istvan. 2015. How does pragmatic competence develop in bilinguals? *International Journal of Multilingualism* 1. 1–16. doi:10.1080/14790718.2015.1071018.
Li, Qiong. 2016. Variations in developmental patterns across pragmatic features. *Studies in Second Language Learning and Teaching* 6 (4). 587–617.
Liu, Jianda. 2006. *Measuring interlanguage pragmatic knowledge of EFL learners*. Frankfurt am Main: Peter Lang.
Liu, Jianda. 2007. Development of a pragmatics test for Chinese EFL learners. *Language Testing* 24 (3). 391–415.
Majer, Jan & Łukasz Salski. 2004. The pragmatics of classroom discourse: Requests and commands. In Janusz Arabski (ed.), *Pragmatics and language learning*,51–67. Kraków: Universitas.
Herraiz Martínez, Ana & Ariadna Sánchez Hernández. 2019. Pragmatic markers produced by multilingual speakers: Evidence from a CLIL context. *English Language Teaching* 12 (2). 68–76. doi: 10.5539/elt.v12n2p68.
Odlin, Terence. 2012. Reconciling group tendencies and individual variation in the acquisition of L2 and L3. In Danuta Gabryś-Barker (ed.), *Cross-linguistic influences in multilingual language acquisition*, 81–98. Berlin Heidelberg: Springer. doi:10.1007/978-3-642-29557-7_5.
Odlin, Terence. 2016. Was there really ever a Contrastive Analysis Hypothesis? In Rosa Alonso Alonso (ed.), *Crosslinguistic influence in second language acquisition*, 1–23. Bristol: Multilingual Matters.
Ogiermann, Eva. 2009a. Politeness and in-directness across cultures: A comparison of English, German, Polish and Russian requests. *Journal of Politeness Research* 5. 189–216.
Ogiermann, Eva. 2009b. *On apologising in negative and positive politeness cultures*. Amsterdam: John Benjamins.
Olshtain, Elite. 1989. Apologies across cultures. In Shoshanna Blum-Kulka, Juliene House & Gabriele Kasper (eds.), *Cross-cultural pragmatics: Requests and apologies*, 155–173. Norwood, NJ: Ablex.
Pienemann, Manfred. 1998. Developmental dynamics in L1 and L2 acquisition: Processability theory and generative entrenchment. *Bilingualism* 1. 1–20.
Pienemann, Manfred. 2015. An outline of processability theory and its relationship to other approaches to SLA. *Language Learning* 65 (1). 123–151.
Ringbom, Håkan. 2006. The importance of different types of similarity in transfer studies. In Janusz Arabski (ed.), *Cross-linguistic influences in the second language lexicon*, 36–45. Bristol: Multilingual Matters.

Ringbom, Håkan. 2007a. *Cross-linguistic similarity in foreign language learning*. Clevedon: Multilingual Matters.
Ringbom, Håkan. 2007b. Actual, perceived and assumed cross-linguistic similarities in foreign language learning. *Suomen soveltavan kielitieteen yhdistyksen julkaisuja* 65. 183–196.
Safont Jordà, Maria-Pilar. 2005. *Third language learners. Pragmatic production and awareness*. Clevedon: Multilingual Matters.
Safont-Jordà, Maria-Pilar. 2008. The speech act of requesting. In Eva Alcón-Soler (ed.), *Learning how to request in an instructed language learning context*, 41–64. Berlin: Peter Lang.
Safont-Jordà, Maria-Pilar. 2012. A longitudinal analysis of Catalan, Spanish and English request modifiers in early third language learning. In Danuta Gabryś-Barker (ed.), *Cross-linguistic influences in multilingual language acquisition*, 99–114. Berlin Heidelberg: Springer. doi:10.1007/978-3-642-29557-7_6.
Schank, Jeffrey C. & William C. Wimsatt. 1986. Generative entrenchment and evolution. *PSA: Proceedings of the Biennial Meeting of the Philosophy of Science Association* 1986 (2). 33–60.
Schauer, Gila A. 2009. *Interlanguage pragmatics development: The study abroad context*. London: Continuum.
Selinker, Larry & Lakshmanan Usha. 1992. Language transfer and fossilization: The 'Multiple Effect Principle'. In Susan Gass & Larry Selinker (eds.), *Language transfer in language learning*, 197–216. Rowley MA: Newbury House.
Sopata, Aldona. 2009. *Erwerbstheoretische und glottodidaktische Aspekte des frühen Zweitspracherwerbs. Sprachentwicklung der Kinder im natürlichen und schulischen Kontext*. Poznań: Adam Mickiewicz University Press.
Sypiańska, Jolanta. 2017. *Cross-linguistic influence in bilinguals and multilinguals*. Poznań: Adam Mickiewicz University Press.
Szczepaniak-Kozak, Anna. 2018. *Interlanguage pragmatic competence. A longitudinal study of 'pragmatic accent' in learning EFL*. Poznań: Adam Mickiewicz University Press.
Taguchi, Naoko. 2017. Interlanguage pragmatics. In Anne Barron, Peter Grundy & Gerard Yueguo (eds.), *The Routledge handbook of pragmatics*, 153–167. Oxford, New York: Routledge.
Tarone, Elaine. 1998. Interlanguage. In Jacob L. Mey (ed.), *Concise encyclopedia of pragmatics*, 389–395. Amsterdam: Elsevier.
Wach, Aleksandra. 2018. Trilingual learners' awareness of the role of L1 in learning target language grammar. In Mirosław Pawlak & Anna Mystkowska-Wiertelak (ed.), *Challenges of second and foreign language education in a globalized world*, 209–226. Cham: Springer.
Włosowicz, Teresa. 2011. Ways of expressing birthday, Christmas and New Year's and Easter wishes in L2 and L3: Cross-cultural transfer and interlanguage pragmatics. In Janusz Arabski & Adam Wojtaszek (eds.), *Aspects of culture in second language acquisition and foreign language learning*, 217–231. Heidelberg: Springer.

Vita Kalnbērziņa
Chapter 9
Curriculum Reform in Latvia: A Move from Multilingual to Plurilingual Education

Abstract: This chapter addresses the issue of multilingualism and plurilingualism in language education. It uses language curriculum reform in Latvia as a research context, to find out if the new 2018 Common European Framework of Reference (CEFR) descriptors can be used in introducing the plurilingualism approach to language education to improve student performance. The present results of school exit examinations in foreign languages in Latvia do not match the existing schools' curriculum achievement target of level B2, as the majority of school graduates do not reach the target in the existing school system where each language is taught separately. Therefore, the state curriculum reform aims at a competence approach which envisages the integration of all subjects into domains, languages included. This plan for curriculum reform matches the approach promoted by the Council of Europe and its plurilingual repertoire level descriptors. This article examines the draft curriculum development process and its preliminary results in relation to CEFR. The findings suggest that the plurilingual aspects of education are easier integrated into the descriptors of the context of language use than the descriptors dedicated to the structural or lexical competence of language.

Keywords: curriculum, multilingualism, plurilingualism, translanguage

1 Introduction

People across the world mix languages every day at home, at work, and in public spaces, but translanguaging (Orellana and García 2018: 386) is generally frowned upon at schools, see, for example, Pētersone (2017 para. 5). As a result, a student who has just learned a new rule for the use of an indefinite article in German after a 10-minute break can be penalized for applying the same rule in an English class. The isolation of languages in the school curricula represents the traditional monolingual approach to language education and is still used in many countries, including Latvia. Indeed, the traditional aim of a curriculum

---
Vita Kalnbērziņa, University of Latvia, Latvia, E-mail: vita.kalnberzina@lu.lv

https://doi.org/10.1515/9781501514692-009

developer is to write a curriculum that states the aims and study objectives for language learners clearly enough to guide the choice of their textbooks, their study trajectory, and the assessment materials in a given language. The Council of Europe has been working for years to change this situation by developing documents and language teaching materials promoting language integration (i.e., plurilingualism), which are challenging to implement as they contradict the nationally legislated language education systems and national language policy objectives. This chapter documents one such attempt to reconcile the Council of Europe's plurilingual language education view and the national legislation in Latvia, first looking at the multilingualism and plurilingualism in European context and then describing the curriculum reform in Latvia. Thus, the research question here is whether the multilingual policies of European Council are compatible with Latvian education system, which elements can be integrated in its documents and how.

2 Curricular and school approaches to plurilingualism in Europe

The term plurilingualism was introduced by the Council of Europe to distinguish between the use of languages by an individual and the use of languages within a society (multilingualism). Beacco et al. (2010: 16) explain the difference between the terms as follows: "Plurilingualism is the ability to use more than one language – and accordingly it sees languages from the standpoint of speakers and learners. Multilingualism, on the other hand, refers to the presence of several languages in a given geographical area, regardless of those who speak them".

This distinction between the use of languages within a society as opposed to the use of languages by individuals introduces a crucial difference for language learning: should languages be taught in isolation or with an integrated approach?

Beacco et al. (2010: 96) provide three different approaches to how plurilingualism can be introduced into schools:
1. Immersion or Content Language Integrated Learning (CLIL): Language across the curriculum: focusing on high achievements in both languages used for immersion as well as subject knowledge;
2. Integrated language didactics (ILD): Teaching all the languages of the curriculum in a systematic manner, introducing the students to the similarities and differences of the languages and thus reinforcing their linguistic competence in general;

3. Language awareness: Introducing into the curriculum not only several languages but also their dialectal variants, their spoken and written peculiarities, sign languages, audio and video recording, seeing languages as semiotic systems.

The first two approaches are focused on the integration of school subjects within the existing school curriculum, and both demand teacher cooperation: either teachers need to coordinate between their subject curricula to integrate, for example, the topics studied in geography and languages (CLIL), or they different language teachers need to cooperate (for example, teachers of Latvian, Russian and English) and agree to when and how to introduce the degrees of comparison in all three languages (ILD). The third approach, that of language awareness, is different as it demands the integration of social aspects into school curricula, the dialects and language varieties – including the use of slang – which are often excluded from academic studies, although they form a large part of student lives.

The availability of the internet has made different language variants and different language symbol systems (e.g. emoticons, abbreviations within text messaging) part of every child's life long before they enter the school system. This kind of language use changes rapidly and cannot be easily introduced in a state curriculum, which takes years to adopt. Therefore, a digitally-inclusive, multimodal approach to language learning requires the cooperation of the teacher, the students, and the parents in curriculum development and implementation. Language teachers would need to carry out a thorough investigation of their student language background, including their everyday language practices to be able to study a student's language repertoire and introduce it into the school routine.

2.1 Plurilingual repertoires versus compartmentalized repertoires

The term *plurilingual repertoire* provides a framework for the competence development of individual learners, who will be the ones to decide the future of their community and their country. The CEFR defines this repertoire as:

> All the resources acquired in each of the languages known or used and the cultures attached to them, collected "under one roof", for example: the majority or official language(s) of schooling and the cultures transmitted in a given educational context; regional and minority or migration languages and the corresponding cultures; modern or classical languages and the cultures taught with them. (Beacco et al. 2010: 16)

The concept of plurilingual repertoire can be further linked to Gumperz's (1968) verbal repertoire, which explains not only the links between the languages, but also the linguistic range of its variants and our need to compartmentalize the different languages and their varieties:

> As an analytical concept the verbal repertoire allows us to establish direct relationships between its constituents and the socioeconomic complexity of the community. We measure this relationship in terms of two concepts: linguistic range and degree of compartmentalization. Compartmentalization refers to the sharpness with which varieties are set off from each other, either along the superposed or the dialectal dimension. We speak of compartmentalized repertoires, therefore, when several languages are spoken without their mixing, when dialects are set off from each other by sharp isogloss bundles, or when special parlances are sharply distinct from other forms of speech.
> (Gumperz 1968: 50)

The language separation versus language integration approach is reminiscent of Cenoz's (2018) distinction between multilingual and monolingual language views: the compartmentalization or monolingual view of languages and dialects, where they contaminate each other, versus the multilingual view of the societies where languages reinforce each other, see Table 9.1.

Table 9.1: Jasone Cenoz (2018) Monolingual versus multilingual views (Language Identity in Education in Multilingual Contexts conference presentation slide).

Monolingual views	Multilingual views
Languages contaminate each other	Languages reinforce each other
The aim is balanced multilingualism for all situations	Multilinguals use their languages for different purposes and have different skills
Non-existing monolingual societies as a reference	Real multilingual societies as a reference

In actual fact, the real societies mentioned in Cenoz's table can also be compartmentalized and insist on keeping languages separate in spite of evermore present networking practices and people switching from one language to another in what is often called translanguaging practice.

2.2 The role of translanguaging in the school curriculum context

The research on translanguaging covers its use in everyday situations as well as language education. For example, Busch (2012: 22) sees translanguaging as part of one's linguistic repertoire: "As a result of varied networking practices – among other things in media spaces – speakers participate in varying and deterritorialized communities of practice. In this context, it seems necessary to re-examine the notion of a linguistic repertoire. This notion is in fact increasingly being referred to, particularly in the current debates around language crossing or translanguaging".

The term translanguaging, or using several languages simultaneously within the same communicative situation, allows us to connect language use in context with the foreign language education context, where teachers and students have been code-switching and code-mixing languages in spite of the stigmatization of the phenomena. The concepts of translanguaging and plurilingual repertoires has finally allowed educators to standardize the practice within the European education setting.

Orellana and García (2018: 386) go even further and say that integrating languages and integrating contexts is how children learn:

> A translanguaging lens really questions the idea that there is a monolingual way of acting. In a sense, it does away with monolingual education. It would mean that teachers would have to acknowledge and work with the language practices that all children bring into classrooms, because the only way to make sense of school language is to start from what one knows and to integrate it. And we do the integration for everything else, right? We know that children learn by integrating contexts. And yet when we think about language, we never think about integration.

Interestingly, the idea of context integration unites the translanguaging at schools with curriculum development at the state level, which can also be seen as working across different contexts. For example, Kirkgoz (2016), talking about curriculum development in Turkey, lists five different aims, covering five levels of context:
- defining an effective approach for teaching and learning (classroom context);
- paying attention to the latest instructional practices in language teaching (professional context),
- as well as local "contextual variables and constraints," (2016: 1200);
- aligning with the national requirements (social, economic and political context);
- and taking into account the ongoing change in the global context.

A multilevel contextual approach seems to be exaggerated and impossible to implement if we are thinking of a monolingual curriculum development situation, or even a bilingual education model, as every language operates within certain limits. If, however, we set an aim for plurilingual language education as described in CEFR (2018), we need to employ not only all five contexts mentioned above, but we also need to add one more context, which is the European context that is specifically concerned with language use in context or communicative situation: " Balanced mastery of different languages is not the goal, but rather the ability (and willingness) to modulate their usage according to the social and communicative situation; barriers between languages can be overcome in communication and different languages can be used purposefully for conveying messages in the same situation" (CEFR2018: 23).Thus, we can see that language use and curriculum development both need to take into account the local, national and international context.

2.3 The integration of plurilingual repertoire in language teaching

The integration of language learners' plurilingual repertoire into language curricula demands changes in language teacher training. Beacco et al. (2010: 39) suggest that language teachers will need new types of expertise: to understand plurilingual people, to learn to develop specific learning objectives, and to manage the learning process using several languages at once. For this they will need:
1. the detailed knowledge of the way in which bilingual/plurilingual people "function";
2. the ability to set realistic targets for acquisition of the plurilingual and intercultural competence;
3. the ability to build on learners' language repertoires;
4. the ability to activate strategies for transfers from one language, competence or subject to another;
5. the ability to manage language alternation in the classroom judiciously and in a controlled manner.

Although many of the teachers in Latvia themselves are plurilingual in their everyday communication and all they would need to do is let their real-life experience into their classroom, without special training, "letting their real-life experience" in can be impossible or even unacceptable to carry out in practice, as can be seen in the recent events that unfolded in a Latvian school:

> A huge uproar was caused in 2015 by a poem titled 'ō,' when a high school teacher Iveta Ratinīka was informally reprimanded for analysing the poem during one of her literature classes. The ban to discuss the poem was due to Russian and Latvian swear words found in the novel, and the so called "decency clauses" demanding that students are to be morally educated by the school system according to the values included in and protected by the Constitution of Latvia, particularly upholding marital and family values.
> (Latvian Literature 2018: para. 2)

The discussion of the use of different language variants and registers provokes a lot of controversy and can endanger the teacher's employability. Therefore, society has to protect its values and the schools' ability to accept and deal with the linguistic reality outside the school walls.

None of the five aims of the teacher training set out by Beacco et al. (2010) mention teachers' ability to explain the national language policy, which may sometimes be necessary. For example, in the case of the Latvian language reform, students can become easy targets, to be rounded up and used in all kinds of protest demonstrations, which we saw in 2004:

> Some 6,000 Russian-speaking teenagers and schoolchildren protested today outside Latvia's parliament as lawmakers prepared to adopt a law limiting the use of Russian in the country's schools. The legislation, expected to pass later today, requires that at least 60 percent of classes in public schools be taught in Latvian, including schools with a majority of Russian-speaking students. (Radio Free Europe 2004: para. 1)

Fifteen years later we have the same kind of news from the BBC (2018), telling us that the Latvian and Russian Parliaments are exchanging resolutions regarding the introduction of Latvian language in Russian secondary schools: "Latvian President Raimonds Vejonis said the language reform would improve equal opportunities for all citizens. In response, the Russian Duma (lower house) resolution called it a violation of internationally recognized rights". The BBC concludes their article entitled "Russia threatens sanctions over Latvian language in schools" with the following statement: "In the Ukraine in 2014 Russian-speakers' fears that their language rights were at risk fueled the ethnic conflict, in which Russia annexed Crimea and helped insurgents in the Donbass region" (2018: para. 16).

Latvian teachers are faced with a choice: to focus on the grammar rules of a given language and ignore the multilingual, plurilingual realities outside the classroom, or get involved. It takes courage to listen to the students, whose lives are affected by these socio-political events. This can be done during language classes (Latvian and Russian), but even better, during the English language class, as it lets in the language used by the BBC and provides an opportunity to look at local events from a foreign perspective.

3 Research context

Latvia is a multilingual country, and so is our system of education: According to the government statistics of 2017, 132,000 students studied in Latvian, 46,000 students studied in Russian, and 16,000 students studied in bilingual Latvian/Russian schools (Government Statistics Bureau n. d.). The current language curriculum is skill-based. It is aimed at level B2 at the secondary level, and it is often test-driven because of the centralized testing of all languages at the end of the secondary school. All students need to take a test in foreign languages, but they can choose between English, Russian, French and German (83% of students prefer testing in the English language). Table 9.2 (below) shows secondary students' main levels of performance: levels B1 and B2. There is a small minority that has reached level C1, and a larger minority, who have not reached the level B1 and thus are not awarded any level.

Table 9.2: Foreign language state examination results in 2017.

	Total	C1	B2	B1	No level
English	11966 (83%)	175	4391	4818	2583
Russian	2388 (16%)	7	1239	963	238
German	86 (0.6%)	17	32	35	2
French	33 (0.4%)	1	21	11	0
Total	14473 (100%)	200 (1%)	5683 (39%)	5827 (40%)	2823 (20%)

The present foreign language curriculum prescribes B1 as the level of achievement for primary school, and B2 as the level of achievement for the secondary school graduates. Nevertheless, we can see that only 40% of students reach the appropriate level of achievement, while 60% of students do not reach their achievement target, which explains the need for changes in the curricula aiming at integrating all the subjects, languages included.

3.1 Description of the reform process

The state curriculum reform started in 2016 with the goal of developing new curricula for all subject areas and all age groups from kindergarten to the upper secondary level. Subject knowledge is to be introduced in an integrated manner on the basis of transversal skills (critical thinking, creativity, cooperation skills and digital literacy). More than 600 teachers and experts participated in the development of all subject curricula from 2016–2018. The language curricula development consisted of 4 stages, as follows:
- Stage 1: Construct conceptualization was carried out by a small expert committee uniting all the languages.

– Stages 2 and 3: The description and validation of the levels using CEFR (2001) was carried out by 5–10 teachers for each language and the Ministry of Education.
– Stage 4: Relating the CEFR plurilingual repertoire descriptors to the curriculum development principles was carried out by a small expert committee consisting of four university professors.

Stage 1: Conceptualization

The process of language education curriculum reform started with negotiations of the type of curricula necessary, and with agreement on four types of language curricula: Latvian as a native language curriculum, state language curriculum (Latvian), minority language curriculum, and foreign language curriculum (for English, German, French and Russian languages). However, because of the common principles of the educational reform project, all the languages were now part of the same language subject domain. The conceptual unity of the language curricula was discussed at length, and it was finally decided that all the language curricula would be based on the functional approach (see Figure 9.1).

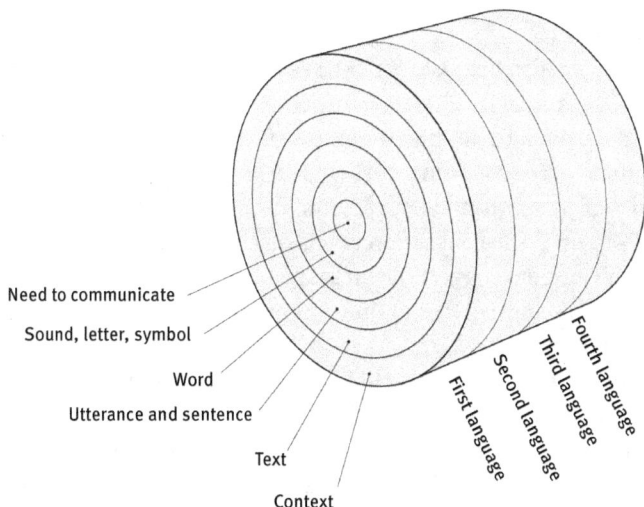

Figure 9.1: The conceptual basis of language curricula (from Curriculum reform development documents).

The construct of the new language curriculum is based on a hierarchical principle: the understanding of contexts allows us to understand and produce texts, which in turn allows us to interpret the sentence structures, words and sounds.

Thus, we arrive at three levels of attainment targets: contextual, textual and language structure, without strict distinction between the languages themselves. The same pattern is observed in everyday life, where languages can often intersect and blend into each other. This approach to curriculum reform provoked protests among Latvian language teachers, as they felt robbed of their unique native language status and downgraded to the position occupied by foreign languages (Pētersone 2017). Incidentally, the author of the article is the same teacher who was described above in connection with the poem containing slang, and fighting for including language variants into the school curriculum (Latvian Literature 2018). This suggests that the need for compartmentalization of language variants can exist separately from the need to compartmentalize languages.

One of the reasons for protests against the "hegemony" of foreign languages in Latvia is the status of the Common European Framework, which has affected all curriculum reform processes. The language education policy (Valsts izglītības satura centrs 2018) in Latvia has been closely linked to the Common European Framework of Reference (2001) levels since its publication, first as the basis for centralized examination development in 1994 and later as the basis for the language curriculum development in 2012 (Valsts izglītības satura centrs 2018).

Stage 2: Description of levels
The new language curricula also used CEFR (2001) as a starting point, following backward design. As Paesan (2017: 2) states, "three elements essential to addressing challenges in curricular reform and program evaluation facing FL [foreign language] programs are: grounding curricula in the concept of literacy, adopting a backward design approach to curriculum revision, and building curriculum from the bottom up". The same approach is also indirectly indicated in CEFR (2018: 42), and the authors suggest the target result as the starting point:

Step 1: Select the descriptor scales that are relevant to the needs of the group of learners concerned.
Step 2: Determine with the stakeholders, for each relevant descriptor scale, the level that the learners should reach.
Step 3: Collate the descriptors for the target level(s) from all the relevant scales into a list. This gives the very first draft of a set of communicative aims.
Step 4: Refine the list, possibly in discussion with the stakeholders.

This framework was applied in integrating the plurilingual repertoire descriptors in the foreign language curriculum, which is described below.

Stage 3: Use of CEFR (2001) language level descriptors in draft curricula

The secondary school curriculum development group consisting of 15 teachers of different languages and all education levels examined the CEFR (2001) descriptors of levels A2, B1 and B2 and found that they could be mapped on the Transversal Skills Framework (we found descriptors addressing critical thinking, creativity, and cooperation skills, as well as digital literacies). On the basis of the formulated hierarchical approach, from context, to text, to language structures, the curriculum development groups developed four draft curricula with common principles for the primary and secondary education:
1. State language curriculum (Latvian)
2. Second language curriculum (Latvian)
3. Minority language curriculum (Russian, Polish, Ukrainian, Belorussian)
4. Foreign language curriculum (English, German, French and Russian).

All the primary education language draft curricula were developed during 2017, and were examined by an expert group in 2018. The preliminary analysis suggests that all the language curricula (Latvian as L1 and L2, the Minority language curriculum, and the Foreign language curriculum) have been implemented in the three domains (context, text and language structure) within 9–11 attainment targets (see the results of the analysis in Table 9.3). This suggests that there are more similarities than differences in the learning outcomes and their levels, thus providing a sound basis for coordination between the different language acquisition and plurilingual education development in Latvia.

This table was developed on the basis of the primary school draft curriculum, and will now be used to develop the secondary school draft curriculum.

Table 9.3: The attainment target grid developed on the basis of all four language curricula drafts.

Contextual level	Text level	Language structures
The role of the language in social context	Recognition of cultural heritage and individual values in texts	Language learning strategies, use of European Language portfolio in self-assessment
Definition of the context (time, space, participants and the function)	Text processing strategies (listening and reading)	Language sounds, pronunciation, language variants and dialects

Table 9.3 (continued)

Contextual level	Text level	Language structures
Seeking factual information	Analysis of text types and text structure (including visual images and graphs)	Orthographic skills and use of symbols in communication
Imparting factual information	Analysis of text contents, evaluation of the quality and reliability of information	Use of morphemes in word building, lexical meaning and style
Expressing and finding out attitudes	Stylistic analysis of the text	Lexical functions in a sentence, syntactic agreement and lexical cohesion
Getting things done	Brainstorming, drafting and planning techniques	Choice of words, their agreement with the intended message, use of dictionaries
Socializing	Cooperation skills in text development	Utterance: word stress, intonation, pausing
Structuring discourse	Editing skills and redrafting skills (including using IT)	Sentence and punctuation (in simple and complex sentences)
Communication repair	Text presentation and feedback elicitation skills	Language use development strategies and self-assessment skills (e.g. ICT tools)

Stage 4: Mapping CEFR (2018) Plurilingual Repertoire Descriptors onto Attainment

The publication of the New Companion Volume CEFR (2018) provides additional input for the secondary school curriculum as it agrees with our perception of the role of the learner: "CEFR broadens the perspective of language education in a number of ways, not least by its vision of the user/learner as a social agent, co-constructing meaning in interaction, and by the notions of mediation and plurilingual / pluricultural competence" (CEFR 2018: 23).

The newly developed attainment target grid (see Table 9.3) was used as a framework to select the plurilingual learning targets from the CEFR descriptors for levels B1 and B2. The following list of descriptors describing the contextual level were discussed by the curriculum expert group (see Table 9.4 below).

As we can see from Table 9.4, appropriate descriptors could be found for all the sections covering the contextual level of attainment targets.

Table 9.4: Results of mapping the contextual level attainment targets with plurilingual repertoire descriptors from CEFR (2018:160–162).

	Contextual level attainment target grid	Plurilingual repertoire descriptors from CEFR (2018)
1	The role of the language	Can explain in simple terms how his/her own values and behaviors influence his/her views of other people's values and behaviors
2	Definition of the context (time, space, participants and the function)	Can discuss in simple terms the way in which things that may look strange to him/her in another sociocultural context may be normal for the other people concerned.
3	Input: imparting and seeking factual information	Can discuss in simple terms the way his/her own culturally-determined actions may be perceived differently by people from other cultures.
4	Output: imparting and seeking factual information	Can exploit creatively his/her limited repertoire in different languages in his/her plurilingual repertoire for everyday contexts, in order to cope with an unexpected situation.
5	Expressing and finding out attitudes	Can balance information and opinions expressed in the media about his/her own and other communities
6	Getting things done	Can identify and reflect on similarities and differences in culturally determined behavior patterns (e.g. gestures and speech volume) and discuss their significance in order to negotiate mutual understanding.
7	Socializing	Can generally act according to conventions regarding posture, eye contact, and distance from others
8	Structuring discourse	Can, in an intercultural encounter, recognize that what one normally takes for granted in a particular situation is not necessarily shared by others, and can react and express him-/herself appropriately.
9	Communication repair	Can generally respond appropriately to the most commonly used cultural cues.

The textual level attainment target mapping, however, was more challenging. We could find the plurilingual descriptors addressing cultural heritage in texts, text contents processing, cooperation skills in text development and text presentation and feedback elicitation skills, but we could not find appropriate descriptors for brainstorming, drafting and planning techniques, or editing and redrafting skills. Altogether we found five out of nine partially matching descriptors (Targets 1, 2, 3, 7, and 9) that were used as a basis for the curriculum attainment target development (see Table 9.5 below).

Table 9.5: Results of mapping of the curriculum attainment principles on plurilingual repertoire descriptors in CEFR (2018:160–162).

	Textual level attainment target grid	Plurilingual repertoire descriptors from CEFR (2018)
1	Recognition of cultural heritage and individual values in texts	Can explain features of his/her own culture to members of another culture or explain features of the other culture to members of his/her own culture.
2	Text processing strategies (listening and reading)	Can extract information from documents written in different languages in his/her field, e.g. to include in a presentation.
3	Analysis of text contents, evaluation of the quality and reliability of information	Can use what he/she has understood in one language to understand the topic and main message of a text in another language (e.g., when reading short newspaper articles on the same theme written in different languages).
7	Cooperation skills in text development	Can make use of different languages in his/her plurilingual repertoire during collaborative interaction, in order to clarify the nature of a task, the main steps, the decisions to be taken, the outcomes expected.
9	Text presentation and feedback elicitation skills	Can make use of different languages in his/her plurilingual repertoire to encourage other people to use the language in which they feel more comfortable

The least successful set of repertoire descriptors was the Language Structure level, as there we could match only three out of nine attainment target principles (Targets 1, 5, and 6) with the CEFR (2018: 160–162) plurilingual repertoire descriptors: those of language learning strategies, lexical functions and lexical meaning.

We were not so successful with the attainment targets for phonological or syntactic competence in plurilingual communication, use of word stress and intonation patterns (see Table 9.6 below).

Table 9.6: Results of mapping the language structure attainment target principles on to CEFR (2018) Plurilingual repertoire descriptors.

	Language structure attainment target grid	Plurilingual repertoire descriptors from CEFR (2018)
1	Language learning strategies, use of European Language portfolio in self-assessment	Can use parallel translations of texts (e.g., magazine articles, stories, passages from novels) to develop comprehension in different languages.
5	Lexical functions in a sentence, syntactic agreement and lexical cohesion	Can introduce into an utterance an expression from another language in his/her plurilingual repertoire that is particularly apt for the situation/concept being discussed, explaining it for the interlocutor when necessary
6	Choice of words, their agreement with the intended message, use of dictionaries	Can recognize similarities and contrasts between the way concepts are expressed in different languages, in order to distinguish between identical uses of the same word root and "false friends".

The attainment targets chosen for the plurilingual repertoire descriptors will now be translated and integrated into the state foreign language curriculum of the secondary education.

4 Conclusion

Language curriculum that integrates all the languages taught at schools is a challenge to develop and implement, not only because of the phonological, lexical or syntactical differences of different languages, but also because it is challenging to overcome the societal compulsion to compartmentalize languages (Gumperz 1968). Not all members of the multilingual society in Latvia share the multilingual view (Cenoz 2018) of language curriculum developers, in spite of the statistics suggesting that studying languages in isolation does not allow students to reach the planned curriculum attainment targets, and in spite of evidence that many policy makers see translanguaging and plurilingual repertoires as a way forward. The descriptors of the CEFR companion volume (2018) partially agree with the Latvian language curriculum developers' view of language learning principles, as they mostly focus on functional and contextual competence and do not contain descriptors addressing phonological and syntactic competence.

Thus, we can answer the research question whether the multilingual policies of European Council are compatible with Latvian education system affirmatively, not only the Council of Europe multilingual policies are compatible with the national language policies, but also useful as a reference framework as they allow the curriculum experts to mediate between the different foreign languages and the native language policies.

The question about which elements of multilingual policies can be integrated in national language policy, is the key concept that connects language learning and language use, namely, that of context. In the case of language learning it is the ability to employ all the languages that are available in the particular context (all one's plurilingual repertoire), but in the case of curriculum development it is the ability to mediate between the classroom, national, and international contexts. As this paper has demonstrated, the contextual aspect of the CEFR was also the most easily integrated in the new Latvian curriculum, and therefore shows the common understanding of the role of context in language education in Europe.

References

BBC (British Broadcasting Company). 2018. *Russia threatens sanctions over Latvian language in schools*. http://www.bbc.com/news/world-europe-43626368 (accessed 15 November 2019).

Beacco, Jeanne-Claude, Byram, Michael, Cavalli, Marissa, Coste, Daniel, Egli Cuenat, Mirjam, Goullier, Francis & Panthier, Johanna. 2010. *Guide for the development and implementation of curricula for plurilingual and intercultural education*. Strasbourg: Council of Europe, Language Policy Division.

Busch, Brigitte. 2012. The linguistic repertoire revisited. *Applied Linguistics* 33 (5). 503–523.

Cenoz, Jasone. 2018. *Focus on multilingualism and translanguaging in language learning in school contexts*. Plenary address in Language, Identity and Education in Multilingual Contexts conference, Dublin Marino Institute, 1–3 February.

Council of Europe. 2001. *Common European framework for language learning, teaching and assessment*. Cambridge: Cambridge University Press.

Council of Europe. 2018. *Common European framework for language learning, teaching and assessment. Companion volume with new descriptors*, Provisional publication.

Strasbourg, https://rm.coe.int/cefr-companion-volume-with-new-descriptors-2018/1680787989 (accessed 15 November 2019)

Orellana, Marjorie Faulstich, & García, Ofelia. 2018. Language brokering and translanguaging in school. *Language Arts* 91 (5). 386–392.

Government Statistics Bureau. (n. d.). https://data.csb.gov.lv/pxweb/lv/iedz/iedz__tau tassk__taut__tsk2000/TSK00-106.px/table/tableViewLayout1/(accessed 15 November 2019)

Gumperz, John. 1968. The speech community. In David L. Sills & Robert K. Merton (eds.), *International encyclopedia of the social sciences*, 381–386. New York: Macmillan.

Kirkgoz, Yassemin. 2016. Laying the theoretical and practical foundations for a new elementary English curriculum in Turkey: A procedural analysis. *Kastamonu Education Journa*, 24 (3), 1199–1212.

Latvian Literature. 2018. *Top 10 most scandalous works of contemporary Latvian literature.* http://www.latvianliterature.lv/en/news/top-10-most-scandalous-works-of-contemporary-latvian-literature (accessed 15 November 2019).

Paesan, Kate. 2017. Redesigning an introductory language program: A backward design approach. *L2 Journal 9* (1). 1–20. http://repositories.cdlib.org/uccllt/l2/vol9/iss1/art1/ (accessed 15 November 2019)

Pētersone, Ilze. 2017, September 29. The reform is killing the Latvian language. *Majas Viesis*. http://www.la.lv/reforma-nogalina-latviesu-valodu/ (accessed 15 November 2019)

Radio Free Europe. 2004. *Russian speakers protest language reform in Latvia.* //www.rferl.org/a/1051443.html (accessed 15 November 2019)

Valsts izglītības satura centrs [*Centre of National Curriculum*]. 2018, April 9. Mācību priekšmetu standarti [School Subject Curricula]. http://visc.gov.lv/vispizglitiba/saturs/standarti.shtml(accessed 15 November 2019)

Antoinette Camilleri Grima
Chapter 10
Pluralistic Approaches in Foreign Language Education: Examples of Implementation from Malta

Abstract: Foreign language pedagogy is witnessing a paradigm shift. During the last decades of the twentieth century, the native-speaker-hearer was retained as the ultimate proficiency target that the foreign language learner was obliged to aim for. Eventually, not only was the notion of native-speaker challenged, but fresh perspectives like those emerging from sociocultural theory, the appreciation of the learner's first language in the classroom, and learner autonomy, brought to the fore a re-consideration of the beliefs about foreign language teaching and learning. Nowadays, the majority of learners arrive in language classrooms already equipped with knowledge of two or more languages and with an experience of cultures different from their own. Given the needs of today's plurilingual learners and societies, and in line with postmodernist theory, there is an appropriate shift toward pluralistic approaches in the foreign language classroom. In this chapter, pluralistic approaches are illustrated with examples from the teaching of Maltese as a foreign language.

Keywords: pluralistic approaches, language education, Maltese as a foreign language

1 Introduction

Up to a few years ago, the literature about foreign language pedagogy focussed largely on foreign languages taught as subjects in the regular school curriculum where the learners were viewed as homogenous monolingual speakers of their first language (Cook 1991; Mitchell, Myles and Marsden 2013). Monolingual attitudes and practices in the classroom thrived in parallel with the biased sociolinguistic perspective of societies as monolingual entities (Ellis, Gogolin and Clyne 2010; Otwinowska 2016). The learner's mind was viewed as coping with

---

Antoinette Camilleri Grima, University of Malta, Malta, E-mail: antoinette.camilleri-grima@um.edu.mt

https://doi.org/10.1515/9781501514692-010

the transfer of elements from their first language, perceived as errors, and much research has been dedicated to crosslinguistic influence in second/foreign language learning (Alonso Alonso, ed. 2016; Yu and Odlin, eds. 2016). While such research is still helpful to learners and teachers (Alfarajat 2019; Cenoz, Hufeisen and Jessner 2001), research has shown that some mistakes learners make cannot be traced back to their L1, and learners with different L1s face similar difficulties (Brown and Larson-Hall 2012). In fact, the Chomskyan notion of the ideal native-speaker-hearer as a universalist view, and used as a model in foreign language learning, has been challenged. Alan Davies (1991, 2003, 2013) argued eloquently that there is no singular model of a speaker, and that there is no clear or definite distinction between a native speaker and a native user. The notion of multi-competence (Cook and Wei 2016) further questions the "ideal, monolingual" native-speaker model, and together with the ever-increasing literature on the advantages of translanguaging in the classroom, the relevance of a paradigm shift is clear (Garcia and Wei 2014).

At present, the sociolinguistic context of foreign language learning and teaching, at least in the Western world, is one where many, possibly the majority of learners in a class, have different first languages, are plurilingual, and have experienced more than one culture (Hélot 2018; Jessner 2008; Piccardo 2017). In this chapter I discuss the paradigm shift in foreign language teaching and learning in the context of high societal mobility. To date, there has been little research on pluralistic approaches for plurilingual language learners. In what follows, I illustrate the implementation of a plurilingual program in Malta, the European Union's smallest state that is currently experiencing an extraordinarily high influx of migrants and young learners in schools. I first present the context of migration in the European Union and in Malta, and after a summary of the literature, I answer the following research questions: (1) How can pluralistic approaches be implemented in a class of plurilingual learners? and (2) What benefits can be accrued from such implementation?

2 Migration in the European and Maltese contexts and the plurilingual learner

European Union (EU) statistics (European Commission 2017) established that in 2015–2016, 35.1 million people living in the EU were born outside its borders. Furthermore, 20.7 million EU citizens were living in a member state different from their country of birth, and 10% of 15-year-old learners in the EU is a second-generation migrant. In 2015–2016, there were more than 2.5 million applicants for asylum in the EU.

The statistics from Malta can be compared and contrasted with the ones published for the EU as a whole. In Malta, from 2004 to 2016 the non-Maltese population increased from 3% to 12% (Jobsplus 2017). In schools, most newcomers arrive from other EU countries at a ratio of 4:1. The largest learner groups (75%) come from the UK and Italy, which is unusual compared with the influx of international migrants in the rest of the EU (Jobsplus 2017). The remaining 25% of learners arrive in Malta from countries like Libya, Serbia, Ukraine, and Pakistan (Ministry for Education and Employment 2019). In some schools, the non-Maltese learner population is about 30%, while in other schools, especially in the coastal areas, the majority (around 80%) of learners in a given class are non-Maltese (Ministry for Education and Employment 2019).

From a foreign language learning (FLL) point of view, it is important to be cognizant of the fact that most learners in this context would be familiar with two or more languages when they join a Maltese language class. Schooling in Malta takes place in a fully bilingual system from the early years through to post-secondary levels (Camilleri Grima 2013a, 2016a), and therefore the Maltese learners themselves are also bilingual. Both local and newly arrived learners are often bi-literate, and in some cases, they are able to read and write in different alphabets. Plurilingual learners normally have a higher level of phonological awareness and visual lexical representation than the traditionally monolingual learners attending FLL classes (for a good overview see Jessner 2008).

In order to draw a realistic picture of FLL, in what follows, I use examples from learners of Maltese as a foreign language (FL). For example, one of the adult learners taking classes at the beginner level arrived in Malta from Finland. Before starting to learn Maltese, in addition to Finnish, Peter (a pseudonym) spoke English, Spanish, and Portuguese fluently, and had knowledge of Swedish and German. He decided to settle in Malta because he had a Maltese girlfriend and wanted to learn Maltese "in order to integrate into Maltese society" (his words, taken from a video-recording that was part of a language course). Peter was a very motivated student. He bought books about Maltese and listened daily to radio programs and news in Maltese. The abilities and needs of learners like Peter call for an appropriate pedagogy that acknowledges, respects, and enhances their already sophisticated metalinguistic abilities. As Cook (2012) argues, multi-competence refers to the knowledge of more than one language in the same brain which, therefore, requires an appropriate pedagogy.

3 A paradigm shift in language teaching and learning

Like Peter, the majority of learners enrolled in FL classes have experienced international travel, migration, and they live in a global village created by social media. The realization that as language educators we need to adjust classroom pedagogy to this type of learner comes in parallel with a theoretical paradigm shift in FL pedagogy. In the 1960s we focused on the four language skills (listening, reading, speaking, and writing), and we taught them as separate, disconnected abilities. The native speaker was set as a model for the learner, and teachers who were native speakers of the FL were normally preferred to those who were not. Language was viewed as a subject like any other subject in the curriculum with an established list of content to be covered. Foreign languages were taught through immersion and the first language of the learner was banned from the classroom; and codeswitching was seen as a hindrance to target language development. Teachers were trained to teach different languages separately, and in some schools, we can still find different rooms assigned to the teaching of different languages in order to make sure that languages do not mix.

In the 1990s, with the advent of the *Common European Framework of Reference for Teaching, Learning, and Assessment* (CEFR) (Council of Europe 2001), language skills came to be understood more realistically as interactive and collaborative activities. Also, in the postmodernist era and through the perspective of sociocultural theory, language is viewed as being created in interaction, between actors in a social setting. The CEFR, for instance, focuses on interactional skills and lists "Can Do" descriptors for areas such as spoken interaction, written interaction, and mediation.

Proponents of pluralistic approaches believe that the learner's first language (L1) scaffolds learning, and that for a plurilingual learner it is best to adopt a plurilingual method (Candelier et al. 2012). The same teacher can, or should, use or allow the use of several languages in the same lesson and in the same classroom. This is an inclusive method and is therefore more ethical because it respects all the learners' previously acquired linguistic knowledge, skills, and experience. In line with sociocultural theory (Lantolf 2000; Lantolf and Poehner 2014; Vygotsky 1986), pluralistic approaches in foreign language education are based on self-mediation, such as talking about one's language knowledge and comparing languages; artefact-mediation, which uses pluralistic tasks such as those in the *Framework of Reference for Pluralistic Approaches to Languages and Cultures* (FREPA) (Candelier et al. 2012); and the scaffolding afforded by the space given to the learners' existing linguistic and cultural knowledge (Baccin and Pavan 2014; Rezaee 2011).

As Gass and Torres (2005) explain, what has changed over the years is not the importance accorded to target language input, but the conception of how input is processed by individual learners and how they assimilate it, because alongside input, interaction plays a crucial role. This paradigm shift has also been supported by research in other pedagogical areas such as learner autonomy. In this regard, Lamb and Murray (2018) explain that in language education the focal space for learning is shifting to include spaces outside the classroom. Learners can meet their learning goals not only in the classroom, but also in libraries, on the internet, and by observing the linguistic landscape in their environment (Chern and Dooley 2014; Sayer 2010; Wilton and Ludwig 2018).

Furthermore, the CEFR introduced *Can-Do* descriptors to help learners monitor their progress. This brought into focus the notion of partial competences in FLL. Thus, a learner could achieve a high C1 level in reading, for example, but only an A2 level in spoken interaction, or vice-versa. And for that particular learner, this might be acceptable and satisfy their communicative needs. Pluralistic approaches retain the same view as the CEFR in terms of the relevance of partial competences so that the learner is encouraged to access several languages without the need for high proficiency in all of the skills in each language.

In the international literature there is evidence of the advantages of plurilingualism and pluralistic approaches in the classroom (Dahm 2017; Hélot 2018; Little and Kirwan 2018; Mary and Young 2018). The *Framework of Reference for Pluralistic Approaches to Languages and Cultures* (FREPA)(Candelier et al. 2012) was developed on the basis of a vast literature review in many languages, around key areas relevant to pluralistic approaches in FLL. I will now highlight some of the key points found in the literature that support the adoption of pluralistic approaches in FLL.

4 Pluralistic approaches in foreign language learning

Festman (2018) reported on a study that investigated the effects of a program uniquely designed for highly heterogeneous learners at the kindergarten level. The multilingual learners' acquisition of vocabulary was compared to the gains made by monolingual German learners, and the aim was to find out which of the two groups made the biggest gains in both German and English. The study concluded that "with the help of this structured program and due to plurilingual experiences, minority children were able to improve language skills in two newly-learned languages, whereas the monolingual children were still consolidating knowledge in their first language and focused on the acquisition of the new language" (Festman 2018: 1–2).

Little and Kirwan (2018) described the interdependent development of language proficiency and language awareness in a linguistically diverse pupil cohort in a primary school in Dublin, Ireland. Most of the pupils in this school came from immigrant homes and lacked fluency in English, the language of schooling. In teaching writing, a school policy was introduced so that pupils were encouraged to write in the language/s they were familiar with, even when these were inaccessible to the teachers. This practice was based on the premise that plurilingual pupils will learn most effectively if they are encouraged to draw on all the languages at their disposal. One measure of this school's success is that its pupils perform above the national average in both English and Math each year. Furthermore, "immigrant pupils' proficiency in the language of schooling is indistinguishable from that of their native speaker peers" (Little and Kirwan 2018: 199).

Piccardo (2017) has made a case for adopting pluralistic approaches in education, especially with a view to developing students' creativity. Although no claim of a causal relationship between plurilingualism and creativity can be made, "embracing plurilingualism can initiate change from the tiniest to the broadest scale, from helping individuals see the interconnections between language systems and discover their full repertoire, thus liberating their plurilingual self, to empowering them in perception, awareness and active exploration of linguistic and cultural diversity, hybridity and interconnections" (Piccardo 2017: 11).

Neuroimaging studies suggest that multiple languages are processed and organized in a single neuroanatomical system in the bilingual brain, although differential activation may be seen. For instance, Mohades et al. (2012) concluded that exposure to two or more languages has an impact on the functional ability and microstructure of the brain and that there are differences between the brains of simultaneous language learners and sequential learners. Through Magnetic Resonance Imaging (MRI) it has been established that "bilinguals receive both common and dedicated cortical areas for their two languages" (Mohades et al. 2012: 72). Also, language learning (and not other types of learning) makes the brain grow. A study conducted in Sweden by Mårtensson et al. (2012) showed, through MRI scans, that the brain structure of university students studying medicine and cognitive science did not change over a period of months. On the other hand, there was an increase in the hippocampus and cortical thickness of the brain of interpreters who attended an intensive three-month foreign language course. These findings confirm the occurrence of structural changes in brain regions known to serve language functions.

Pluralistic approaches take a holistic view of language and such approaches are adopted in the pedagogy proposed here. Rather than considering each language as a separate entity, each with its own compartment, there is a global approach to all languages, especially those present in the experience of the learners. This global approach takes into consideration the language/s of schooling, the languages spoken at home by the learners, the languages learned as subjects at school, and any other languages in the environment. Relatedly, plurilingual repertoires are understood as partial competences to varying degrees. It is believed that there is an underlying language proficiency (Cummins 2016) that supports further language learning. As a result of plurilingual competences, learners will be better able to face different cultures, new work environments, changing opportunities for employment, and further study. Additionally, there is evidence that pluralistic approaches contribute to social integration in the school environment (Camilleri Grima 2013b; Mary and Young 2018).

Pluralistic approaches include different learning procedures, activities, and techniques involving several varieties of languages and/or cultures during any one teaching event (Candelier, Daryai-Hansen and Schröder-Sura 2012). These teaching methods have been implemented in a number of European countries (e.g. Dahm 2017; Daryai-Hansen et al. 2015), and can be considered as a major pedagogical development (Derenowski 2014; Le Pichon-Vorstman, Siarova, and Herzog-Punzenberger 2017).

The primary instrument detailing what is to be achieved through pluralistic approaches is the Council of Europe's framework of reference, known as the FREPA. The framework is available in English, French, Italian, and Arabic (see https://carap.ecml.at/Accueil/tabid/3577/language/en-GB/Default.aspx). It was developed over a period of six years by a team of experts. The coordinator of the project was Michel Candelier from France, and the other team members who worked on the publication were Antoinette Camilleri Grima from Malta, Véronique Castellotti from France, Jean-François de Pietro from Switzerland, Ildikó Lörincz from Hungary, Artur Noguerol from Spain, and Franz-Joseph Meissner and Anna Schröder-Sura from Germany. The publication was the result of an international project hosted by the European Centre for Modern Languages in Graz, Austria, which is part of the Language Policy Division of the Council of Europe. The FREPA is based on a multilingual literature review of publications in the area of plurilingualism and intercultural competence. The FREPA project team identified the competences and intellectual resources available to plurilingual and multicultural persons in modern day society. The intellectual resources, referred to here as descriptors, are presented in the FREPA in three sets: Knowledge, Attitudes, and Skills. The list of descriptors is a hierarchy of main and secondary (or sub-) descriptors. The descriptors can be transformed into attainment targets or lesson objectives, and the teacher and the learners are free to identify which, and how many, descriptors suit their context and needs. Pluralistic approaches do not replace other FL teaching and learning methods, but they provide an added value through the conscious and explicit promotion of awareness about language learning, a respect for everyone's plurilingualism, culture and cultural identities, and a global and holistic view of language education.

The FREPA is closely linked to the four pluralistic approaches known as, Intercomprehension, the Integrated Approach, Awakening to Languages, and the Intercultural Approach. These approaches are described below, and some practical examples from the teaching of Maltese as a FL are given in the section that follows.

4.1 Intercomprehension

Intercomprehension is "a communicative process which refers to the communication strategies used more or less consciously by speakers who do not speak the same languages, yet they are languages that provide sufficient transparency (for their speakers) to understand each other" (Dufour 2018: 71). Since the 1990s, Intercomprehension has been implemented with the aim of developing speakers' communicative competence (Capucho 2013; Capucho 2016). It gives a lot of attention to the deveopment of receptive skills, first of all in languages of the same language family, but also beyond (Dabène 1995; Melo-Pfeifer 2012; Ollivier 2013). It helps the learner focus on understanding a text in a language they have not yet studied in order to acquire information (Capucho 2013; Capucho 2016). In the classroom, the learners build on their capacity to develop receptive proficiency on the basis of lexical transparency and the underlying language proficiency and cross-lingual dimensions discussed by Cummins (2016) and others (Blanche-Benveniste 2008; Degache and Melo 2008). Intercomprehension has been developed in tertiary education institutions where learners who speak languages different from the medium of instruction, but which belong to the same language family, take the same university course, such as Economics (e.g. Castagne 2007; Cojocariu 2017; Dufour 2018; Felicia and Rodica 2012).

4.2 The Integrated Didactic Approach

The aim of the Integrated Didactic Approach is for learners to make an explicit comparison between a few languages present in the curriculum. It is a text-genre-based approach and relies on cross-linguistic transfer. It targets specific skills such as the organization of content in different languages (Esteve et al. 2015). Following Hufeisen's important work (e.g. Hufeisen 2018), the integrated didactic approach is based on the notion that languages are learned in interaction with each other, and that there is some knowledge that can be transferred between languages. A didactic sequence in the integrated approach is normally constituted by three sequential steps (Manterola 2014). The first step or point of departure is a communicative function, like making a proposition, compromising with a partner, or expressing likes and dislikes. The students start by producing a text that fulfills that function in two or three languages. This is followed by a metalinguistic activity, guided by the teacher, in order to discuss the difficulties identified in the production of the texts, such as differences in grammatical gender or pragmatic issues. The final step consists in the production of a refined text.

4.3 Awakening to Languages

Intercomprehension and the Integrated Didactic Approach are implemented with adult learners. On the other hand, Awakening to Languages is widely practiced with young learners. It originated from the Eric Hawkins Language Awareness movement in the UK in the 1980s and became widespread under the direction of Michel Candelier (2003a, 2003b). It is known in French as *Éveil aux langues*. The general aim is to expose learners to as many languages as possible, including those not normally encountered at school (Martins, Andrade, Pinho and Simões 2015). Such activities are meant to encourage positive attitudes toward language diversity and to stimulate an interest in FLL. It is meant for young learners to become aware of linguistic and cultural diversity in their environment and around the world, to develop attitudes of openness and respect, and also to encourage the acquisition of linguistic concepts and an aptitude for language learning (Martins, Andrade, Pinho and Simões 2015).

4.4 The Intercultural Approach

The Intercultural Approach aims to develop in the learner an ability to perform effectively and appropriately when interacting with others who are linguistically and culturally different from oneself (Byram 1997), and this applies to all age groups (Gürsoy 2014). It has evolved from the traditional thinking of culture in terms of national symbols, important personalities, iconic buildings, and typical food, and has moved toward the understanding of culture in terms of activities by which habits, behavior, and ways of life are compared, contrasted, and interpreted (Byram 2014; Corbett 2010; Liddicoat 2004). I define Intercultural Competence as the ability to transcend the limitations of one's own worldview, to interpret another way of life, and then explain that way of life to those who do not live that way. This involves many attitudes related to otherness, such as sensitivity, interest, respect, empathy, acceptance, and a disposition to engage and to share with others.

UNESCO (2013) presents a visual conceptualization of intercultural competences in the shape of a tree with roots, a trunk, branches, and leaves representing various aspects of culture and communication. The roots stand for identity, values, attitudes, and beliefs and for language and dialogue. The trunk represents cultural diversity, human rights, and intercultural dialogue which, in turn, open into branches that clarify, teach, enact, support, and promote intercultural competence. There are many leaves flourishing as a result, such as intercultural responsibility, conviviality, semantic availability, and multilingualism.

5 Pluralistic approaches in the teaching of Maltese as a foreign language

The four pluralistic approaches are transparent in the FREPA. The FREPA presents teachers, teacher educators, and learners with a set of competences and descriptors that are valid for all languages. Competences are listed as a small set of complex units which mobilize different intellectual resources grouped as Knowledge, Attitudes, or Skills. The ultimate aim of the FREPA is to help the individual manage "linguistic and cultural communication in a context of otherness" and "to ensure the construction and widening of a pluralistic linguistic and cultural repertoire" (15). The next section presents examples from the FREPA and then explains how they were implemented in foreign language teaching in Malta.

5.1 Knowledge

In the FREPA, the section on Knowledge relevant to pluralistic learning is divided into 15 sections, with the first seven referring to Language and the rest to Culture (Table 10.1). In each section, there are descriptors followed by sub-descriptors (see examples in Table 10.2).

Table 10.1: FREPA sections on Knowledge.

Section Language	Area of Knowledge	Number of descriptors
1	Language as a semiological system	15
2	Language and society	15
3	Verbal and non-verbal communication	14
4	The evolution of languages	8
5	Plurality, diversity, multilingualism, and plurilingualism	11
6	Similarities and differences between languages	35
7	Language and acquisition/learning	12
Culture		
8	Cultures: General characteristics	17
9	Cultural diversity and social diversity	8
10	Cultures and intercultural relations	22
11	The evolution of cultures	14
12	The diversity of cultures	15
13	Resemblances and differences between cultures	10
14	Culture, Language, and Identity	10
15	Culture and acquisition/learning	5

The first area of Knowledge shown in Table 10.1, *Language as a Semiological System*, is organized into descriptors and sub-descriptors (see Table 10.2).

A very successful activity related to K1.2 and K1.2.1 (Table 10.2) was implemented with young learners in Malta based on animal sounds. In Table 10.3, taken from the textbook for teaching Maltese as a FL (Camilleri Grima 2016b: 228), I listed a number of animals and their sounds in Maltese, English, and

Table 10.2: Examples of Knowledge descriptors relating to language as a semiological system.

K1	Knows some of the principles of how languages work
K1.1	Knows that language is/languages are composed of signs which form a semiological system
K1.2	Knows that the relationship between words and their referent (the reality which they designate)/between the signifier (the word, the structure, the intonation . . .) and the meaning is *a priori* an arbitrary one
K1.2.1	Knows that even cases of onomatopoeia, where a link does exist between word and referent, retain a degree of arbitrariness and vary from one language to another
K1.2.2	Knows that two words which may have the same form/look alike in different languages do not automatically mean the same thing
K1.2.3	Knows that grammatical categories are not the replica of reality but one way of organizing this in language
K1.2.3.1	Knows that grammatical gender and sexual gender are not the same things

Table 10.3: Animal sounds (Camilleri Grima 2016b: 228).

	Animal	Maltese	English	Italian	other
	baqra – *cow*	mu mu	moo moo	muuu	
	hmar – *donkey*	hi llo	bray bray	i-oo i-oo	
	serduq – *cock*	quqqu qu qu	cock-a doodle-doo	pio pio	
	papra – *duck*	kwakk kwakk	quack quack	qua qua	
	qattus – *cat*	mjaw mjaw	meow meow	miao	
	kelb – *dog*	baw waw	woof woof	bau bau	

Table 10.3 (continued)

	Animal	Maltese	English	Italian	other
	naghga – *sheep*	beq beq	baa baa	beee	
	hanzir – *pig*	ojnz ojnz	oinkoink	oink	

Italian (because these are the two largest groups of migrant children in Maltese schools), and in the last column I left space for whichever other languages the learners wish to include. In class, the learners discussed the similarities and differences between onomatopoeic sounds in various languages and the arbitrariness that clearly arises. This discussion was then transposed to human languages (see K1.2.2 and K1.2.3 in Table 10.2). In our case, this activity was accompanied by a visit for newly arrived children from Italy, Serbia, Libya, and Pakistan to a farm. At the farm, the children enjoyed watching animals such as sheep, pigs, cows, hens, and horses. They were offered free rides on a donkey, and they also had a writing activity about animal sounds and language. In this way, as Piccardo (2017: 8) argues, "language learning is seen as an active, reflexive process," and the environment provides affordances that are particularly useful when they are action-oriented. Incidentally, this activity had much-added value because the newly arrived children became friends during this outing, and subsequently enjoyed attending classes together at school.

In teaching Maltese as a FL to adults, for example, I chose to work on K1.2.3 and K1.2.3.1 (Table 10.2). This provides a platform for learners to discuss the distinction between biological sex and linguistic gender (M for masculine and F for feminine), and how grammatical gender differs from one language to another (Table 10.4).

In the case of language lessons for adults, a pluralistic approach like the one based on the activity shown in Table 10.4 engages learners in exercising their agency by comparing languages, thus making full use of their metalinguistic abilities. This is one way of exploiting their plurilingual knowledge for more effective and efficient acquisition of yet another language.

Table 10.4: Grammatical gender (Camilleri Grima 2016b: 261).

Kliem Words in Italian & Maltese	bit-Taljan in Italian		bil-Malti in Maltese		Add a language of your choice	
	M	F	M	F	M	F
sole – xemx	x		x			
luna – qamar		x	x			
casa – dar		x		x		
giorno – ġurnata	x			x		
paese – pajjiż	x		x			

5.2 Attitudes

When learning to communicate in a new language one needs to be prepared to face otherness. It is impossible to acquire a whole language, and therefore, the learner needs to develop the right attitudes to different ways in which languages work and people behave. Table 10.5 lists the key attitudes identified in the FREPA, and Table 10.6 provides a few examples from the first section on Attitudes.

Table 10.5: FREPA sections on Attitudes.

Section	Attitudes	Number of descriptors
1	Attention/sensitivity/curiosity/positive acceptance/openness/respect/valorization with respect to languages, cultures, and the diversity of languages and cultures	60
2	Disposition/motivation/will/desire to engage in an activity related to languages/cultures and to the diversity of languages and cultures	30
3	Attitudes/stances of: questioning – distancing – decentring – relativizing	33
4	Readiness to adapt/self-confidence/sense of familiarity	17
5	Identity	11
6	Attitudes to learning	19

Table 10.6: Examples of Attitude descriptors from Section 1 (see Table 10.5).

A 2.2	Sensitivity to linguistic/cultural differences
A 2.5.2	Being sensitive to/aware of the linguistic/cultural diversity of the classroom
A 3.2.1	Being curious about and wishing to understand the similarities and differences between one's own language/culture and the target language/culture
A 4	Positive acceptance of linguistic/cultural diversity
A 5.3.3	Openness towards the unfamiliar (linguistic or cultural)
A 6.2	Valuing/appreciating linguistic/cultural contacts

In teaching Maltese as a FL at an intermediate level of proficiency, the descriptors in Table 10.6 were implemented when working on the topic of food, and more specifically on bread. First, the teacher asked each of the learners in the class to tell her the word for bread in their own language or any other language they were familiar with. Then she looked for pictures illustrating the topic and prepared a handout for use in the next lesson, showing the word for bread in the different languages alongside the relevant pictures. In this particular class, there were learners from Poland, Germany, France, Finland, and Kenya. The learners were encouraged to talk about the type of bread they were familiar with, and about how it was consumed in their respective cultures. They managed this activity through Maltese as they spoke about customs in their home country. The teacher then introduced the vocabulary related to the different types of bread in Malta and the various ways in which it is prepared and served. The learners worked on a simple reading and writing activity at this stage in order to familiarize themselves with the relevant vocabulary. They also participated in a hands-on activity that involved the preparation of a Maltese sandwich called *ftira* (or *ħobż biż-żejt*). In this way, they practiced their listening skills by following the instructions given by the teacher. Although the activity was mainly intended for listening, the learners were so enthusiastic that they also expressed their likes and dislikes for food like fish and meat, and discussed healthy and unhealthy eating habits. This indicates that implementing the FREPA will (1) provide an opportunity to practice authentic language, (2) motivate intercultural interest, and (3) reduce stress in the acquisition of interactive skills.

5.3 Skills

Most of the skills related to pluralistic approaches in language learning are also lifelong learning skills and help the learners to develop autonomous learning skills. Table 10.7 lists the sections dealing with Skills in the FREPA, and Table 10.8 gives examples of descriptors.

Table 10.7: FREPA sections on Skills.

Section	Skills	Number of descriptors
1	Can observe/can analyze	30
2	Can recognize/identify	25
3	Can compare	36
4	Can talk about languages and cultures	6
5	Can use what one knows of a language in order to understand another language or to produce in another language	12
6	Can interact	19
7	Knows how to learn	25

Table 10.8: Examples of descriptors from the sections on Skills.

S 3	Can compare linguistic/cultural features of different languages/cultures
S 3.4	Can perceive lexical proximity
S 3.6	Can compare the relationships between sounds and script in different languages
S 4.3	Can explain one's own knowledge of languages

For plurilingual learners and users, it is natural to compare linguistic elements from the languages they know (Festman 2018). However, this ability has been ignored and even reprimanded in the past. The FREPA, on the other hand, recognizes that it is an advantage and an asset that teachers and learners ought to capitalize on. In the Maltese as a FL class, I provide several opportunities for learners to compare linguistic and cultural features from the different languages and cultures they are familiar with (see S 3 in Table 10.8). For example, in relation to culture, one popular activity is to discuss the daily timetable in different cultures. Learners are asked questions like: At what time do people normally wake up in country X, Y, Z? What do they eat for breakfast? At what time do they start school or work? At what time do they have lunch and dinner? At what time do shops open and close? And above all, the more significant questions are those that start with Why, such as: Why do people finish work early in Scotland, in comparison with people in Spain, who finish work later? These questions lead to a discussion on factors like climate and geographical features that influence different cultures.

An activity linked to the issues discussed above was very successful in a class of teenage boys from different countries that attended a school in an under-resourced area of Malta. Each of the boys enjoyed narrating his experience about, for instance, how to get to the beach, e.g., on foot in Malta, but in a two-hour car journey in Bulgaria; or to school, e.g., by train in the Czech Republic and in Sweden. This was very surprising for the Maltese boys because there are no trains in Malta and distances are very short. The boys worked in international groups on an activity to describe an imaginary country. They were asked to hypothesize about its typical dish, means of transport, and daily timetable. The boys thoroughly enjoyed this activity as they imagined themselves enjoying very short school days, owning transport companies, driving luxurious cars, and so on. In this way, the students started with personal experience, moved on to collaborative production and finally to creative writing in the target language, describing their life in the imagined country. Both cognitive and affective dimensions of learning were catered for, and negative judgment was avoided because the culture was imagined and not pertaining to any of the boys (Camilleri Grima 2013b).

From a linguistic point of view, in order to compare lexical proximity (see S 3.4 in Table 10.8), the Maltese language provides excellent opportunities for learners who are familiar with Semitic and/or Romance languages. Table 10.9 shows Maltese lexical items that originate from Italian or from Arabic. Learners' attention is drawn to the spelling system of Maltese and they are invited to talk about lexical proximity among various languages. Maltese is a mixed language described by Mifsud (1995) as having a Semitic stratum of phonology, morphology, and to a lesser extent, syntax; a Romance super-stratum of a large stock of lexical, syntactic, phonological, and some morphological accretions; and an English ad-stratum that consists mainly of lexical material. This makes Maltese fairly transparent to learners who already know Italian and/or Arabic.

An activity related to lexical comparison was developed with young learners on the topic of shopping. The learners in the class were asked to find out which food items from their own culture were available in Maltese supermarkets or shops. Then the teacher prepared a shopping list together with the learners, that

Table 10.9: Lexical items in Maltese related to Italian and Arabic (adapted from Camilleri Grima 2016b: 196).

Maltese words of Italian origin		
klinika *(clinica)*	ambulanza *(ambulanza)*	emerġenza *(emergenza)*
segretarja *(segretaria)*	mediċina *(medicina)*	vista *(visita)*
Maltese words of Arabic origin		
triq *(road)* t-r-q طري	siġra *(tree)* s-ġ-r شطرة	qatra *(adrop)* q-t-r قطرة
ħabb *(to love)* ħ-b-b حب	tagħlim *(teaching)* għ-l-m تعليم	ktieb *(book)* k-t-b كتاب

included the various items mentioned by the students, such as pasta (suggested by an Italian student), garam masala (suggested by a Pakistani student), and noodles (suggested by a Chinese student). In the list, next to the words written out in Maltese, the children put the word in their own language in brackets. Then they wrote a dialogue between a customer and a shopkeeper in order to practice using these lexical items in a communicative context. In the following lesson, the teacher created a make-believe shop and the students practiced the dialogues in a role play. In this way, the learners were very motivated to learn these and other lexical items that are more typical of Maltese culture.

6 Conclusion

The literature confirms that pluralistic approaches are advantageous in language learning. Some of the advantages are cognitive and others are motivational (Dmitrenko 2017; Festman 2018; Hélot et al. 2018; Little and Kirwan 2018; Piccardo 2017; Romanowski 2017). In answer to my two research questions–(1) how can pluralistic approaches be implemented in a class of plurilingual learners? and (2) what benefits can be accrued from such implementation?–the examples provided above in the context of teaching and learning Maltese as a FL show that pluralistic approaches can be fun and very motivating. They provide added value in terms of language awareness, respect for everyone's plurilingualism, and heightened intercultural competence.

However, in spite of the strong international evidence from multiple areas of research in support of pluralistic approaches, I can see a number of challenges ahead for practitioners. Unfortunately, such approaches are not always easy or straight-forward to implement (Piccardo 2017). For instance, in school settings difficulties arise due to curricular and examination pressures, and the training of teachers in monolingualizing strategies. First, teacher educators need to become more aware and appreciative of pluralistic approaches so that they are able to educate teachers on how to move away from singular to pluralistic methodologies whenever these are deemed appropriate (Laurenço, Andrade and Sá 2018; Pinho and Andrade 2009). This means a reconsideration of how teacher education courses are structured and delivered, and possibly the inclusion of the role of intercultural mediator in teachers' professional development (Meier 2014; Siek-Piskozub 2014). Second, curriculum designers also need to take note of the paradigm shift in science and academia, and of the plurilingual experiences of the majority of learners, in order to transform the curricular frameworks in ways that are more ethical and inclusive. As Beacco et al. (2010) explain, for innovation in the area of pluralistic approaches to be successfully implemented, there needs to be a coherent curricular policy at all levels: at the supra- (international), macro- (national), meso- (school), micro-(class) and nano-(individual) levels. Given the incongruences in several contexts between the national syllabus (which is still based on the monolingual approach), and the growing support for pluralistic approaches in research, much more policy work needs to be done. For example, there is a clear need for appropriate teaching materials and textbooks that are based on one or more of the pluralistic approaches, and that provide opportunities for the learners to be creative (Król-Gierat 2014). Lastly, more research is needed in areas like the impact of pluralistic approaches for social cohesion outside the school setting, which, if shown to be successful, could be an important catalyst for change in education.

References

Alfarajat, Raid. 2019. L'interférence entre les langues, difficulté majeure d'apprentissage.
    Le français dans le monde 423 (mai-juin 2019). 44–45.
Alonso Alonso, Rosa (ed.). 2016. *Crosslinguistic influence in second language acquisition.*
    Bristol: Multilingual Matters.
Baccin, Paola & Elisabetta Pavan. 2014. Developing intercultural awareness – an ongoing
    challenge in foreign language teaching. In Piotr Romanowki (ed.), *Intercultural issues in*

the era of globalization, 8–21. Warsaw: Wydawnictwo Naukowe, Instytutu Komunikacji Specjalistycznej i Interkulturowej, University of Warsaw.

Beacco, Jean-Claude, Michael Byram, Marisa Cavalli, Daniel Coste, Mijam Egli Cuenat, Francis Goullier & Johanna Panthier. 2010. *Guide for the development and implementation of curricula for plurilingual and intercultural education*. Strasbourg: Council of Europe.

Blanche-Benveniste, Claire. 2008. Aspetti lessicali del confronto tra lingue romanze. Esiste un lessico europeo? In Monica Barni, Donatella Troncarelli & Carla Bagna (eds.), *Lessico e apprendimenti: il ruolo del lessico nella linguistica educativa* 47–66. Milan: FrancoAngeli.

Brown, Steven & Jenifer Larson-Hall. 2012. *Second language acquisition myths*. Michigan: Ann Arbor.

Byram, Michael. 1997. *Teaching and assessing intercultural competence*. Bristol: Multilingual Matters.

Byram, Michael. 2014. Twenty-five years on – from cultural studies to intercultural citizenship. *Language, Culture and Curriculum* 27 (3). 209–225.

Camilleri Grima, Antoinette. 2013a. A select review of bilingualism in education in Malta. *International Journal of Bilingual Education and Bilingualism* 15 (5). 553–569.

Camilleri Grima, Antoinette. 2013b. Fostering plurilingualism and intercultural competence: Affective and cognitive dimensions. In Sandro Caruana, Liliana Coposescu & Stefania Scaglione (eds.), *Migration, multilingualism, and schooling in Southern Europe*, 74–94. Newcastle upon Tyne: Cambridge Scholars.

Camilleri Grima, Antoinette. 2016a. Young children living bilingually in Malta. *Lingwistyka Stosowana* 17 (2). 1–13.

Camilleri Grima, Antoinette. 2016b. *Bil-Qatra l-Qatra. Learning Maltese as a foreign language*. Malta: Miller.

Candelier, Michel (ed.). 2003a. *Evlang – L'éveil aux langues à l'école primaire – Bilan d'une innovation européenne*. Brussels: De Boek – Duculot.

Candelier, Michel (ed.). 2003b. *Janua Linguarum – La Porte des Langues – L'introduction de l'éveil aux langues dans le curriculum*. Graz and Strasbourg: ECML, Council of Europe Publishing.

Candelier, Michel, Antoinette Camilleri Grima, Véronique Castellotti, Jean-François de Pietro, Ildikó Lőrincz, Franz-Josef Meissner, Artur Noguerol & Anna Shröder-Sura. 2012. *A framework of reference for pluralistic approaches to languages and cultures*. Graz: Council of Europe/European Centre for Modern Languages.

Candelier, Michel, Petra Daryai-Hansen & Anna Schröder-Sura. 2012. The framework of reference for pluralistic approaches to languages and cultures – a complement to the CEFR to develop plurilingual and intercultural competences. *Innovation in Language Teaching and Learning* 6 (3). 243–257.

Capucho, Filomena. 2013. De la didactologie des langues et des cultures à l'intercompréhension. *Synergies Portugal* 1. 131–144.

Capucho, Filomena. 2016. Les politiques linguistiques européens. Un plus pour le Français? *Carnets* 2 (8). 1–13.

Castagne, Eric. 2007. *Les enjeux de l'intercompréhension*. Reims, France: Epure.

Cenoz, Jasone, Britta Hufeisen & Jessner Ulrike (eds.). 2001. *Cross-linguistic influence in third language acquisition*. Bristol: Multilingual Matters.

Chern, Chiou-lan & Karen Dooley. 2014. Learning English by walking down the street. *ELT Journal* 68 (2). 113–123.

Cojocariu, Andreea Manuela. 2017. Intercomprehension in the foreign language class. *Revista de Pedagogia* LXV (2). 27–40.
Cook, Vivian. 1991. *Second language learning and language teaching*. London: Edward Arnold.
Cook, Vivian J. 2012. Multi-competence. In Carol A Chapelle (ed.), *The encyclopaedia of applied linguistics*, 3768–3774. New York: Wiley-Blackwell.
Cook, Vivian & Li Wei (eds.). 2016. *The Cambridge handbook of linguistic multi-competence*. Cambridge: Cambridge University Press.
Corbett, John. 2010. *Intercultural language activities*. Cambridge: Cambridge University Press.
Council of Europe. 2001. *Common European framework of reference: Language, teaching, assessment*. Cambridge: Cambridge University Press.
Cummins, Jim. 2016. Reflections on Cummins (1980), "The cross-lingual dimensions of language proficiency: Implications for Bilingual Education and the Optimal Age issue". *TESOL Quarterly* 50 (4). 940–944.
Dabène, Louise. 1995. Learning to understand a related language. What are the curricular concepts? *Études de Linguistique Appliqée* 98 (Issue Apr-June). 103–112.
Dahm, Rebecca. 2017. Can pluralistic approaches based upon unknown languages enhance learner engagement and lead to active social inclusion? *International Review of Education* 64 (4). 521–543.
Daryai-Hansen, Petra, Brigitte Gerber, Ildikó Lörincz, Michaela Haller, Olga Ivanova, Hans-Jürgen Krumm & Hans H Reich. 2015. Pluralistic approaches to languages in the curriculum: The case of French-speaking Switzerland, Spain, and Austria. *International Journal of Multilingualism* 12 (1). 109–127.
Davies, Alan. 1991. *The native speaker in applied linguistics*. Edinburgh: Edinburgh University Press.
Davies, Alan. 2003. *The native speaker: Myth and reality*. Clevedon: Multilingual Matters.
Davies, Alan. 2013. *Native speakers and native users: Loss and gain*. Cambridge: Cambridge University Press.
Degache, Christian & Silvia, Melo. 2008. Introduction. Un concept aux multiples facettes. *L'Intercompréhension. Les Langues Modernes. Revue de l'APLV* 1. 7–14.
Derenowski, Marek. 2014. Developing learners' intercultural awareness through the use of projects. In Piotr Romanowki (ed.), *Intercultural issues in the era of globalization*, 47–56. Warsaw: Wydawnictwo Naukowe, Instytutu Komunikacji Specjalistycznej i Interkulturowej, University of Warsaw.
Dmitrenko, Violetta. 2017. Language learning strategies of multilingual adults learning additional languages. *International Journal of Multilingualism* 14 (1). 6–22.
Dufour, Marion. 2018. Intercomprehension: A reflexive methodology in language education. *Educazione e Società Plurilingui* 44. 71–84.
Ellis, Elizabeth, Goglin, Ingrid & Michael Clyne. 2010. The Janus face of monolingualism: a comparison of German and Australian language education policies. *Current Issues in Language Planning* 11 (4). 439–460.
Esteve, Olga, Francisco Fernandez, Ernesto Martin-Peris & Encarna Atienza. 2015. The integrated plurilingual approach: A didactic model providing guidance to Spanish schools for reconceptualizing the teaching of additional languages. *Linguistics and Human Sciences* 11 (1). 1–23.
European Commission. 2017. *Rethinking language education and linguistic diversity in schools*. Brussels: European Commission.

Felicia, Constantin & Bogdan Rodica. 2012. Les approches plurielles dans le modèle CARAP: Savoirs acquis par l'intercompréhension. *Annals of the University of Ovadea: Economic Science* 1 (1). 176–182.

Festman, Julia. 2018. Vocabulary gains of mono- and multilingual learners in a linguistically diverse setting: Results from a German-English intervention with the inclusion of home languages. *Frontiers in Communication* 3(Article 26). 1–15.

Garcia, Ofelia & Li Wei. 2014. *Translanguaging. Language, bilingualism and education*. Basingstoke: Palgrave Macmillan.

Gass, Susan & Maria José Alvarez Torres. 2005. Attention when?: An investigation of the ordering effect of input and interaction. *Studies in Second Language Acquisition* 27 (1). 1–31.

Gürsoy, Esim. 2014. Intercultural awareness and its integration to young learner classes: Prospective teachers' views. In Piotr Romanowki (ed.), *Intercultural issues in the era of globalization*, 65–73. Warsaw: Wydawnictwo Naukowe, Instytutu Komunikacji Specjalistycznej i Interkulturowej, University of Warsaw.

Hélot, Christine. 2018. A critical approach to language awareness in France: Learning to live with Babel. In Christine Hélot, Carolien Frijns, Koen Van Gorp & Sven Sierens (eds.), *Language awareness in multilingual classrooms in Europe* 117–142. Berlin: De Gruyter.

Hélot, Christine, Carolien Frijns, Koen Van Gorp & Sven Sierens (eds.). 2018. *Language awareness in multilingual classrooms in Europe*. Berlin: De Gruyter.

Hufeisen, Britta. 2018. Models of multilingual competence. In Andreas Bonnet & Peter Siemund (eds.), *Foreign language education in multilingual classrooms* 173–189. Hamburg: Hamburg Studies on Linguistic Diversity.

Jessner, Ulrike. 2008. Teaching third languages: Findings, trends, and challenges. *Language Teaching* 41 (1). 15–56.

Jobsplus. 2017. *Foreign nationals employment trends*. https://jobsplus.gov.mt/resources/publication-statistics-mt-mt-en-gb/labour-market-information/foreigners-data#title2.1 (7 April 2019).

Król-Gierat, Werona. 2014. Intercultural issues raised in selected EFL course books: Early English education in Poland. In Piotr Romanowki (ed.), *Intercultural issues in the era of globalization*, 100–108. Warsaw: Wydawnictwo Naukowe, Instytutu Komunikacji Specjalistycznej i Interkulturowej, University of Warsaw.

Lamb, Terry & Garold Murray. 2018. Space, place, and autonomy in language learning: An introduction. In Garold Murray & Terry Lamb (eds.), *Space, place, and autonomy in language learning* 1–6. London: Routledge.

Lantolf, James P. (ed.) 2000. *Sociocultural theory and second language learning*. Oxford: Oxford University Press.

Lantolf, James P & Matthew E. Poehner. 2014. *Sociocultural theory and the pedagogical imperative in L2 education*. London: Routledge.

Laurenço, Mónica, Ana Isabel Andrade & Susana Sá. 2018. Teachers' voices on language awareness in pre-primary and primary school settings: implications for teacher education. *Language, Culture and Curriculum* 31 (2). 113–127.

Le Pichon-Vorstman, Emmanuelle, Hanna Siarova & Barbara Herzog-Punzenberger. 2017. *Multilingual education in the light of diversity: Lessons learned. NESET II report*. Luxembourg: Publications Office of the European Union.

Liddicoat, Anthony J. 2004. Intercultural language teaching: principles for practice. *New Zealand Language Teacher* 30. 17–24.

Little, David & Deirdre Kirwan. 2018. From plurilingual repertoires to language awareness: Developing primary pupils' proficiency in the language of schooling. In Christine Hélot, Carolien Frijns, Koen Van Gorp & Sven Sierens (eds.), *Language awareness in multilingual classrooms in Europe* 169–206. Berlin: Walter de Gruyter.

Manterola, Ibon. 2014. Bilingual education searching for promising didactic proposals. *Frontiers in Psychology* 5. 1–3.

Mårtensson, Johan, Johan Eriksson, Nils Christian Bodammer, Magnus Lindgren, Mikael Johansson, Lars Nyberg & Martin Lövdén. 2012. Growth of language-related brain areas after foreign language learning. *Neuro Image* 63 (1). 240–244.

Martins, Filomena, Ana Isabel Andrade, ana Sofia Pinho & Ana Raquel Simöes. 2015. Éveil aux langues et place de langues minorisées dans des projets de recherche-action en contexte scolaire portugais. *Migration Société* 162 (6). 155–176.

Mary, Latisha & Andrea Young. 2018. Black-blanc-beur: Challenges and opportunities for developing language awareness in teacher education in France. In Christine Hélot, Carolien Frijns, Koen Van Gorp & Sven Sierens (eds.), *Language awareness in multilingual classrooms in Europe* 275–300. Berlin: De Gruyter.

Meier, Ardith J. 2014. Developing negotiation skills as part of intercultural communicative competence. In Piotr Romanowki (ed.), *Intercultural issues in the era of globalization*, 147–161. Warsaw: Wydawnictwo Naukowe, Instytutu Komunikacji Specjalistycznej i Interkulturowej, University of Warsaw.

Melo-Pfeifer, Silvia. 2012. Intercomprehension between Romance languages and the role of English: a study of multilingual chat rooms. *International Journal of Multilingualism* 11 (1). 120–137.

Mifsud, Manuel. 1995. *Loan verbs in Maltese: A descriptive and comparative study*. Leiden: E. J. Brill.

Ministry for Education and Employment. 2019. *Unpublished School Statistics*. Malta: Ministry for Education and Employment.

Mitchell, Rosamund, Myles, Florence & Marsden, Emma. 2013. *Second language learning theories*. London: Routledge.

Mohades, Seyede Ghazal, Esli Struys, Peter Schuerbeek, Piet Van De Crain & Robert Luypaert. 2012. DTI reveals structural differences in white matter tracts between bilingual and monolingual children. *Brain Research* 1435. 72–80.

Ollivier, Christian. 2013. Tensions épistémologiques en intercompréhension. *Recherches didactique des langues et des cultures* 10 (1). 1–16.

Otwinowska, Agnieszka. 2016. *Cognate vocabulary in language acquisition and use*. Bristol: Multilingual Matters.

Piccardo, Enrica. 2017. Plurilingualism as a catalyst for creativity in super-diverse societies: A systemic analysis. *Frontiers in Psychology*, 8. 1–13.

Pinho, Ana Sofia & Ana Isabel Andrade. 2009. Plurilingual awareness and intercomprehension in the professional knowledge and identity development of language student teachers. *International Journal of Multilingualism* 6 (3). 313–329.

Rezaee, Mehrdad. 2011. Sociocultural theory revisited: What are the educational implications? *BRAIN: Broad Research in Artificial Intelligence and Neuroscience* 2 (4). 62–67.

Romanowski, Piotr. 2017. *Intercultural communicative competence in English language teaching in Polish State Colleges*. Newcastle upon Tyne: Cambridge Scholars.

Sayer, Peter. 2010. Using the LL as a pedagogical resource. *ELT Journal* 64 (2). 143–154.

Siek-Poskozub, Teresa. 2014. Educating FL teacers for the role of intercultural mediators – challenges and options. In Piotr Romanowki (ed.), *Intercultural issues in the era of globalization*, 191–199. Warsaw: Wydawnictwo Naukowe, Instytutu Komunikacji Specjalistycznej i Interkulturowej, University of Warsaw.

UNESCO. 2013. *Intercultural competences. Conceptual and operational Framework*. Paris: UNESCO.

Vygotsky, Lev Semyonovich. 1986. *Thought and language*. Translation newly revised and edited by A. Kozulin. Cambridge, MA: MIT Press.

Wilton, Antje & Christian Ludwig. 2018. Multilingual linguistic landscapes as a site for developing learner autonomy. In Garold Murray & Terry Lamb (eds.), *Space, place, and autonomy in language learning* 76–94. London: Routledge.

Yu, Liming & Odlin, Terence (ed.). 2016. *New perspectives on transfer in second language learning*. Bristol: Multilingual Matters.

Natalia Barranco-Izquierdo, M. Teresa Calderón-Quindós
Chapter 11
Interlingual Education in the Classroom: An Action Guide to Overcoming Communication Conflicts

Abstract: Society's linguistic and cultural diversity transfers, unavoidably, to schools. For this reason, teachers need to consider linguistic and cultural diversity as a learning tool, and children need to be trained to deal with interpersonal communication barriers that sometimes arise from linguistic and cultural diversity. This chapter addresses issues related to diversity in schools mainly from a communicative perspective, placing "interlingual" education (as correlated to "intercultural" education, vs. the use of multi- and pluri- terms) at the forefront of these issues. The first sections (2–4) of this chapter present the importance of developing intercultural and (the newly-coined concept) "interlingual education" at school, based on European policies on education and immigration. Section 5 focuses on how communication conflicts at school can be dealt with through oral mediation. And section 6 attempts to provide school teachers with an action guide to minimize these conflicts. This action guide addresses three basic issues: First, some generic measures regarding backgrounds and families; second, clues to foster "interlingual education" through the inclusion of all the languages present in the class; and third, oral mediation strategies to overcome the communication conflicts that sometimes take place in a multicultural classroom due to the presence of two or more mother tongues and home cultures.

Keywords: interlingual education, communication conflicts, inclusive education

> Education shall be directed to the full development of the human personality and to the strengthening of respect for human rights and fundamental freedoms. It shall promote understanding, tolerance and friendship among all nations, racial or religious groups, and shall further the activities of the United Nations for the maintenance of peace.
> (United Nations 2015: 54, Article 26)

Natalia Barranco-Izquierdo, M. Teresa Calderón-Quindós, University of Valladolid, Spain, Email: natalia.barranco@uva.es, Email: calderon@fing.uva.es

https://doi.org/10.1515/9781501514692-011

1 Introduction

Social and political situations force many migrants, refugees, and asylum seekers to seek new homes in Europe. At the same time, European policies encourage the mobility of workers, who bring their families with them. Thus, increasing numbers of children are coming to European schools from other cultural and national backgrounds. It is, therefore, necessary that schools and educational institutions work towards the development and implementation of teaching approaches and strategies that promote communication, understanding, and learning. European policies are working on the implementation of measures to promote inclusive education where no child is left behind, however, this must be necessarily materialised in schools through know-how strategies. In this sense, the chapter addresses questions or issues of concern to which we intend to give some answer:

- Q.1: Are national curricula, schools, and teachers sufficiently prepared to deal with cultural and linguistic variety in a class in such a way that no child is left behind in every area of the curriculum?

In section 2 we will explore how different European policies prepare the ground for inclusive plurilingual schools. What remain to be seen and deeply studied at a large scale is how actually these policies are implemented at national and local levels.

- Q.2: In a narrower sense, can linguists and language teachers provide support to curriculum developers for the purpose of cohesion and knowledge building in plurilingual classes?

Sections 3–5 deal with social inclusion in education from a linguist point of view, drawing attention onto the communication conflicts that may rise in plurilingual school contexts, presenting the newly-coined concept "interlingual[1] education" at the base of healthy plurilingual classes and schools, and considering "linguistic mediation" as the main language activity for achieving social cohesion and actual knowledge building.

- Q.3: Are there any down-to-earth recommendations that can facilitate inclusion in plurilingual classes and schools?

Section 6 provides an action guide that covers the issue, from day-to-day concerns to more specific actions and strategies regarding interlingual education

---

[1] Not to be confused with "interlanguage" (Selinker 1972). For other uses of the term "interlingual" see Guardado (2017) and Tsushima and Guardado (2019).

and mediation. This guide bases on American and European perspectives on the matter (including previous work by Barranco-Izquierdo 2014, 2017).

2 European policies on inclusive migrant education

The European policies aimed at the inclusion of diversity in education originate from the rather ambitious objective of promoting mutual understanding across languages and cultures, and preventing xenophobia and marginalization. Thus, the first basic principle of *Recommendation No. R (82) 18 of the Committee of Ministers to Member States Concerning Modern Languages* establishes that "the rich heritage of diverse languages and cultures in Europe is a valuable common resource to be protected and developed" and, more specifically, that "a major educational effort is needed to convert that diversity from a barrier to communication into a source of mutual enrichment and understanding" (Council of Europe 1982: 1).

In fact, the first general measure set out in the Appendix to *Recommendation No. R (82)18* is "To ensure, as far as possible, that all sections of their populations have access to effective means of acquiring a knowledge of the languages of other member states (or of other communities within their own country) as well as the skills in the use of those languages that will enable them to satisfy their communicative needs" (Council of Europe 1982: 2).

This general measure aims to achieve "a wider and deeper understanding of the way of life and forms of thought of other peoples and of their cultural heritage" (Council of Europe 1982: 2, measure 1.3). It is vital, then, that educators work for the promotion of "democratic values and cultural diversity" as put forward by the Second Summit of Heads of State's Action Plan (Council of Europe 1997), so people can be educated in such a way that they are able to overcome communication barriers, and deal with plurilingual and intercultural experiences productively. Schools are the places where relationships of this kind should be encouraged, experienced, and appreciated from a constructive learning perspective.

Documents, such as the *Common European Framework of Reference for Languages* (Council of Europe, 2001), *Recommendation CM/Rec (2008) 4 of the Committee of Ministers to Member States on Strengthening the Integration of Children of Migrants and of Immigrant Background*(Council of Europe, 2008) and *Guide for the Development and Implementation of Curricula for Plurilingual and Intercultural Education* (Beacco et al. 2010), grow from an understanding of Europe as an in-motion, multicultural, plurilingual society in which language learners are "social agents" (Council of Europe 2001: 9) who use foreign languages in social situations. This idea of a borderless Europe where migration, interculturality, and plurilingual relations are seen as common and beneficial must be transferred to education at all levels.

Recommendation CM/Rec (2008) 4 of the Committee of Ministers to Member States on Strengthening the Integration of Children of Migrants and of Immigrant Background particularly addresses the need to include core contents related to the teaching of children of migrants and immigrants in professional training programs for schools and social and health services:

> At every stage of the professional qualification process for teachers, social and health workers and other professionals working with children of migrants and of immigrant background there should be learning opportunities to develop and test the special skills that they require. These include intercultural competence skills, skills to manage cultural differences in the classroom, peaceful conflict resolution skills, diagnostic skills to differentiate language problems from learning deficiencies, and skills to develop didactic instruments and learning strategies aimed at supporting children whose mother tongue is not that of the majority of society and/or the receiving country. (Council of Europe 2008: 3–4)

According to the *Guide for the Development and Implementation of Curricula for Plurilingual and Intercultural Education* (Beacco et al. 2010), these are some of the facts and preconceptions about young migrants that current European education encounters:

- Young migrants are from different backgrounds. We need to use strategies that are useful in all cases and can be adapted to each student's origin and first language.
- All schools should be inclusive, which means that any actions should benefit the whole group to avoid the stigmatization of students, or the dilution of the curriculum.
- Young migrants should be given the chance to develop literacy in their mother tongue for their social, emotional, and professional benefit, but also because there are psycho-linguistic arguments supporting the connection between first language development and second language learning benefits.
- Plurilingual contexts should be considered as an opportunity to educate future citizens with the intention of fostering cultural and linguistic flexibility.

European documents that provide general outlines of how school curricula and language programmes should be sensitive to diversity from a plurilingual intercultural perspective have proliferated in the past few years. This current concern at the higher levels of educational policy is also shared by many school teachers. Many school teachers believe that spurring the development of plurilingual and intercultural skills at school is beneficial for all students regardless of national background. However, the European approach towards inclusive education involves dramatic changes in the teacher's role. Teachers are now being asked to make understanding and learning possible for all students in a plurilingual and intercultural social context. This multifaceted ideal school teacher will not only need to deal with subject content, syllabi, key competences, updated methodologies, special needs, meetings with parents, and playground supervision; but also with the management of successful learning in a plurilingual class and the communication conflicts that may arise. This will be challenging for teachers coming from monolingual backgrounds. A relevant question is also whether teachers are given the necessary tools to tackle cultural and linguistic diversity in their classes.

In this chapter, we mean to partially respond to the following European principles:

- "convert diversity from a barrier to communication into a source of mutual enrichment and understanding" (*Recommendation No. R (82)18*'s general principle, quoted in Council of Europe 1982: 1).
- "ensure that our diversity becomes a source of mutual enrichment, *inter alia*, by fostering political, inter-cultural and inter-religious dialogue" (Council of Europe 2005a: 2).
- "enhance all opportunities for the training of educators, in the fields of education for democratic citizenship, human rights, history and intercultural education" (Council of Europe 2005b: section III.3).

Throughout this chapter we describe, from the communicative point of view, what makes a multicultural class an ideal context for learning, pondering on the new concept "interlingual education" and the use of "oral mediation" (Council of Europe 2001) as language activity. The term "interlingual education" will be defined and clarified in the following sections.

3 Orientations to benefitting from inclusive migrant education at different levels

In order to ensure inclusion of migrants at school, and the enrichment of society through diversity, actions at different educational levels should be taken (Beacco et al. 2010): at the international level (supra); in the national education systems (macro); in schools and institutions (meso); in teaching and learning sequences (micro); and throughout individual learning experiences (nano). For the purpose of this chapter, we will focus on the lower levels, where down-to-earth struggles in cultural linguistic education take place. Nevertheless, we will still be mindful of some of the general supra guidelines that contribute to the development of strategies at the meso, micro, and nano levels.

In general terms, every idea suggested at the supra level works towards the understanding of the individual learner in holistic and social terms. In other words, the student is seen as a multi-competent social agent at school, and social experiences and transferences between skills build their education. Following this idea, throughout all the different approaches mentioned by Beacco et al. (2010), we can find some down-to-earth orientations that seem to benefit migrant inclusion in class and which can enhance all learners' language and plurilingual skills. We have grouped our orientations into three categories:

- Transferability. Transference of skills and competences should be encouraged through the crossover linking of subjects. Strategies and skills developed for a language in a subject can and should be transferred to communication and learning activities in another language or subject. For this reason, coordination between teachers becomes essential.
- Exposure to cultures and languages. Diversity of plurilingual and intercultural experiences progressively enlarges the repertoire of skills and strategies that can be transferred, which makes plurilingual learning and interculturalism an asset in education. For this reason, activities that involve experiencing other cultures and languages should be promoted in the classroom.
- Language awareness. Perceiving variations in terms of language (discourse genres, subject-specific language peculiarities, registers, dialects, similarities, and contrasts) allows learners to adopt a standpoint outside their own.

National education systems in Europe warrant analysis concerning whether European policies on language and cultural diversity at school are being implemented or not. Consequently, this chapter will discuss the micro and nano levels. In particular, we mean to provide some guidelines on how school teachers can effectively contribute to linguistic and cultural inclusion in their classes.

Begioni et al. (1999) have stated the need for teachers to possess and develop proficiency competences to foster interpersonal relations among students from different language backgrounds and cultures. This proficiency is intrinsically linked to four of the 40 elements described in the *European Profile for Language Teacher Education: A Frame of Reference* (Kelly et al. 2004). This report proposes a European profile for foreign language teachers that serve as a checklist for existing training programs and serve as a guide for those yet to be developed:

> 22. Training in ways of adapting teaching approaches to the educational context and individual needs of learners.

26. Training in the development of independent language learning strategies.
36. Training in the diversity of languages and cultures.
37. Training in the importance of teaching and learning about foreign languages and cultures. (Kelly et al. 2004: 6)

In the same line of thought, the Director General for Education, Culture, Youth and Sport, Battaini-Dragoni (2006), has argued that all languages are necessary in promoting social inclusion. She asserted that, beyond being merely a linguistic matter, promoting the use of different languages is a means towards a more inclusive Europe. As such, teachers are urged to work for the promotion of linguistic/cultural sensitivity and awareness in their classrooms.

4 Interlingual education in the classroom

The *DeSeCo Project* (Organisation for Economic Co-operation and Development, 2005) considers three main competences as necessary for a person to participate appropriately in social contexts: use a range of tools for interacting effectively (use of language); interact in heterogeneous groups; and act autonomously. On a daily basis, all three competences are necessary for the successful handling of diverse interactions in schools. However, these competences raise several questions: What is the meaning of "adequate" in school contexts? In which sense do we understand "effective" when it comes to managing language diversity in a class? Do we, as teachers, want our students to "interact" through competition or through collaboration? These are some questions teachers need to face before attempting to design a lesson plan addressing democratic social and communicative competences.

Multilingual/multicultural classrooms offer a place where linguistically and culturally heterogeneous groups can coexist, but this heterogeneity does not necessarily turn them into environments where healthy democratic interactions are taking place, i.e., where interactions are intended for "the understanding between the citizens of the North and the South" and for the promotion of "mutual respect and solidarity among peoples" (Council of Europe 1997: 2). Migrant students' languages and cultures, apart from coexisting, should be promoted and displayed in the classrooms. In addition, there should be a relationship between individuals, and mutual benefits should be obtained from that relationship (Abdallah-Pretceille 2001).

To foster this type of classroom interaction, European policies refer to plurilingual education as an adequate method of teaching in this culturally and linguistically diverse social context. Beacco and Byram (2007: 116) have remarked that plurilingual education:

> (. . .) is not necessarily restricted to language teaching, which aims to raise awareness of each individual's language repertoire, to emphasize its worth and to extend this repertoire by teaching lesser used or unfamiliar languages (. . .) [Plurilingual education] also aims to increase understanding of the social and cultural value of linguistic diversity in order to ensure linguistic goodwill and to develop intercultural competence.

Therefore, to achieve maximum benefits and democratic success, further elaborated education strategies should be displayed: namely, the promotion of intercultural competences, and what we call "interlingual education". "Interlingual education" goes beyond "plurilingual education" mainly in the sense that in the former, language competence is used during the teaching and learning process in order to build knowledge and a more cohesive interrelated class atmosphere; while in the latter the focus is placed on the personal cognitive equipment that allows an individual to manage in situations when their whole linguistic knowledge needs to be put to work. Consequently, "interlingual education" is understood as the social process of facilitating the building of knowledge, competences and values through the active use of several languages in the learning process. In order to construe a clearer definition of "interlingual education", we will start from the terms: "intercultural competence" and "intercultural approach".

Intercultural competence was defined by Meyer (1991: 137) as:

> (. . .) the ability of a person to behave adequately and in a flexible manner when confronted with actions, attitudes and expectations of representatives of foreign cultures. *Adequacy* and *flexibility* imply an awareness of the cultural differences between one's own and the foreign culture and the ability to *handle cross-cultural problems* which result from these differences. Intercultural competence includes the capacity of stabilising one's self-identity in the process of *cross-cultural mediation* and of helping other people to stabilise their self-identity. (emphasis ours)

The ideas described by this definition are shared by the *Common European Framework of Reference for Languages* (Council of Europe 2001) which adds that we need to know how to deal effectively with intercultural misunderstandings and conflict situations. Relatedly, Candelier et al. (2008) have presented the "intercultural approach" as one of the pluralistic approaches to languages and cultures. As stated previously, the mobilization of the intercultural education that underlies these approaches should not be exclusive to those school contexts with a migrant population. In this case, we would be denying the rest of the educational community knowledge of cultural diversity. Thus, intercultural education should offer valid and appropriate responses to the challenges presented by the cultural coexistence in our classrooms. Students are taught to interact with others, accept others' perceptions of the world, and mediate between different perspectives. A person who possesses these abilities is interculturally competent (Byram, Nichols, and Stevens 2001).

If these insights are transferred to language learning, we need to be talking about the development of interlingual education. It is extremely necessary to highlight the importance of teaching tools and strategies which will incorporate all students' mother tongues. Therefore, when discussing interlingual education, we are not just considering the presence of different mother tongues in the classroom as an opportunity to enrich and benefit the whole group. We are referring to the teachers' capacity to increase and diversify how they approach languages, not just in order to attend to migrant students' necessities but, as said before, to prepare the whole group to address language contact outside the scope of the classroom. Teachers need to forget about the governance of duality (mother tongue and foreign language) and start planning, among other things, ways to foster the performance of all the languages in the classroom.

Interlingual education at school, as we understand it, involves meeting at least four complementary demands: 1) enlarging the children's capacity (cognitive-linguistic skills) to deal with languages different from their own through frequent exposure to other languages; 2) helping children to use their own literacy competence in their mother tongues as a base for the development of literacy strategies in other languages; 3) encouraging empathy and awareness of otherness through mutual linguistic and cultural understanding in the languages they may encounter at school or in society; 4) using language communication skills in a group to build knowledge and more cohesive class atmospheres.

Developing interlingual education is not just a matter of being able to communicate and feel at ease in different linguistic contexts or act as language mediators. When it comes to migration, developing interlingual education is also a matter of providing individuals with the necessary tools to receive basic education. A research study carried out by the European Commission (2019) on the social and school integration of migrant students specifically advises that schools tackle the teaching of language(s) of origin because of its multiple benefits. The European Commission (2019: 19) argues that:

> Proficiency in their language of origin is widely considered to be of great importance for immigrant students. Proficiency can make it easier for these students to learn the language of instruction and thus stimulate their development in all areas. In addition, the manner in which their mother tongue is viewed in the host community helps secure the self-esteem and identity of immigrant children and their families.

Indeed, the promotion of interlingual education in the classroom can provide tools and strategies to overcome or even avoid potential communication conflicts.

5 Overcoming communication conflicts in the classroom through oral mediation

In this interlingual learning scenario, interpersonal barriers which occur in verbal and nonverbal communication put spoken interaction at risk (Malik Liévano and Herraz Ramos 2005). This risk is linked to the notion of communication conflict during the teaching and learning process. Teachers must use appropriate strategies and techniques so students can attain the two key "communication" competences identified in the *Recommendation of the European Parliament and of the Council of 18 December 2006 on Key Competences for Lifelong Learning* (2006/962/EC):

> Communication in the mother tongue is the ability to express and interpret concepts, thoughts, feelings, facts and opinions in both oral and written form (listening, speaking, reading and writing), and to interact linguistically in an appropriate and creative way in a full range of societal and cultural contexts; in education and training, work, home and leisure. (. . .) Communication in foreign languages broadly shares the main skill dimensions of communication in the mother tongue (. . .) [and] also calls for skills such as mediation and intercultural understanding. (Official Journal of the European Union 2006: 14)

Throughout this communication process, the classroom environment is characterized by functional interdependence among its members and the verbal or nonverbal social interaction (Puren 2002). In this environment, new knowledge is generated, so the more students' contributions are produced, the more possibilities there are to enlarge knowledge. Therefore, students with different mother tongues and cultures potentially enrich the general knowledge.

Oral mediation serves as the backbone of communication and enables this enrichment to occur (Barranco-Izquierdo and Guillén Díaz 2017). Oral mediation implies spoken interaction between at least two people with their own linguistic, cultural, and personal backgrounds. For Coste and Cavalli (2015), the concept of "mediation" involves ideas such as overcoming obstacles and dealing with problem areas, etc. In this case, the teacher will need to tackle communication conflicts produced by the presence of different languages and cultures in a learning environment and, consequently, by how those languages and cultures influence each child's perspective on reality, personal relationships, teaching and learning.

The *Common European Framework of Reference for Languages* says that "In mediation activities, the language user (. . .) act(s) as an intermediary between interlocutors who are unable to understand each other directly – normally (but not exclusively) speakers of different languages" (Council of Europe 2001, 87). In this reference document, we find the following examples of oral mediation: simultaneous interpretation, consecutive interpretation, and informal interpretation. Cantero Serena and De Arriba García (2004) refer to oral mediation as a verbal or nonverbal language activity of negotiation and interaction in a communicative context where speakers must be able to understand each other. For the performance of oral mediation articulated in the teaching and learning process, the mobilization of different strategies or intellectual operations is also required. They list the following strategies related to oral mediation: intermediate, summarize, synthesize, paraphrase, and apostille (or clarify).

Oral interactions between teachers and students or students and students may generate communication conflicts that should be solved at that very moment through oral mediation. It is in these situations of communication conflict that students need to deal with their own frustrations, apply flexibility of thought, appreciate one's own and their peer's diverse intelligences (Gardner 1999), or ask for and recognize help. Thus, through oral mediation as a communicative language activity, social, and emotional education is also taking place, as it fosters collaboration, engagement, conflict resolution, diversity awareness, negotiation, resilience, empathy, etc. We can, therefore, affirm that mediation in oral communication contexts, besides improving children's communicative skills, ensures their training as citizens in a global society. Adopting this activity enhances the development of soft skills, as face-to-face interaction occurs between peers and between the students and their teacher.

As we focus on the conflicts preventing successful communication, a teacher or student might perform the role of a social mediator who knows the rules to follow, or the role of a cognitive mediator who knows how to communicate their understanding (Vez, Guillén, and Alario 2002). These social and cognitive mediators facilitate the necessary interrelationships to make the classroom a place based on communication and on the social and spoken interactions of the individuals involved. In this sense, Uranga (1994) has indicated that the use of mediation in schools and in classrooms has a very positive impact in developing soft skills, since:

- It creates a more relaxed and productive environment.
- It contributes to the development of respect for the other.
- It helps to recognize and value one's own and others' feelings, interests and needs.
- It contributes to the development of the capacity for dialogue and the improvement of communicative skills, especially active listening.

A teacher, as a social and cognitive mediator, regulates class communication exchanges by controlling, directing, and reorienting interactions. The three main mediation functions, which may be interpreted as an action guide for teacher mediators, are: planning, execution, and evaluation (Council of Europe, 2001). As these functions are carried out during the teaching and learning process, the mediator must display an intentional purpose of solving the communication conflict. This intentional purpose shows a positive attitude towards its resolution and, hence, it is the first step for schools to develop interlingual and intercultural education.

6 Action guide for school teachers

The guide presented below is addressed to those teachers who have migrant students in their classes, but it can also be useful for those who believe in the necessity of integrating intercultural and interlingual methodologies and materials into their classrooms. Some of these ideas have been taken and rephrased from: Council of Europe (2008), Beacco et al. (2010), Genzuk (2011), Barranco-Izquierdo (2014), and Meyer, Halbach, and Coyle (2015).

Before going deeply into the linguistic issue, it may be necessary to present some general clues for a convenient education frame.

6.1 General recommendations for teachers towards the inclusion of migrant children in their classrooms

- Make an effort to recognize and address the learning needs of migrant children (assess proficiency in the language of schooling, talk with family, and social services, etc.)
- Provide migrant families with important information about issues relevant to their child (services, etc.). It can also be useful for those who believe in them. If necessary and possible, make this information available in their mother tongue or any other additional language they may understand well.
- Foster the collaboration of families to promote respect for other languages and cultures.
- Differentiate learning problems from the lack of language skills. Do not assume children are not learning because they are not able to express content in the language of schooling.
- Facilitate access to the whole curriculum. Sometimes learning resources in the migrant child's mother tongue may be needed.
- Provide a "buddy" to newcomers. It can be another migrant who has successfully engaged in school life, a peer who has already developed intercultural

and interlingual communication competences, or someone who is likely to develop such competences.
- Coordinate with other teachers in order to encourage the development of learning skills and the transference of skills and competences through crossover linking of subjects (use of cognitive maps, notebook strategies, etc.)
- Help migrant children to develop a positive image of themselves and their identification with their new country. Support the self-esteem and identity of immigrant children and their families.
- Encourage a respectful and tolerant classroom atmosphere.
- Promote links between children of different origins.
- Educate future citizens to foster cultural and linguistic flexibility.
- Assess the benefits of including the languages and cultures present in the classroom.

Language:
- Allow the use of mother tongues in your class, it should be seen as a learning opportunity from the linguistic and cultural point of view.
- Assist migrant children in acquiring proficiency in the language of schooling. Whatever the subject you are teaching, include appropriate language objectives in your classes, from specialized vocabulary to discourse organization when writing or talking about the lesson topic.
- Focus on the cognitive operations related to language (e.g., identifying, locating, recounting, describing, arguing) and have migrant students use them throughout the learning process depending on their level of proficiency in the language of schooling.
- Use metacommunicative activities, which focus on the language to be used to perform a task. You will find this not only helps migrant students but also domestic students. Being a native speaker in a language does not automatically imply having the skills for elaborate intelligible and coherent oral or written discourse on a complex topic or task.
- Change your register when speaking. Explain things in different ways. Repeat. Focus on key concepts.
- Provide mediation to overcome communication conflicts and make sure that understanding is successful.
- Assist children in the development of literacy in their mother tongue. Studies have shown that positive literacy experiences in one's first language have a positive influence on second language acquisition.
- Show a positive attitude towards the students' errors in the language activities.

Methodology:
- Build on students' previous knowledge and use scaffolding.
- Encourage teamwork and collaboration. Design cooperation activities, which involve the participation and engagement of all the students.
- Design strategies to support learning for students whose mother tongue is not the language of schooling.
- Design strategies that are useful in any situation and can adapt to each student's cultural background and mother tongue.
- Use visual aids and hands-on demonstrations to support your explanations.
- Focus on key concepts and facilitate understanding through different media (visual supports, manipulation, comparisons, etc.). Do not reduce your teaching to oral explanations and reading alone.
- Do not overload migrant students with written material in the language of schooling. Make sure written material is actually necessary and can be understood with the help of oral mediation. Provide the same information through other means.
- Design ways in which children can show their understanding and learning. In most cases, traditional exams will mainly test their language proficiency and not their actual learning in a subject.
- Teaching materials should reflect the diversity of the society.

Intercultural Competence:
- Develop positive attitudes and openness to linguistic and cultural diversity in the classroom.
- Increase your knowledge of the cultures of origin in your class. In this way you may foresee reactions or avoid misunderstanding. Offer this knowledge in class to promote an inclusive classroom environment.
- Address migration and cross-cultural knowledge and its benefits through the curriculum.
- Design activities aimed at promoting awareness of cultural, religious, and linguistic diversity.
- Address communication conflict with a constructive attitude. Consider communication conflict as an opportunity for learning.

6.2 Guidelines for interlingual education

- Plan activities that involve exposure to other cultures and languages.
- Use alternation between languages in the teaching and learning process, for example using plurilingual aids.

- Allow migrant students to use material in their own language and share the information with their classmates.
- Prepare real-life activities where two or more languages are needed. For example, you can involve your class in e-twinning – a free online community to find schools to collaborate with other schools on projects – especially with those schools in the countries of origin of the migrant children in your class. Use videos or podcasts by people from different origins talking about the topic you are studying. Include videos in the languages of the migrant students and encourage them to explain to their classmates the information provided.
- Have students from different origins work together for a purpose. Keep in mind that language interaction is necessary to complete the task and permit students to express themselves using any language resource.
- Encourage students to reflect on the linguistic dimension of all the languages present in the class. You can look for similarities and differences, research the common origin of terms in different languages, etc.
- Incorporate drama and role plays in your lessons to create situations in which students need to take the role of a person from a different origin. Have students cooperate in writing their own plays and encourage them to include interactions in two or more languages in their scripts. Local and migrant students will both profit from plurilingual performance rehearsals.
- Open the door to imagination. Let students play on the aesthetic dimension of the languages by having them create puns, riddles, rhymes, stories or songs.
- Start the process of overcoming a communication conflict or even prevent it from arising.
- Use oral mediation to address conflicts.

6.3 Guidelines for mediation

6.3.1 Planning: Considering interlocutors' needs

- Plan, elaborate, and select teaching strategies, types of activities, and class materials.
- Design activities aimed at developing oral communication in all the students' mother tongues.
- Establish individual plans regarding linguistic competence for those students who need it.

- Prepare a glossary of terms: general functional terms and subject content terms.
- Provide authentic language samples.
- Plan strategies to develop skills and competences to overcome possible communication conflicts during lessons.

6.3.2 Execution: Processing input and bridging communicative gaps

- Use non-verbal communication to support the verbal message in order to minimize communication conflict, such as gestures, paralinguistic actions, and paratextual characteristics.
- Use body language and dramatization as communicative resources.
- Produce clear instructions.
- Intermediate. Be an interpreter. Explain, summarize or paraphrase the message.
- Summarize. Transmit the meaning of the message by adapting it to the interlocutor's needs.
- Synthesize. Reduce the message to essential data by adapting the message to the interlocutor.
- Paraphrase. Change the way you phrase the message to make it more understandable.
- Apostille. Clarify, comment, explain, amplify or give extra information that the interlocutor requires to understand what is being said.
- Help to solve the internal group divisions that cause communication conflict.

6.3.3 Evaluation: Checking congruence and consistency of usage

- Evaluate the students' previous knowledge and needs, introducing different strategies that take into account the characteristics of the educational context.
- Control behavior after overcoming a communication conflict.
- Report on the progress of migrant students.
- Offer new information, ideas, theories, and options to overcome communication conflicts.

Above, we offer what means to be a useful tool for teachers who want to perform inclusive education in classes with the presence of migrant students. Having migrant students in the class may cause a lack of understanding due to language communication conflicts. The appropriate and flexible management of these communication conflicts suggests the need for adequate teacher training. This training should focus on the benefits for and enrichment of the whole class by incorporating all students' mother tongues into the teaching and learning process, thereby fostering interlingual education. Oral mediation might be necessary for the resolution of potential language communication conflicts that could take place because of the inclusion of diverse languages and cultures. We are mainly addressing the use of oral mediation in the classroom as a communicative language activity, which involves the awareness of both verbal and nonverbal elements to manage classroom diversity. It is very important to know how to mobilize oral mediation strategies and to have the ability to bring the different languages and cultures into conversation with each other.

7 Conclusions

The presence of different languages and cultures in the classroom is now a fact in European contexts. Schools must make an effort to profit from this new learning scenario by using the variety of languages and cultures as a basis for knowledge and competence building. European policy (supra) on migrant education at Primary and Secondary levels gives the general frame in this direction; yet, in other levels (macro, meso, micro and nano) measures must still be implemented.

In this chapter we have focused on how communication conflicts in the classroom can be dealt with through the use of mediation as a language activity. And, in a more holistic way, we suggest that what we call "interlingual education", as defined in section 4, can be the first step towards knowledge and competence building.

From an integrated educational perspective, including migrants' languages in the learning process cannot be attained only by paying attention to languages, but dealing with other variables, such as: families and students' mentoring; teachers' coordination regarding curriculum development; encouraging positive attitudes, self-perception and appreciation of otherness; methodology; and the development of intercultural competence, among others. Therefore, in section 6, we offer an action guide for those teachers who want to create more inclusive learning environments and do not know how to begin.

References

Abdallah-Pretceille, Martine. 2001. *La educación intercultural*. Barcelona: Idea Books.
Barranco-Izquierdo, Natalia. 2014. *La mediación oral en el contexto escolar con alumnado extranjero. Su impacto en el aula de inglés en Educación Primaria*. Valladolid: Universidad de Valladolid dissertation.
Barranco-Izquierdo, Natalia & Carmen Guillén Díaz. 2017. Efectos de la mediación oral para la resolución de conflictos comunicativos en aulas de inglés de Educación Primaria con presencia de alumnado extranjero. *Revista Electrónica Interuniversitaria de Formación del Profesorado* 20. 159–172.
Battaini-Dragoni, Gabrielle. 2006. *Languages of schooling: Towards a framework of reference for Europe*. Strasbourg: Council of Europe.
Beacco, Jean-Claude & Michael Byram. 2007. *From linguistic diversity to plurilingual education: Guide for the development of language education policies in Europe*. Strasbourg: Council of Europe.
Beacco, Jean-Claude, Michael Byram, Marisa Cavalli, Daniel Coste, Mirjam Egli Cuenat, Francis Goullier & Johanna Panthier. 2010. *Guide for the development and implementation of curricula for plurilingual and intercultural education*. Strasbourg: Council of Europe.
Begioni, Luis, Edvige Costanzo, Fátima Ferreira & Clara Ferrao. 1999. Para una formación europea de los formadores de lenguas: enfoque accional y multimodalidad. *Lenguaje y textos* 13. 29–39.
Byram, Michael, Adam Nichols & David Stevens (eds.). 2001. *Developing intercultural competence in practice*. Clevedon: Multilingual Matter.
Candelier, Michel (coord.), Antoinette Camilleri-Grima, Véronique Castellotti, Jean-François de Pietro, Ildikó Lörincz, Franz-Joseph Meissner, Anna Schröder-Sura & Artur Noguerol. 2008. *Framework of reference for pluralistic approaches to languages and cultures*. Strasbourg: Council of Europe.
Cantero Serena, Francisco Javier & Clara de Arriba García. 2004. Actividades de mediación lingüística para la clase de ELE. *Didáctica. Lengua y Literatura* 16. 9–21.
Coste, Daniel & Marisa Cavalli. 2015. *Education, mobility, otherness: The mediation functions of schools*. Strasbourg: Council of Europe.
Council of Europe. 1982. *Recommendation no. R (82) 18 of the committee of ministers to member states concerning modern languages*. Strasbourg: Council of Europe.
Council of Europe. 1997. *Second Summit of Heads of State and Government: Final declaration and action plan*. Strasbourg: Council of Europe.
Council of Europe. 2001. *Common European framework of reference for languages: Learning, teaching, assessment*. Strasbourg: Council of Europe.
Council of Europe. 2005a. *Third Summit of Heads of State and Government of the Council of Europe. Warsaw declaration*. Warsaw: Council of Europe.
Council of Europe. 2005b. *Third Summit of Heads of State and Government of the Council of Europe. Action plan*. Warsaw: Council of Europe.
Council of Europe. 2008. *Recommendation CM/Rec (2008) 4 of the committee of ministers to member states on strengthening the integration of children of migrants and of immigrant background*. Strasbourg: Council of Europe.

European Commission/EACEA/Eurydice. 2019. *Integrating Students from Migrant Backgrounds into Schools in Europe: National Policies and Measures. Eurydice Report*. Luxembourg: Publications Office of the European Union.

Gardner, Howard. 1999. *Intelligence reframed: Multiple intelligences for the 21st century*. New York: Basic Books.

Genzuk, Michael. 2011. *Specially designed academic instruction in English (SDAIE) for language minority students*. California: University of Southern California.

Guardado, Martin. 2017. Heritage language development in interlingual families. In Peter Trifonas & Themistoklis Aravossitas (eds.), *Handbook of research and practice in heritage language education*, 1–17. New York: Springer.

Kelly, Michael, Michael Grenfell, Rebecca Allan, Christine Kriza & William McEvoy. 2004. *European profile for language teacher education: A frame of reference*. Luxembourg: European Commission.

Malik Liévano, Beatriz & Mercedes Herraz Ramos. (eds.). 2005. *Mediación intercultural en contextos socio-educativos*. Málaga: Aljibe.

Meyer, Martine. 1991. Developing transcultural competence: Case studies of advanced foreign language learners. In D. Buttjes & M. Byram (eds.), *Mediating languages and cultures*, 136–158. Clevendon: Multilingual Matters.

Meyer, Oliver, Ana Halbach & Do Coyle. 2015. *A pluriliteracies approach to teaching for learning: Putting a pluriliteracies approach into practice*. Strasbourg: Council of Europe.

Organisation for Economic Co-operation and Development. 2005. *The definition and selection of key competencies. Executive summary*. Paris: OCDE.

Official Journal of the European Union. 2006. *Recommendation of the European parliament and of the council of 18 December 2006 on key competences for lifelong learning (2006/962/EC)*. Strasbourg: Council of Europe.

Puren, Christian. 2002. Perspectives actionnelles et perspectives culturelles en didactique des langues-cultures: vers une perspective co-actionnelle co-culturelle. *Langues modernes* 3. 55–71.

Selinker, L. 1972. Interlanguage. *IRAL; International Review of Applied Linguistics in Language Teaching* 10:3.

Tsushima, Rika & Martin Guardado. 2019. "Rules . . . I want someone to make them clear": Japanese mothers in Montreal talk about multilingual parenting. *Journal of Language, Identity, and Education* 18:5. 311–328. DOI: 10.1080/15348458.2019.1645017

United Nations. 2015. *Universal declaration of human rights*. https://www.un.org/en/universal-declaration-human-rights/ *(28 October 2019)*

Uranga, M. 1994. *Transformación de conflictos y mediación como propuesta de desarrollo de la educación para la paz en el sistema educativo vasco*. Guernica: Guernica Gogoratuz.

Vez, José Manuel, Carmen Guillén & Ana I. Alario. 2002. *Didáctica de la lengua extranjera en educación infantil y primaria*. Madrid: Síntesis.

Vimbai Mbirimi-Hungwe
Chapter 12
Transcending Linguistic Boundaries in Higher Education Pedagogy: The Role of Translanguaging and Lecturers

Abstract: Whereas modernist sociolinguists advocate for the separation of languages especially for purposes of teaching and learning, critical post-structural sociolinguists of the 21st century are calling for the disruption of language boundaries and allowing multilingual students to utilize languages as they feel appropriate. Thus, languages have been reframed to depart from the position of some languages as superior to others. Instead, fluid language practices are being advocated for in pedagogical contexts. The concept of translanguaging has been at the heart of this recent shift. With this backdrop, this study seeks to investigate how lecturers from maths, statistics, physics and computer science view the use of translanguaging for pedagogic purposes. Knowing what these lecturers believe about translanguaging could assist us in convincing them to accept and use translanguaging in their teaching for the benefit of the students. Responses from lecturers were solicited using an open-ended questionnaire, and recurring themes were uncovered during data analysis. Results show that the majority of science lecturers firmly believe that English is the only language that should be used for academic purposes.

Keywords: translanguaging, multilingualism, language, language boundaries

1 Introduction

This chapter will outline a general overview of the South African multilingual nature. It will present a literature review analysis on translanguaging pedagogy. The study is presented thereafter where data is presented consequently followed by the analysis of the data.

It is well-known that South Africa is a multilingual country with diverse cultural practices. This diversity makes it known as the Rainbow Nation. Social

---
Vimbai Mbirimi-Hungwe, Sefako Makgatho University of Health Sciences, South Africa,
E-mail: vimbai.hungwe@smu.ac.za

rights activist Archbishop Desmond Tutu first called South Africa the Rainbow Nation at the dawn of its democracy in 1994 (Kellerman 2014). Ultimately, the term Rainbow Nation was intended to capture the diversity in both language and culture in South Africa (Kellerman 2014). In addition to the 11 official languages, South Africa is home to different cultures whose heritages include Malay travelers, indigenous African and Khoi San tribes, Asian emigrants, as well as Dutch and British settlers, making it one of the most linguistically and culturally diverse nations in the world. In addition, due to the movement of people in search of better economic prospects, South Africa is now home to people from different parts of the world who speak different languages.

Linguistic diversity in South Africa seems to be most recognized at a macro level, namely, the constitution and related legislation. According to the Department of Education (2002), the language policy for higher education mandates universities to embark on projects that focus on the development of all South African languages such that they can be used across disciplines and as formal academic languages. Although there is policy that caters to multilingualism in South African higher education institutions, the policy is at a macro level, and as Baldauf (2010) explains, policies at the macro level are somewhat stagnant. That is, the South African government has a policy, which supports its 11 indigenous languages, but there is no policy framework to support those who contribute to the Rainbow Nation, especially in higher education. Due to the prevalence of linguistic diversity, lecturers are left with what Baldauf (2010) refers to as meso and micro level language policies: the meso level policies are those provided at the institutional level whereas the micro level policies are those designed for the classroom level. These policies are of an ephemeral nature since they can be changed to suit the needs of the participants.

The research reported on in this chapter sought to uncover whether the use of translanguaging at the micro level is possible at Sefako Makgatho University of Health Sciences (SMU). Specifically, I investigated whether lecturers concede to the use of translanguaging based on the linguistically diverse nature of students found in the classrooms. The research does not focus on the meso level because the university is a newly established university. Founded in 2015 following a separation from the University of Limpopo, SMU does not yet have a formal language policy. However, the university uses English as the de facto official language as well as the medium of instruction. It is important to mention that the university admits students of diverse multilingual repertoires.

Because SMU does not have a language policy at the institutional level (meso level), this chapter examines the micro level language policy, to find out from lecturers especially from the basic sciences (mathematics, statistics, computer science and physics) about their views on using translanguaging in their classrooms. The other reason is that I would like to make them aware of the benefits of translanguaging as a follow up on their responses. I have called for the use of translanguaging to be introduced to all members of the faculty and not to be used by language lecturers only (Mbirimi-Hungwe 2016).

2 Nation state ideology and monolingualism

How did the English language acquire the high status it holds, especially in institutions of higher learning, if South Africa is a multilingual country and a Rainbow Nation? The answer to this question can be unearthed by tracing the origins of monolingual ideologies. Critical post-structural sociolinguists (García, Flores and Spotti 2017; Makalela 2016; Makoni 2017; Makoni and Pennycook 2007; May 2017) trace the origins of monolingual ideology and observe that monolingualism was designed by those in power who wanted to create a nation-state ideology. According to García (2014), monolingualism dictated by a nation-state ideology was first evinced in 1469 in Spain. Through the marriage of Ferdinand and Isabella from the royal families of Aragon and Castile, the two kingdoms were unified. The Crown viewed the local linguistic diversity as a threat to political stability, which prompted the imposition of Spanish as the only language to be used in their kingdom and their colonies in the Americas. Ferdinand of Aragon and Isabella of Castile believed that bringing all of the different groups together under one language, Castilian (Spanish), would create a stable nation. May (2017) adds that the French revolution upheld the monolingual ideology. In 1789, France pursued the banishment of all minority languages and cultures to pave the way for the monolingual use of French. May (2017) writes that the basis of the nation-state ideology was French leaders' perception that unity of speech would unite the Republic of France. However, he remarks that this was an imagined construct of one nation, one language and one culture.

The arrival of missionaries in America, Africa and Asia extended the idea of nation-state ideology when they categorized the fluid language practices of indigenous communities into named, bound languages (Lane and Mikihara 2017). In the southern part of Africa, there existed the Kingdom of Mapungubwe. This kingdom flourished in the area of modern-day Zimbabwe, Botswana, and South Africa from the 10th to the 13th centuries. Makalela (2016) provides an analogy of how the people from this kingdom used to trade, conduct business, and inter-marry using language systems that overlapped without boundaries. The kingdom traded in gold and ivory with China, Egypt, and India (South African

History Online [SAHO] 2011). There was no official language with which to conduct business, but business was surely carried out using fluid language practices amongst the traders. These fluid language practices were disrupted by the nation-state ideology brought by Dutch, British, and Afrikaner colonizers (Makalela 2016). Their mission was to impose the nation-state ideology and ultimately the concept of divide and rule. In South Africa, Makalela (2016) mourns the disruption of mutually intelligible languages by the foreign missionary linguists who assigned different orthographic representations to those languages, thus resulting in languages being assigned to "boxes" (Makalela 2015), "enumerable entities" (Makoni 2007) and "monolithic entities" confined within a boundary (García et al. 2017).

It is imperative to explain how nation-state ideologies contributed to the creation of the field of sociolinguistics. The field of sociolinguistics was established in the 1960s when many states gained independence from their colonial masters and sociolinguists began to use the nation-state ideologies to study the positivist, modernist approach to the study of language (García et al. 2017). At the time, this field of study advanced the notion of the standardization of languages. Ndlhovu (2017) refers to this as part of the "standard ideology". Thus, sociolinguists utilized corpus planning strategies and helped the newly established nation states with the standardization of languages (García et al. 2017). Through the standardization of languages came the separation of dominant languages from non-dominant languages. This resulted in the "minoritization" of languages – especially indigenous – and those speaking such languages were to be considered as backward and in need of civilization (Ndlhovu 2017).

In order to perpetuate the standard ideology, the education system was instrumental in promoting standard languages at the expense of the "non-standard" languages. The education system predominantly used English as the standard language for academic purposes. This resulted in indigenous languages being positioned as inferior to English, especially in higher learning institutions. As mentioned earlier, South Africa does have policies that recognize and encourage multilingualism. However, these policies are not being implemented at the institutional (meso) level. Some universities have allowed the use of English and Afrikaans (which are colonial languages) for the purposes of teaching and learning (Makalela and McCabe 2013). Nonetheless, there has not been any attempt in universities to allow students to learn and utilize their home languages for the purposes of learning the same way Afrikaans and English have been allowed to be used for teaching and learning in many historically white universities. The reason for this is to avow the standard use of these languages to support nation-state ideologies. Thus, an English monolingual status quo has been maintained in several universities and SMU is one of them.

3 Translanguaging framework

Translanguaging is a term that was coined by Williams (1996) from the Welsh word *trawsieithu* to describe complex discursive practices used for pedagogical purposes in Wales. Developments since then have disrupted the notions of additive bilingualism as well as diglossic pedagogical practices (García et al. 2017). Indeed, translanguaging is a theory that evolved from post-structural linguistics (García and Wei 2014) and is located within the critical post-structural sociolinguistics movement. This movement is represented by a growing number of linguists (e.g., García 2014; García and Wei 2014; Makalela 2015, 2016; Makoni and Pennycook 2007; May 2017) who question the use of languages as bound entities that should be separated for purposes of teaching and learning. According to critical post-structural sociolinguists, languages were named for the sake of nation-state ideologies (Makoni and Pennycook 2007) as seen in the few examples of Spain, France, and modern-day Zimbabwe, Botswana, and South Africa. Thus, critical post-structuralist sociolinguists argue that language belongs to the speaker rather than to nation-states (Flores and García 2013). With this view, critical post-structural sociolinguists aim to disrupt conceptions of language that keep power in the hands of a few actors.

Translanguaging has become a suitable paradigm with which to enact linguistic social justice by working against the linguistic hierarchies created by nation-state ideologies (Otheguy et al. 2015). Translanguaging disrupts the linguistic hierarchies that were accentuated by nation-state ideologies, and places languages into what García and Wei (2014) refer to as integrated social spaces that were formerly practised separately in different places. Scholars who propagate the concept of translanguaging have argued that boundaries separating one language from another fail to accurately reflect the fluid nature of language (García and Wei 2014). Importantly, translanguaging questions some teachers' belief that language separation will prevent the cross-contamination of languages.

According to García and Wei (2014), translanguaging is based on the premise that individuals (i.e., students) do not draw from two separate languages but from a single linguistic repertoire accommodating different languages and language varieties. Thus, a translanguaging lens posits that multilinguals possess one linguistic repertoire from which they select features prudently in order to communicate effectively (García and Wei 2014). In other words, translanguaging considers the language practices of multilinguals to be the norm. As such, limiting multilingual students to one language stifles their ability to make meaning and to understand their surroundings. Thus, a translanguaging trajectory views multilingualism from an advantageous point of view where multilingual students have the benefit of utilizing the different linguistic resources that they possess in order to make meaning. Bock and Mheta (2014) offer the analogy of multilingualism as a large cooking pot where multilinguals store their language knowledge, repertoires of language, and language resources. When the need arises, they dip into the pot and take out what they need. Instead of viewing multilinguals from a deficit point of view, translanguaging leverages the abilities of multilinguals by acknowledging the rich linguistic resources that they possess. In fact, translanguaging paves the way for multilinguals to utilize their funds of knowledge (Moll et al. 1992) for purposes of learning. Simply expressed, translanguaging works against the ideologies of homogeneity in that it represents ideologies where different linguistic resources are acknowledged and valued (Paulsrud et al. 2018).

The fact that languages have no boundaries and languages are not compartmentalized should prompt lecturers to adopt a translanguaging model of teaching by allowing students to utilize all the linguistic resources at their disposal. In this chapter, I argue that students enter into classrooms with rich linguistic repertoires (Carroll and Morales 2016) that require recognition and utilization for meaning-making and understanding academic material. The importance of recognizing, valuing and utilizing students' linguistic repertoires is emphasized by García and Kleyn's (2016) call for educators to start looking at language from the point of view of the multilingual students in their classrooms. As such, lecturers are encouraged to leverage students' full repertoires in their pedagogy, and to ensure that students understand the learning material. In addition, García, Johnson and Seltzer (2016) call for the creation of translanguaging classrooms. A translanguaging classroom is any classroom in which students are allowed to deploy their full linguistic repertoires and not just particular language/s that are used for instructional purposes (García, Johnson, and Seltzer, 2016). A translanguaging classroom is a space built collaboratively by the teacher and multilingual students as they use their different language practices to teach and learn.

The aim of this research was to find out from lecturers from the School of Science and Technology at SMU about their views on the use of translanguaging in their classes. Although many language teachers and lecturers in South Africa have embraced translanguaging as a pedagogical practice, there is a dearth of research documenting translanguaging being used by other members of the faculty besides those involved in language teaching. In order to introduce translanguaging to my colleagues from the Science and Technology disciplines, I decided to solicit their views on the use of translanguaging for pedagogical purposes.

4 Research method

This qualitative research used an open-ended questionnaire consisting of four questions and was designed to solicit science lecturers' views on the use of translanguaging in their classes. The questionnaire was open so that respondents could provide as much information as possible in their responses. Since respondents were not familiar with the term "translanguaging" I had to briefly explain the general definition of the term. This was included in the introductory part of the questionnaire. Responses were analyzed according to recurring themes from each question. An inductive analysis approach was used to analyze the data. According to Bhattacharya (2017), inductive analysis is the process where a researcher categorizes chunks of data and identifies patterns, which are called themes. Bhattacharya (2017) asserts that categorization can be based on meaning, critical incidents, theoretical constructs, or patterns from the existing literature. In this case, themes from the data were categorized according to the implied meaning that is, the responses to the questionnaire were matched to the theoretical concepts of translanguaging.

4.1 Participants

The research focused on lecturers from the School of Science and Technology who teach mathematics (2), computer science (4), physics (2), and statistics (3). These lecturers were asked to participate because my department, Language and Proficiency, is situated in the School of Science and Technology as a service department, which facilitated recruitment. The questionnaire was distributed to all lecturers in the school. However, only 11 out of 57 lecturers in the school were willing to participate in this survey. There were six male participants and five female participants. Nine of these participants are speakers of more than three South African languages, Setswana being the predominantly spoken language by these lecturers. Two lecturers who participated could speak only two languages: English and Shona, a Zimbabwean language.

5 Results and analysis

An open-ended questionnaire was administered to 20 lecturers from the science department and 11 were completed. Results from the four open-ended questions were analyzed by paying attention to recurring themes from the responses. These themes were classified based on the questions from the questionnaire.

In general, lecturers concur that students understand concepts better when they are allowed to use their own languages. However, many of them still believe in the use of English only for the purposes of teaching and learning. In what follows, I will present common themes featuring the responses for each question.

Question 1 asked: What are your views about the use of English only as the language for teaching and learning? The majority of participants (from surveys 1, 3, 4, 5, 6, 8, 9, 10) indicated that English should be used as the only language for teaching and learning because English is a "common language" for communication purposes. Some participants, 3 of them were concerned about international students, and felt that the use of English would accommodate those students who cannot speak any of the South African indigenous languages. In addition, most respondents indicated that South Africa has too many languages and allowing these languages to be used in the classroom for teaching and learning would cause confusion among students, so to avoid confusion it is best to use English. Among these respondents, one strongly felt that English should continue to be used for pedagogical purposes in order to fortify their understanding of the language. This respondent wrote: "The use of English emphasizes and fortifies the understanding of English". On the other hand, another respondent felt that using English only for teaching and learning stifles students' ability to grasp concepts. The respondent referred to the sole use of English as deficit-based because it does not consider meaning inherent in the social and cultural background of other languages. The respondent wrote: "It [the use of English only] limits students' understanding and grasping of concepts. It is a deficit-based approach, as it does not consider social, cultural inherent meaning in other languages used by the students".

The second question asked: Do you think that allowing students to use their various linguistic resources during discussions (either group/class) would enhance their understanding of concepts? The majority of responses showed that lecturers agree that if students are allowed to use their entire linguistic repertoire, they should be able to understand concepts better than when they use English only to try and make meaning. However, among the responses, lecturers expressed their scepticism about allowing students to translanguage when assessments are always in English. In particular, one respondent wrote: "For understanding yes, it is a good idea but I do not support the idea because students are assessed in English". In addition to concerns regarding the English language being the language of assessment, some indicated that they allow students to use other languages to discuss concepts in group discussions. However, they would not allow translanguaging to be done during class discussion in order to cater to those students who do not speak any of the South African languages. One of the respondents wrote: "Yes, I do allow them to discuss in their own languages so they can understand concepts well. However, when they address the class I encourage them to use English in order to accommodate some foreign students". Two lecturers responded to the second question by providing personal experiences with students when they used translanguaging during class discussions. Both respondents pointed to the benefits of allowing students to utilize other languages besides English. These respondents conceded that students showed a better understanding of concepts. One of them wrote: "Yes, I think it helps. I have observed during my statistics lectures that students understand concepts better they ask questions in their MT [mother tongue] (mostly Sepedi) and I respond in Sepedi. Those who would have understood tend to explain to the rest of the class in both English and Sepedi".

Question 3 requested respondents' views on the use of translanguaging during group and class discussions, and many participants responded from a personal standpoint by stating whether they allowed translanguaging or not in their classrooms. These responses overlapped with Question 4, which specifically asks the lecturers if they insist on the use of English only during group discussions. The intention of this question was to learn about lecturers' practices concerning language in their classrooms. The majority indicated that they insist on students using English during discussions. These respondents justified their practice for various reasons, the most common reason being that English is a common language that accommodates all students despite their linguistic backgrounds. Others indicated that they insist on using English because the English language needs to be practised in order to be perfect. Some respondents insisted that English is the business language of today and, of course, it is the language of teaching and learning in the university.

Two respondents indicated that they do not insist on the use of English during discussion in class or in groups. It should be noted that these respondents showed that they supported the use of translanguaging in teaching. Their reasons for allowing a translingual approach during class discussion were because students find it easy to express themselves in the languages that they understand better. Among these responses, they emphasized that even if they allow students to translanguage, it should be recognized that English is always the language of teaching and learning in the university. One respondent wrote: "I am not strict if a student finds it difficult to express a concept in English I allow them to use languages they are comfortable with. However, English should always be used as a medium of instruction."

6 Discussion

The research intended to find out two things from the science lecturers: (1) Do they see the need to allow students to utilize their linguistic repertoires for meaning-making and understanding of concepts? And (2) What are their perceptions about using translanguaging in their classrooms? I will now discuss the findings of this research based on these two questions.

6.1 Do lecturers see the need to use translanguaging?

There was a general consensus among participants that many students struggle with using English in their formal learning. However, due to the fact that English has been elevated to a higher status than all other languages, they felt that students should be encouraged to use English frequently in order to strengthen their English language skills. Most of the lecturers believed in English monolingualism for learning purposes. They believed that English is the standard language that is suitable to be used as a medium of instruction. To these lecturers, English should be the only language in the students' repertoire and thus they should eliminate all the other languages. This line of thinking is ill-informed because all multilinguals possess a linguistic repertoire from which they draw when the need arises (García and Wei 2014). Thus, creating linguistic boundaries in a multilingual individual is a futile exercise. It is in the best interest of the students for lecturers to allow the full use of their linguistic repertoires to enhance their learning.

These lecturers did not see the need to use translanguaging because they believed that, for students to be proficient in English, they need to discard all the other languages and focus on learning English as well as trying to understand concepts in English. Again, this is not a true reflection of multilinguals. In fact, if multilingual students are allowed to use translanguaging they will benefit from the fact that the weaker language will be supported by the stronger language, resulting in better understanding of concepts (Lewis, Jones and Baker 2011). Thus, I call on lecturers to see translanguaging as a benefit to the students and not a liability to them.

Most importantly, lecturers do not see the benefits of using translanguaging because they strongly believe, or they have been made to believe, that English is the only language for business. Such beliefs do not consider the fact that business was conducted successfully during the pre-colonial era without the use of English (or any one language) as the official business language. For example, in the Mapungubwe settlement of the 10th century, trade was conducted successfully between Africans, Indians, Egyptians, and the Chinese (SAHO 2011) without any dominant language being used for transactions. The idea of a business language or standard language only came as a result of colonization. Admittedly, colonization came to disrupt translingual societies by introducing English as "the standard language". I, therefore, concur with Makalela (2015) when he refers to the need for a multilingual return. Lecturers need to recognize that multilingualism is not a new phenomenon. It has been in existence and society was able to survive without a single business language for a long time. Communication was done through translanguaging where fluid language practices were utilized for meaning making and, above all, trading. Thus, if fluid language practices are allowed in multilingual classrooms, it will result in students understanding concepts better, which will enhance their learning.

Responses from the lecturers indicated a genuine concern for international students who are enrolled at the university. The lecturers felt that allowing students to use their home languages in class would exclude those students who cannot speak any of the South African languages. However, it should be noted that many international students are multilingual. Thus, in order to accommodate them, lecturers can allow these students to use their home languages to understand concepts. This actually means that even though the students are not originally from South Africa, they can be allowed to use their language practices to understand concepts thus assimilating them with their linguistic repertoires. I argue that lecturers could allow students both local and international to translanguage for meaning-making. Lecturers can use translanguaging as a micro-level response to the linguistic diversity that they find in the classroom. Because lecturers are the ones who are in contact with the students, and they are familiar with the academic challenges many students face due to the use of English only for learning, they should create translanguaging classrooms and allow students to fully utilize their linguistic repertoire (García et al. 2016).

6.2 What are lecturer's perceptions about using translanguaging in their classrooms?

Lecturers agreed that when students are allowed to use languages besides English, they understand concepts better. However, lecturers were concerned about the language for assessment. Their argument is that even if students are allowed to use translanguaging for discussion, assessments will always be in English. Therefore, they would rather insist on using English in order to adequately prepare students for assessments. Many lecturers, including those who did not participate in this research, have always raised this concern.

If translanguaging is a means of understanding concepts, lecturers can allow students to access examination papers in two languages. One paper can be in English and the other can be in the home language of the student. Translanguaging has the capacity to break the barrier caused by the nation-state ideology of one nation, one language, especially for academic purposes (Otheguy et al. 2015). Translanguaging is a vehicle towards social justice because it nullifies the standard language ideology (Ndhlovu 2017) which declares those not competent in the standard language (English) to be in need of remedial teaching. Rather, translanguaging transcends all linguistic boundaries and considers all languages suitable for education. Thus, when students are afforded the opportunity to utilize language in rich and meaningful ways without boundaries, their academic performance is enhanced. All that is required is for lecturers to acknowledge and respect students' linguistic repertoires in their teaching and allow students to excel academically using their complex language practices.

7 Conclusion

The purpose of this research was to investigate science lecturers' perceptions of the use of translanguaging in their teaching. Although lecturers who participated in this study acknowledge that students benefit from using their home languages to understand concepts, they are mostly against the use of any language besides English in their classrooms. Many of the respondents justified such teaching practices by saying that English is the medium of instruction of the university. In reality, the university does not yet have a written language policy but due to the symbolic language boundaries and hierarchies that were created by social actors (Valdés 2017), English has become the language of teaching and learning. Therefore, I call upon lecturers to embrace multilingualism and avert dominant language ideologies for the sake of the students instead of insisting on the use of English. Due to the lack of policy at the university, I cannot enforce the use of multilingualism in teaching as a policy, I can however continue to advocate and encourage lecturers to use the strategy. Further research also is also recommended especially on how to transform lecturer's mind frame in terms of translanguaging.

Lecturers cited their belief that English is the language of business as well as the fact that English is the language of assessment at SMU. In this chapter, I have argued that insisting on the use of English in multilingual classrooms disregards students' multilingual abilities. I, therefore, urge science lecturers to move away from the colonial ideology of dominant language vs. non-dominant language. There is no doubt that languages have no inherent hierarchy in relation to each other, nor do they have boundaries. There is a need for greater awareness to be raised among the faculty so that translanguaging pedagogy can be embraced. This can be done through workshops and conferences to sensitize colleagues about the importance of using translanguaging practices in their role teaching multilingual students. It is important to mention that among the science lecturers who participated in this study there are a few who have acknowledged multilingualism and have embraced translanguaging in their teaching. These well-meaning lecturers need support so that they can continue to embrace and utilize translanguaging in their teaching practices. Lastly, it is important to acknowledge that it will take time for translanguaging to be an acceptable practice, especially among members of the faculty. Further research on translanguaging attitudes and practices will no doubt benefit multilingual learners.

References

Baldauf, Richard. 2010. Rearticulating the case for micro language planning in a language ecology context. *Current Issues in Language Planning* 7 (2–3). 147–170.
Bhattacharya, Kakali. 2017. *Fundamentals of qualitative research: A practical guide*. London: Routledge.
Bock, Zannie & Gift Mheta. 2014. *Language, society and communication: An introduction*. Pretoria: Van Schaik.
Carroll, Kevin. S. & Astrid Sambolin Morales. 2016. Using university students' L1 as a resource: Translanguaging in a Puerto Rican ESL classroom. *Bilingual Research Journal* 39 (3). 248–268.
Department of Education. 2002. *Language policy for higher education*. Pretoria, RSA: Government Printers.
Flores, Nelson & Ofelia García. 2013 Linguistic third spaces in education: Teachers' translanguaging across the bilingual continuum. In David Little, Constant Leung & Piet van Avermaet (eds.), *Managing diversity in education: Key issues and some responses*, 243–256. Clevedon, UK: Multilingual Matters.
Garcia, O. & Wei, Li. 2014. *Translanguaging language, bilingualism and education*. New York: Palgrave Macmillan.
García, Ofelia. 2014. U.S. Spanish Education: Global and local intersections. *Review of Research in Education* 39 (1). 58–80.
García, Ofelia, Nelson Flores, & Massimiliano Spotti. 2017. Introduction. Language and society: A critical poststructuralist perspective. In Ofelia García, Nelson Flores & Massimiliano Spotti (eds.), *The Oxford handbook of language and society*, 1–16. New York: Oxford University Press.

García, Ofelia, Susan Ibbara Johnson & Kate Seltzer. 2016. *The translanguaging classroom: Leveraging student bilingualism for learning*. New York: Caslon Publishing.

García, Ofelia & Tatyana Kleyn. 2016. Translanguaging theory and project. In Ofelia García & Tatyana Kleyn (eds.), *Translanguaging with multilingual students: Learning from classroom moments*, 9–34. New York: Routledge.

García, Ofelia & Li Wei. 2014. *Translanguaging language, bilingualism and education*. New York: Palgrave Macmillan.

Kellerman, Stephen 2014. *Dreams to reality*. http://www.dreamstoreality.co.za/the-rainbow-nation/ (accessed 19 June 2017).

Lane, Pia & Miki Mikihara. 2017. Language and indigenous minorities. In Ofelia García, Nelson Flores & Massimiliano Spotti (eds.), *The Oxford handbook of language and society*, 299–230. Oxford: Oxford Press.

Lewis, Gwyn, Byron Jones & Colin Baker. 2011. Translanguaging: developing its conceptualization and contextualization. Educational Research and Evaluation: An *International Journal on Theory and Practice* 18 (7). 655–670.

Lopez, Alexis, Daniel Guzman-Orth & Sultan Turkan. 2014. *Study on the use of translanguaging to assess the content knowledge of emergent bilingual students*. Paper presented at the annual meeting of the AAAL Annual Conference, Portland, OR, 23–25 March.

Makalela, Leketi. 2015. Moving out of linguistic boxes: The effects of translanguaging strategies for multilingual classrooms. *Language and Education* 29 (3). 200–217.

Makalela, Leketi. 2016. Translanguaging *practices* in a South African institution of higher learning: A case of Ubuntu multilingual return. In Cathy M. Mazak & Kevin S. Carroll (eds.), *Translanguaging in higher education*, 65–78. Bristol: Multilingual Matters.

Makalela, Leketi & Rose-Marie McCabe. 2013. Monolingualism in a historically black South African University: A case of inheritance. *Linguistics and Education* 24. 406–414.

Makoni, Sinfree. 2017. From elderspeak to gerontolinguistics: Sociolinguistic myths. In Ofelia García, Nelson Flores & Massimilano Spotti (eds.), *The Oxford handbook of language and society*, 350–369. New York: Oxford University Press.

Makoni, Sinfree & Alistair Pennycook. 2007. *Disinvesting and reconstituting languages*. Clevedon, England: Multilingual Matters.

May, Stephen. 2017. Language, imperialism and the modern nation-state system: Implications for language rights. In Ofelia García, Nelson Flores & Massimilano Spotti (eds.), *The Oxford handbook of language and society* 35–54. New York: Oxford University Press.

Mbirimi-Hungwe, Vimbai. 2016. Translanguaging as a strategy for group work: Summary writing as a measure for reading comprehension among university students. *Southern African and Linguistics Studies* 34 (3). 241–249.

Mbirimi-Hungwe, Vimbai & Taurai Hungwe. 2018. Translanguaging for epistemic access to computer science concepts: A call for change. *Per Linguam: A Journal of Language Learning* 34 (2). 97–111.

Moll, Luis C., Cathy Amanti, Deborah Neff & Norma Gonzalez. 1992. Funds of knowledge for teaching: Using a qualitative approach to connect homes and communities. *Theory and Practice* 31. 132–141.

Ndlhovu, Finex. 2017. Language, migration, diaspora: Challenging the big battalions of groupism. In Ofelia García, Nelson Flores & Massimilano Spotti (eds.), *The Oxford handbook of language and society*, 141–160. New York: Oxford University Press.

Otheguy, Ricardo, Ofelia García & Wallis Reid. 2015. Clarifying translanguaging and deconstructing the named languages: A perspective from linguistics. *Applied Linguistics Review* 6 (3). 281–307.

Paulsrud, Beth Anne, Jenny Rosén, Boglarka Strasser & Asa Wedin (eds.). 2018. *New perspectives on translanguaging and education*. Bristol: Multilingual Matters,

South African History Online [SAHO]. 2011. *Mapungubwe*. www.sahistory.org.za/article/mapungubwe. (accessed 26 June 2017).

Valdés, Guadalupe. 2017. Entry visa denied: The construction of ideological language borders in educational settings. In Ofelia García, Nelson Flores & Massimilano Spotti (eds.), *The Oxford handbook of language and society*, 321–348. New York: Oxford University Press.

Williams, Cen. 1996. Secondary education: Teaching in the bilingual situation. In Cen Williams, Gwyn Lewis & Colin Baker (eds.), *The language policy: Taking stock*, 39–78. UK: CIA Publishers.

Martin Guardado
Chapter 13
Bringing it all Together: Multilingualism in Family, Society and Education

1 Introduction

There is currently an increasing awareness of multilingualism across the globe, which includes a recognition of its complexity as a social phenomenon, as well as of its relentless cultural-political situatedness. It has therefore become commonplace to examine the factors affecting multilingualism using a variety of heuristic scales (e.g., micro, meso, macro, etc.) and even emerging alternate timescales (e.g., Wortham 2012). All of these factors provide an arguably infinite constellation of possible directions for investigation and theorization. The preceding chapters constitute a clear example of the issues that surround multilingualism, whether the social focus of the discussion is the individual, the family, the larger society, or the education system. As such, one of the strengths of the foregoing papers taken together is in their diversity, not only in terms of the multiplicity of factors and topics discussed, but also in terms of the wide range of geographical, social, cultural, economic, and political realities in which the authors work and study. Admittedly, the majority of the authors are located in the global North. However, many are originally not from the global North or focused on participants from other settings. Arguably, these other contexts are often less visible in the academic literature, and thus, less available for examination and debate within the scholarship on multilingualism – particularly when compared with the work of those from institutions in the global North with significantly more access to research and research resources (Lillis and Curry 2010) – and linguistic resources; that is, the means to develop sufficient English proficiency (Curry and Lillis 2004).

2 Multilingualism efforts and realities in family and society

Families can be seen as societies in miniature. Indeed, family settings are *de facto* "training grounds" for individuals as they prepare for participation in

---

Martin Guardado, University of Alberta, Canada, E-mail: guardado@ualberta.ca

https://doi.org/10.1515/9781501514692-013

communities and broader societies. This progressive socialization trajectory gives newcomers (by age or by immigration) the opportunity to learn to interact with others and follow rules (Durkheim 1972), co-construct meaning, and to produce culture, skills, and processes that will likely become more in demand as they assume increasingly more complex subject positions and enter broader social circles. Thus, much of what individual family members experience at home is often also a reflection of broader societal attributes and processes. This is clearly reflected in my contribution (Chapter 4), which engages with the multifaceted strategies deployed by the parents with the goal of fostering the socialization of Spanish as a heritage language in different sites, including home, community, and even in transnational spaces. Thus, the ideologies of language espoused by the family participants are acted upon at the individual, family, and community levels.

In his vast scholarship on multilingualism and heritage languages, Joshua A. Fishman reminded us time and time again that there is no substitute for family when it comes to heritage language development, maintenance, and the pursuit of multilingualism. But due to a variety of circumstances, often families find themselves unable to achieve their intergenerational language transmission goals. This is particularly true in linguistic minority settings such as Indigenous communities. Peres, Finardi and Calazans discuss the contact situation between Guarani and Portuguese in the state of Espírito Santo, Brazil, and make a direct connection from the micro setting to the macro. Through interviews with Guarani speakers, they offer rare insights into the processes of language maintenance and loss in that community from the perspective of its speakers. While the authors found Guarani to be holding relatively strong in the face of language shift to Portuguese, they also identified threats to its maintenance, such as the influence of various media, the location of their schools outside of Guarani villages, and the frequent contact with Portuguese-dominant urban centres. It is clear that in the face of rapidly advancing national contexts, exacerbated by strong globalizing and technologizing forces, Indigenous and other ethnolinguistic communities find themselves strongly impacted by societal factors that limit their familial and community linguistic agency. Duranti, Ochs and Schieffelin (2012) have highlighted the "complex networks of informal and formal social institutions that regiment, or attempt to regiment, cultural and symbolic values associated with different linguistic varieties and discursive expressions" (485), which might help explain the social reality of the Guarani speakers in Brazil. It is also possible to extend this argument to the issues Romanowski raises in his comprehensive overview of the linguistic minority picture of Poland (Chapter 2), revealing how the promotion of national languages has been prioritized over mother tongue development. Importantly, this volume raises issues about the common disconnect between the linguistic rights mandates of international organizations such as UNESCO, and the disregard for such rights in educational contexts. Further research into this disconnect would be a possible way to help ensure linguistic rights are upheld in practice. As argued in Chapter 2, despite the favourable conditions for the promotion of minority languages that the Polish government offers, in practice the situation of linguistic minorities is not as promising. For some groups, increased mobility and other social conditions are disrupting intergenerational language transmission practices and possibilities, and languages with the fewest speakers, such as Czech, Slovak, Yiddish, and Hebrew, are at risk, while others, such as Tatar and Karaim, no longer have speakers. In some cases, it is not only that social institutions attempt to regulate linguistic ideologies and practices, but that the general Polish population is not even aware of, or is conveniently oblivious to, the existence of linguistic minorities in their national territory.

3 The multilingual speaker in context

While analyses of familial and societal aspects of multilingualism provide a big picture view of groups of multilingual speakers and their desires, challenges, and the contexts in which they live, analyses at the individual level shed light on, among other factors, the identity development trajectories and moment-by-moment communicative practices of existing or aspiring multilingual speakers. This book includes insightful studies in English as a *lingua franca* contexts from the perspectives of conversation analysis, pragmatics, as well as identity formation in study abroad. In their chapter, Martínez-Arbelaiz and Pereira examine the relationship between identity development and second language proficiency for four US undergraduate students studying abroad in Spain. They found that the two students with stronger Spanish language competence also had greater investment in the target language and culture, and seized opportunities for interaction with locals more enthusiastically than the two students who did not. The authors call for further research into this under-examined area of study abroad identity development and second language (L2) proficiency attainment. Their recommendations to language instructors in study abroad contexts include designing activities that not only require students to interact with locals and thereby enhance their communication strategies, but that also validate their L2 identities. Work in study abroad reminds us that theoretical and empirical developments that are nuanced and flexible are needed in order to achieve a deeper understanding of these issues. Language acquisition concerns itself with the development of communicative skills, but does not account for the process of identity formation that language learning in study abroad might entail. Language socialization (Schieffelin and Ochs 1986) provides the missing piece of this puzzle by accounting for how novices and others are constructed as members of social communities and as particular kinds of people. Furthermore, given that increasingly, one of the stated primary goals of study abroad is global competence and global citizenship (see Guardado and Tsushima forthcoming 2021), important questions can be raised around who accesses study abroad programs in higher education, and therefore, who is included in definitions of "cosmopolitanism" in this sociocultural, institutional milieu. Long (2013) points out that study abroad programs often tend to focus on nurturing the individual's identity development, and argues that such programs would do well to foster "the interpersonal features of life which shape us as individuals and define how we are able to build community" (31) on a global scale. Indeed, research around study abroad experiences needs to move beyond promoting tolerance of cultural differences and into the realm of "how we engage strangers" as we work toward universal goals of peace and justice (Appiah 2006: 32).

While multimodal analysis, such as gesture, has a long research tradition in the field of intercultural communication (see Kim and Lausberg 2018, Lin 2017), arguably, this is an area that has been long neglected in applied linguistics and related multilingualism research areas (Sueyoshi and Hardison 2005). Therefore, it is refreshing to see Hanamoto's analysis of interactions between Japanese university students and Filipina English instructors focusing on the role of gesture in building rapport and addressing communicative difficulties. He found that gesture is a useful modality through which participants in an English as a *lingua franca* language learning context make meaning and achieve mutual understanding, both related to spoken language and independent of/in addition to it. His research lends insight into the little understood role of gesture in English as a *lingua franca* language learning contexts, and as such, offers a way forward for researchers interested in multimodal communication strategies in similar *lingua franca* contexts. This is a fertile area of research within multilingualism studies and related areas.

An analytic focus that has been used productively in multilingual interactions since the inception of sociolinguistics, language socialization, and the ethnography of communication, is the linguistic analysis of natural conversation. A much more recent focal and methodological development concerns the phenomenon of linguistic transfer in institutional multilingual interactions and in the acquisition of pragmatics in an L2. Chapter 6, for instance, examined code alternation in institutional enrollment consultations between multilingual, *lingua franca* speakers of German and English. Khalizova found competence-related code-switching to be the most common strategy for negotiating or securing understanding, occurring particularly in situations with multiple students or when counsellors answered questions quickly in one language and did not shift immediately back to the *lingua franca* of the main interaction. This chapter contributes to the burgeoning line of research into the role of code alternation between *lingua franca* speakers in institutional settings. Szczepaniak-Kozak (Chapter 8) employed a discourse completion task to investigate the ways in which her participants' L1 (Polish) and L3 (German) affected their acquisition of pragmatics in their L2 (English as a foreign language). Echoing Ringbom (2007), the main finding of her research was that the students' strongest language (Polish) seemed to have much more impact on interference errors in their English pragmatics than did their less proficient language (German). She concludes by calling for more research into this phenomenon from different perspectives (e.g., different languages, relationships between the languages themselves, expanding the speech acts or pragmatic features under examination).

4 Critical multilingualism approaches in educational settings

The contributors to this volume provide a wide range of insights into the role of education in developing multilingualism in a variety of instructed settings. Although this volume was not conceptualized as a guide to curriculum design or pedagogy, the contributions in Part II offer well-considered theoretical and practical discussions of topics of relevance to multilingual education, and each chapter suggests ways for teachers and other practitioners to improve their particular learning contexts. Successful approaches, including plurilingualism (Chapters 9 and 10), interlingualism (Chapter 11), and translanguaging (Chapter 12) will prove particularly helpful. For instance, Kalnberzina's work in the Latvian context describes the recent draft language curriculum development process, which culminated in mapping the new *Common European Framework of Reference for Languages* (CEFR) descriptors (2018) onto Latvian curricular attainment targets. One of the goals of this reform process was to examine the usefulness of the descriptors in introducing plurlingualism to a context where languages are typically treated and taught separately. The area of greatest synergy in the mapping exercise was "context" (e.g., getting things done, structuring discourse) – a finding that Kalnberzina argues reflects "the common understanding of the role of context in language education in Europe." Mapping exercises like this would undoubtedly be useful in other European contexts as well, in order to cast into sharper relief the areas of resonance and dissonance between local language teaching curricula and the CEFR descriptors. Likewise, in Chapter 10 Camilleri Grima notes several barriers to the implementation of the *Framework of Reference for Pluralistic Approaches to Languages and Cultures*. This highlights the need for a coherent, plurilingually-informed policy at all levels of education, and a critical engagement with the productive possibilities that a deeper understanding of the effects of plurilingual approaches to language learning might have on social cohesion outside of the classroom. These are fruitful areas for future research on plurilingualism. Given the one-size-fits-all curricula that dominates in many parts of the world, work such as that described in Chapters 11 and 12 offers productive possibilities for change and innovation. Barranco Izquierdo and Calderón Quindós offer an action plan to help teachers create more inclusive, linguistically supportive learning environments through the implementation of interlingual strategies in their classrooms. Along similar critical lines, based on her research in South Africa, Mbirimi-Hungwe advocates for more supports for faculty who do use or allow for translanguaging in their classroom, as well as further research in this area in order to persuade faculty who do not yet see its benefits for multilingual learners.

The terms pluralingualism, translanguaging, and interlingualism as they are used in the chapters mentioned above have more in common than it might appear at first glance. The differences, at least in my understanding, are rather subtle. For instance, the key defining factor of plurilingualism is that it distinguishes between individual or societal language use, and as such is contrasted with multilingualism. Translanguaging emerged from the post-structural turn in linguistics that challenged the rigid separation of languages found in traditional theories of language such as structuralism. Interlingualism highlights its relationship to other terms, such as interculturalism. All terms see languages as integrated and subscribe to linguistic ideologies of integration rather than separation, and pursue an agenda of social justice. Therefore, what they share is the keen recognition that the ability of individuals to function in several languages can and should be capitalized on in the classroom in order to enhance learning. Thus, the common core that brings together all chapters drawing on these terms is that all intend to enhance different aspects of learning by recognizing and using several languages in learning contexts.

5 Moving the multilingualism agenda forward

As the title of the book proclaims, its chapters purport to provide a diversity of perspectives on multilingualism across various populations, contexts, and topics. To be sure, a common thread running throughout the volume in terms of the agenda forward is an appeal for expanded diversification of research around multilingualism. Most authors call for the expansion of the scope of multilingualism research in relation to their own research focus. The urgent questions at hand, according to several of the authors, can be fruitfully addressed by broadening the participant pool. For instance, Peres, Finardi and Calazans posit that there is a need for sociolinguistic studies of Guarani language use among children and youth in situations of contact with Portuguese language speakers. Along similar lines, Guardado argues in Chapter 4 that the perspectives of children and youth, and perhaps also the impact of social networks (friendships) in conjunction with those of adults would provide a fuller picture of heritage language development. Similarly, but in classroom settings, Hanamoto proposes that his research on the role of gesture in addressing communication challenges should move from small group interactions to large classrooms, and perhaps also address the topic with populations living in contexts of English as a *lingua franca*.

Camilleri Grima (Chapter 10) suggests that research should be amplified to include not only school settings but also the community in order to better understand the impact of plurilingual approaches to education in Malta. Indeed, this type of research broadening, such as small to large scale, is found in several chapters, including Martínez-Arbelaiz and Pereira's study abroad research in Spain (Chapter 7); and micro/ utterance-level to speech events in the analysis of how pragmatic features are transferred from one language to another in Poland. An increase in the diversity of research variables has been proposed as well, as in Barranco Izquierdo and Calderón Quindós' work on interlingual education (Chapter 11). Finally, a widening of the ideological stances from traditional colonial ideologies of linguistic dominance to post-structuralist transformational ideologies is found particularly in Mbirimi-Hungwe's work in relation to translanguaging in South Africa. To conclude, the goal of the book to present and propose diverse ways forward in the study of multilingualism is indeed accomplished, and the authors furthermore also collectively called for greater scholarly efforts in those regards, a commitment that is also realized in the majority of chapters.

It is fitting to reiterate the fact that several contributors to the present volume are working or conducting research in and/or hail from the global South. Indeed, not only is multilingualism the focus of the book, but all of its authors are multilingual. I argue that these attributes in and of themselves make this volume a valuable one. Although English has been the language of scientific and scholarly dissemination in recent history, many scholars have strongly critiqued this practice particularly in the last two decades on the grounds of equity (Gazzola and Grin 2007, Van Parijs 2007) and related social justice concerns (Clavero 2010, Hyland 2019). The most common themes found in these discussions include the lack of access to scientific knowledge by those who do not use English academically, as well as greatly reduced opportunities to disseminate their own research more widely. Indeed, the reality has been that those who do not work in English are effectively excluded from global academic conversations. It is also possible that in an increasingly interconnected world, this reality will only intensify in the years ahead as English continues to solidify its stronghold on global academic communications. An interesting twist, however, was provided by Fishman (1999) who declared that English monolingualism negatively affects global business practices, clearly rejecting the idea that globalization makes local languages irrelevant. On the contrary, he argued that just as Latin, an international language in its time, became irrelevant because of the emergence of local languages, so can English. We wonder, then, if our communication within, across, and outside of our academic circles will be strengthened because of – and not in spite of – our linguistic diversity.

An argument can be made that scholars working in the global South are a sub-segment of those neglected groups of people, as described by Hardt and Negri (2005), who constitute a productive force that can be understood as a potential resisting "multitude" (their term) against the tyrannical global capitalist processes of what they refer to as "Empire." Hardt and Negri argue that the contemporary scene of production has been transformed by labour that produces immaterial products such as ideas and knowledge, processes that can be easily extended to academic work. It is clear that equitable access to the scholarly literature, as well as the ability of scholars working in non-Anglophone contexts to broadly disseminate the products of their scholarship, remain key challenges of the 21st century academy.

References

Appiah, Kwame Anthony. 2006. *Cosmopolitanism: Ethics in a world of strangers*. New York: W. W. Norton & Co.
Clavero, Miguel. 2010. "Awkward wording. Rephrase": Linguistic injustice in ecological journals. *Trends Ecology Evolution* 25, 552–553.

Curry, Mary J. & Theresa Lillis. 2004. Multilingual scholars and the imperative to publish in English: Negotiating interests, demands, and rewards. *TESOL Quarterly* 38 (4). 663–688.
Duranti, Alessandro, Elinor Ochs & Bambi B. Schieffelin. 2012. Language and culture contact. In Alessandro Duranti, Elinor Ochs & Bambi B. Schieffelin (eds.), *The handbook of language socialization*, 485–491. West Sussex, UK: Wiley-Blackwell.
Durkheim, Emile. 1972. *Selected Writings*. Edited, translated and with an introduction by Anthony Giddens. Cambridge, England: Cambridge University Press.
Fishman, Joshua A. 1999. *Handbook of language and ethnic identity*. Toronto: Oxford University Press.
Gazzola, Michele, & François Grin. 2007. Assessing efficiency and fairness in multilingual communication: Towards a general analytical framework. In Augusto Carli & Ulrich Ammon (eds.), *Linguistic Inequality in Scientific Communication Today. AILA Review* 20, 87–105. Amsterdam: John Benjamins.
Guardado, Martin & Rika Tsushima. Forthcoming 2021. *Global Jinzai* and short-term study abroad: Expectations, readiness and realities. In Sandra R. Schecter & Carl E. James (eds.), *Critical approaches toward a cosmopolitan education*. New York, NY: Routledge.
Hardt, Michael & Antonio Negri. 2005. *Multitude: War and democracy in the age of empire*. New York, NY: Penguin.
Hyland, Ken. 2019. Participation in publishing: The demoralizing discourse of disadvantage. In Pejman Habibie & Ken Hyland (eds.), *Novice writers and scholarly publication*, 13–22. Cham: Palgrave Macmillan.
Kim, Zi Hyun & Hedda Lausberg. 2018. Koreans and Germans: Cultural differences in hand movement behaviour and gestural repertoire. *Journal of Intercultural Communication Research* 47 (6). 439–453. DOI: 10.1080/17475759.2018.1475296
Lin, Yen-Liang. 2017. Co-occurrence of speech and gestures: A multimodal corpus linguistic approach to intercultural interaction. *Journal of Pragmatics* 117. 155–167.
Ringbom, Håkan. 2007. *Cross-linguistic similarity in foreign language learning*. Clevedon: Multilingual Matters.
Schieffelin, Bambi B. & Elinor Ochs. 1986. Language socialization. *Annual Review of Anthropology* 15. 163–191.
Sueyoshi, Ayano & Debra M. Hardison. 2005. The role of gestures and facial cues in second language listening comprehension. *Language Learning* 55(4). 661–699.
Lillis, Theresa & Mary Jane Curry. 2010. *Academic writing in a global context: The politics and practices of publishing in English*. New York: Routledge.
Long, Theodore E. 2013. From study abroad to global studies: Reconstructing international education for a globalized world. *Frontiers: The Interdisciplinary Journal of Study Abroad*, 22. 25–36.
Van Parijs, Phillipe. 2007. Tackling the Anglophones' 'free ride': Fair linguistic co-operation with a global lingua franca. In Augusto Carli and Ulrich Ammon (eds.), *Linguistic inequality in scientific communication today. AILA Review 20*, 72–86. Amsterdam: John Benjamins.
Wortham, Stanton. 2012. Introduction to the special issue: Beyond macro and micro in the linguistic anthropology of education. *Anthropology & Education Quarterly* 2 (43). 128–137.

Subject Index

attitudes 163, 170, 176

Canada 44
Canadian identity 54
catchment 65, 79
codeswitching 89
communication conflicts 196, 203
community 45
contextualization cue 88
conversation analysis 88
cosmopolitanism 226
Council of Europe 166, 169
critical multilingualism 227
critical post-structural sociolinguistics 209, 211
cultural awareness 49
culture 26, 28, 30, 32, 33, 35
curricula, curriculum 147, 152, 159

discourse analysis 42
discursive expressions 224
dominant language 219
dominant language ideologies 218

Empire 230
English as a lingua franca, ELF 63, 66
enrollment consultation 85
Espirito Santo 29, 33, 34
ethnic minorities 11, 13, 15
ethnographic 43

Filipina 67
Fishman, Joshua 224

German 137
Gesture 65
global citizenship 226
global North 223
global South 229
globalization, globalizing 224, 230
Guarani 27–29, 31, 33, 34

heritage language, HL 32, 39, 42–43, 224

heritage language socialization 40, 42, 43, 56, 57
heuristic scales 223
Hispanic 43, 44
home culture 51

identity 40, 42, 52, 53, 57, 112, 226
inclusive education 188, 191, 202
inclusive migrant education 189, 191
Indigenous 224
indigenous language 32, 36, 210
intercultural communication 226
interlanguage pragmatic competence 129
interlingual 188
interlingual education 191, 194, 195, 203
interlingualism 227
item transfer 130, 135, 138

Japanese students 67

Kashubian 12, 14, 16, 17, 21
knowledge 166, 170, 172

L2 identity 110, 123
L2-mediated identities 113, 122
language 25
Language awareness 49
language boundaries 218
language change 88, 95
language contact 27, 28, 35
language dominance 55
language loss 28, 31
language maintenance 33
language policies 25, 27, 35
language vitality 26, 29, 31, 33
Latin American culture 52
Latin American identity 58
Lemkian 17, 21
lingua franca 89, 225
lingua franca speakers 92
linguistic diversity 230
linguistic repertoire 212, 217
literacy 50

Lithuanian 14, 16–17, 19, 21
loss 25
loss of their language 26

Malta 4, 6, 164, 165, 169, 172, 173, 177, 179
Maltese 165, 170, 173, 175, 177, 179
mediation 196, 197, 199, 203
Mexican-Canadian 39
Mexico 44
minorities 12
minority language 12, 14, 22
mother tongue 58
multimodal analysis 64, 68, 79
multimodality 65
Multiple Effect Principle 132
multitude 230

narrative 111, 114, 118, 121
national minorities 14
nation-state ideologies 211
negative pragmatic transfer 129
negative sociopragmatic transfer 139
negative transfer 129, 136–138, 140
NVivo 44

oral mediation 191, 196, 200, 201, 203
overgeneralization 140

pedagogy 207
Philippines 66
pluralistic 166, 167, 169, 170, 228
plurilingual 1, 6, 90, 146–151, 153–156, 158–160, 164, 166–169, 175, 178, 180–181, 188–190, 192–194, 200–201, 228–229
plurilingualism 146, 227
Polish 136
positive transfer 140
pragmatic 129
pragmatic accent 141

pragmatic competence 130, 133, 140, 141
pragmatic transfer 9
pragmatic transfer 135
procedural transfer 130, 138
processability theory 131
proficiency 111, 115, 118, 122

Rainbow Nation 208
regional languages 14, 20
role of school 53

semi-structured interview 43
skills 166, 170, 178
social distance 140
social justice 230
social networks 229
socialization 224
sociolinguistics 210
sociopragmatic transfer 137
South Africa 207, 212, 214
Spanish 44, 46, 47
standard ideology 210
standard language ideology 218
study abroad, SA 110, 111, 112, 114, 122, 124, 226

that language change 103
the estimation of future social distance 140
the process of understanding 95, 103
transfer 88, 89, 96, 98, 100
translanguaging 145, 148, 211, 213, 217, 218, 227
translanguaging classrooms 212
transnational spaces 224

Ukrainian 14, 17, 21

Vancouver 44
verbosity 131
verbosity effect 135

www.ingramcontent.com/pod-product-compliance
Lightning Source LLC
Chambersburg PA
CBHW070800230426
43665CB00017B/2435